# Cooking Light

# GLUTEN-FREE
# BAKING

# Cooking Light

## ROBERT LANDOLPHI

# GLUTEN-FREE
# BAKING

**Delectable from-scratch
sweet and savory treats**

Oxmoor
House

For millions of people, the gluten-free diet is not a fad or a trend. Rather, it's a mandatory lifestyle, which must be adhered to in order for them to regain their health and maintain their wellness. My family is no stranger to the gluten-free lifestyle. In fact, we're ardent promoters of wheat- and gluten-free cuisine. Why? In 2000, my wife was diagnosed with celiac disease/gluten intolerance after a three-year battle with multiple symptoms that left a previously healthy, active, and vibrant young woman feeling ill, fatigued, in pain, and fighting neurological symptoms, malabsorption, and infertility. Going gluten free changed her health, my career, and every aspect of our lives. By 2004, we were able to have the first of our three beautiful sons, without doctors or drugs, but simply by adhering to a gluten-free diet! Our gluten-free inner circle now includes my wife, two of my sons, my mother-in-law, brother-in-law, nephew, and dozens of friends and co-workers.

As the culinary development manager for a large university, I meet on a weekly basis with college students who are newly diagnosed with gluten intolerance. They're often overwhelmed by the thought of their new diet, but then pleasantly surprised at how easily we can accommodate them, even on the commercial dining level. They are comforted by how many choices they have, and leave our meetings without a care in the world—nor an inkling of what it used to be like in the "days of old" when gluten-free products were hard, if not impossible, to find, and those that were available were *not good.*

Thankfully, gluten-free foods are more widely available than they used to be. A trip to our favorite restaurant, a local bakery, or the neighborhood grocery store yields many options. I have written this cookbook for the home baker who is longing for heavenly baked items that will be enjoyable for everyone and still provide healthy choices. The 150 from-scratch gluten-free recipes in this book are indeed nutritious and, even more importantly, are absolutely delicious. I hope you love them as much as the Landolphi family does!

Many thanks to Janine and Michael Callahan and the Willimantic Food Co-op for their accommodation and assistance during the photo shoot in Connecticut. Heartfelt gratitude to our family and friends for their continued encouragement, support, and enthusiasm; and to Mary, for all her love and guidance.

—Robert Landolphi, "The Gluten-Free Chef"

*Robert with his wife, Angela, and his sons,*
*Stephen, Andrew, and Joseph*

# CONTENTS

# chapter 1

# KITCHEN
# BASICS

Gluten-free baking is both an art and a science. Unlike traditional baking, where you can pick up a bag of all-purpose wheat flour and use it to make almost any baked good, in gluten-free baking, there isn't an equivalent. Instead, you have to rely on a mix of flours and starches that each have different flavor profiles and varying levels of protein and starch that affect the structure and tenderness of the baked goods. Gluten-free pancakes need a different mix of flours than a hearty bread to achieve the right texture.

This chapter is your starting point. You'll learn the basics of how to create gluten-free versions of all the delicious baked goods you crave: quick breads, yeast breads, cookies, muffins, cakes, pies, cobblers, pizzas, and more. You'll learn what flours work best and in what ratios and how to substitute ingredients when you need a dairy-free option. I share tips that I've learned over the years that will ensure your success and garner wonderful reactions from your family and friends.

# WHAT IS GLUTEN?

As a chef and culinary arts instructor who lectures on the art of gluten-free cuisine all across this fine nation, I inevitably field the same question from people in the audience who believe they are having difficulty digesting or processing wheat and gluten-laden foods: "What is gluten, and where is it found?"

Gluten is the general name for specific proteins found in wheat, barley, and rye. It provides bread, pizza crust, bagels, muffins, etc., with their characteristic chewy texture—it's essentially what gives bread its "breadness." Most people can eat gluten without any ill effects, but it's a serious health hazard for millions of others.

One of the big misconceptions about gluten is that it's only found in bread products. It's true—you'll find it in breads, pastas, crackers, and cereals that have been made with grains—but it can also be found in many prepared foods, such as stocks, sauces, salad dressings, malt vinegars, chips, spices, deli meats, fast-food items, and candy. It also shows up in beauty products like makeup, shampoos, soaps, and moisturizing lotions.

Whether you decide to embark on a gluten-free diet because of a diagnosis by your doctor or your own personal choice, there are a couple of habits you'll have to adopt: reading food labels and ingredient lists, and checking manufacturers' websites or calling them directly to determine whether or not an item is safe. A good example is oatmeal. Even though oats are a naturally gluten-free grain, they're very often cross-contaminated with wheat during the planting and harvesting process. Before puchasing, you need to check that the container you're buying contains only pure oats, certified as gluten-free through testing by the manufacturer, which are the only ones guaranteed as safe for a gluten-free diet.

# WHO NEEDS TO AVOID GLUTEN?

There are a number of conditions that require people to follow a gluten-free lifestyle: celiac disease, gluten intolerance, gluten sensitivity, and a wheat allergy. Here's a brief primer on the differences:

**CELIAC DISEASE** is a genetic disorder also known as coeliac, celiac sprue, and gluten-sensitive enteropathy. For those who have celiac disease, gluten damages the villi—the small hair-like protrusions lining the intestines that are responsible for absorbing a variety of vital nutrients. These flattened, compromised villi can lead to a number of physical and neurological symptoms that vary from person to person, including bloating, irritable bowel, infertility, muscle cramps, skin rashes, nerve damage, abdominal pain, bruising, and anemia. Once a celiac disease diagnosis is confirmed, gluten has to be avoided for life. This means adhering to a strict gluten-free diet, which allows the intestines to heal and, in most cases, for the symptoms to subside. It is important to remember that anyone diagnosed with celiac disease is, by definition, gluten intolerant and has a gluten sensitivity as well.

**GLUTEN INTOLERANCE (GI) AND GLUTEN SENSITIVITY (GS)** are two terms often used interchangeably. They're similar to celiac disease in that individuals have trouble digesting gluten and don't feel well after eating it. While these two conditions share some of the same symptoms as celiac disease, including irritable bowel, abdominal pain, fatigue, headaches, joint pain, and rashes, GI and GS are not as severe as celiac disease because patients with these conditions have not shown damage in the lining of their small intestines. Unlike for celiac disease, there is no diagnostic test to confirm GI or GS. However, after people with GI or GS implement a gluten-free diet, the symptoms disappear, and the person's body begins to heal and to function properly again.

**A WHEAT ALLERGY** causes an allergic reaction to foods or products containing wheat, but people with a wheat allergy may be able to tolerate other grains, such as oats, rye, and barley, since the allergy is not in response to gluten. This is very different from celiac disease in that symptoms can develop within a few hours, minutes, or even seconds after exposure, and they don't necessarily affect the gastrointestinal system. With a wheat allergy, the whole immune system responds and can produce symptoms such as nausea; hives; bloating; breathing difficulties; swelling of the eyes, face, or throat; and even anaphylaxis. Wheat is one of the Food and Drug Administration's top eight food allergens in the United States. A wheat allergy can be diagnosed by an allergist with a skin prick or blood test.

# KITCHEN ESSENTIALS

Here's a list of the items you'll need to create delicious gluten-free baked products at home. A note on kitchen safety: If you also prepare foods that contain gluten in your kitchen, preventing cross-contamination is key. You'll need to thoroughly clean dishes, counters, cooking surfaces, and kitchen utensils and appliances after any of them have come into contact with foods containing gluten. (In a perfect world, separate appliances and small wares, such as cutting boards and flour sifters, would be best.)

**KITCHEN SCALE:** Because each person scoops flour into a measuring cup differently, a kitchen scale is ideal because it allows for accurate measurements every time. A digital scale is the easiest to use, but a top-loading or hanging scale will also work.

**LIQUID MEASURING CUPS:** Liquid measuring cups are usually made of glass, plastic, or stainless steel and are used to measure ingredients such as water, juices, milks, oils, and honey. (See Measuring Dry and Wet Ingredients on page 30 for other tips and how-to instructions.)

**DRY MEASURING CUPS:** Dry measuring cups are usually made of plastic or stainless steel and are used to measure ingredients like flour, sugar, dried fruits, and nuts. (See Measuring Dry and Wet Ingredients on page 30 for other tips and how-to instructions.)

**MEASURING SPOONS:** Measuring spoons are usually made of plastic, metal, stainless steel, or porcelain. They're used to measure smaller amounts of ingredients such as spices, herbs, sugar, vanilla extract, baking soda, baking powder, xanthan gum, and yeast.

**MIXERS:** The three most popular baking mixers include the stand mixer, hand mixer, and stick mixer. Electric mixers are designed to do the work for you, and ensure that all the ingredients get mixed evenly and uniformly. They also have different speeds that allow you to whip delicate ingredients such as egg whites or thick ingredients such as brownie batter or marshmallows. Hand and stick mixers are ideal for smaller jobs that don't involve mixing heavy batters or doughs.

**FOOD PROCESSOR:** The food processor is a must-have, multi-tasking tool vital for every kitchen. It slices, chops, shreds, purees, grinds, and mixes a variety of ingredients—it is the most versatile piece of equipment in the kitchen, and a huge time-saver when prepping ingredients.

**BLENDER:** A blender is used to mix, blend, or emulsify food. It is great for pureeing fruit for pie fillings or toppings, or blending batters for pancakes, crepes, or waffles.

**KNIVES AND CUTTING BOARDS:** A high-quality chef's knife and a sturdy cutting board are important purchases for a well-stocked kitchen. Together, they provide a quick and easy way to chop, dice, slice, and mince ingredients. If you prepare foods that contain gluten, it would be smart to purchase a cutting board specifically for prepping gluten-free ingredients since cutting boards made of wood or bamboo have porous surfaces, which are hard to clean and have nooks and crannies where gluten can adhere.

**GRATER AND ZESTER:** These two essential pieces of equipment come in handy for grating a variety of ingredients like cheese, carrots, and zucchini. They are also needed to achieve the right texture, weight, and consistency when grating fresh nutmeg or citrus rinds, which add bursts of flavor to baked goods.

**BAKING PANS:** If you bake often, you'll find it helpful to assemble a small arsenal of baking pans, including baking sheets, jelly-roll pans, muffins tins, Bundt pans, baking pans (square, rectangle), round cake pans, springform pans, pie plates, and loaf pans.

# FLOURS

There is a host of flours that don't contain gluten. Each has unique flavors and properties that work particularly well in certain baked goods. Here's a short glossary to help you make sense of all your options and also guidelines about how to store them properly.

**1. ALMOND MEAL FLOUR:** Ground from whole, blanched almonds, this high-protein flour adds a superb texture and nutty flavor.
**SHELF LIFE:** Store in an airtight container in refrigerator or freezer up to six months.
**BEST FOR:** biscuits, pancakes, waffles, muffins, cookies, piecrusts, cakes, and cobblers

**2. ARROWROOT STARCH:** This tasteless white flour derived from the base of the arrowroot plant is an excellent substitute for cornstarch in baked goods.
**SHELF LIFE:** Store in an airtight container in a cool, dry place up to six months.
**BEST FOR:** breads and biscuits

**3. OAT FLOUR:** Oat flour is made from very finely ground oats. It adds a robust taste and hearty texture to baked goods. To avoid cross contamination, purchase oat flour that's certified gluten free.
**SHELF LIFE:** Store in an airtight container in a cool, dry place up to three months or in refrigerator or freezer up to six months.
**BEST FOR:** muffins, breads, cookies, and cakes

**4. SWEET POTATO FLOUR:** When added to baked goods, sweet potato flour helps them retain moisture, while enhancing nutrition and adding richness.
**SHELF LIFE:** Store in an airtight container in a cool, dry place up to one year.
**BEST FOR:** pancakes, crepes, breads, and muffins

**5. FLAXSEED MEAL:** Made from flaxseeds that have been ground into a dark, dense flour, flaxseed meal works best when blended with other gluten-free flours.
**SHELF LIFE:** Store in an airtight container in refrigerator up to six months or freezer up to one year.
**BEST FOR:** pancakes, waffles, muffins, and breads

**6. CORN FLOUR:** Corn flour is ground from whole corn kernels into a texture much finer than traditional cornmeal. Variations include masa harina, which is ground from white or yellow corn, and harinilla, which is ground blue corn.
**SHELF LIFE:** Store in an airtight container in refrigerator up to six months or freezer up to one year.
**BEST FOR:** breads, pizza crusts, muffins, pancakes, cakes, and tortillas

**7. HAZELNUT FLOUR:** This sweet, tawny, high-protein flour is made from finely ground hazelnuts.
**SHELF LIFE:** Store in an airtight container in refrigerator up to six months.
**BEST FOR:** breads, muffins, cookies, and cakes

**8. QUINOA FLOUR:** Ground from seeds, quinoa flour is a nutritious, high-protein flour that has a slightly nutty flavor.
**SHELF LIFE:** Store in an airtight container in refrigerator up to six months.
**BEST FOR:** biscuits, muffins, cookies, breads, and cakes

**9. TAPIOCA FLOUR (STARCH):** A light, powdery, tasteless flour, tapioca flour adds body and chewy texture to baked goods. It works best when combined with other gluten-free flours.
**SHELF LIFE:** Store in an airtight container in a cool, dry place up to two years.
**BEST FOR:** pancakes, muffins, biscuits, cookies, cakes, and breads

**10. SORGHUM FLOUR:** Sorghum flour is ground from a high-protein, high-fiber cereal grain. It is heavy and should be blended with lighter, starchier flours.
**SHELF LIFE:** Store in an airtight container up to three months, in refrigerator up to six months, or in freezer up to one year.
**BEST FOR:** muffins, pancakes, biscuits, cookies, cakes, and breads

**11. CORNMEAL:** Ground from whole corn kernels into a gritty meal, cornmeal is much coarser than corn flour. It adds a sweet, nutty flavor to a variety of baked goods.
**SHELF LIFE:** Store in an airtight container in a cool, dry place up to two months or in refrigerator up to six months.
**BEST FOR:** breads, muffins, pizza crusts, and tortillas

**12. TEFF FLOUR:** This finely textured flour is milled from a grain named teff.
**SHELF LIFE:** Store in an airtight container in refrigerator up to six months.
**BEST FOR:** pancakes, muffins, breads, and tortillas

**13. COCONUT FLOUR:** Coconut flour is ground from dried, defatted coconut meat. It works best when combined with other gluten-free flours.
**SHELF LIFE:** Store in an airtight container in refrigerator or freezer up to six months.
**BEST FOR:** pancakes, cakes, muffins, and breads

**14. CORNSTARCH:** This is a flavorless, fine white powder that adds airiness to gluten-free baked goods. It works best when blended with other gluten-free flours.
**SHELF LIFE:** Store in an airtight container in a cool, dry place up to two years.
**BEST FOR:** pancakes, muffins, biscuits, breads, and cakes

**15. POTATO FLOUR:** This flour is made from cooked, dehydrated, milled potatoes.
**SHELF LIFE:** Store in an airtight container in refrigerator or freezer up to six months.
**BEST FOR:** breads, pancakes, waffles, and cakes

**16. POTATO STARCH:** Potato starch is a powdery flour derived from cooked potatoes that are washed to remove excess starch. It's commonly blended with heavier, whole-grain flours to add lightness to baked goods. It is not a substitute for potato flour.
**SHELF LIFE:** Store in an airtight container in a cool, dry place up to one year.
**BEST FOR:** cookies, biscuits, cakes, and breads

**17. WHITE RICE FLOUR:** This flour is derived from white rice that has been ground into a light, powdery flour. It is a gluten-free baking staple. Use it interchangeably with brown rice flour.
**SHELF LIFE:** Store in an airtight container in a cool, dry place up to one year.
**BEST FOR:** pancakes, waffles, crepes, piecrusts, biscuits, muffins, cookies, brownies, cakes, and pastries

**18. BUCKWHEAT FLOUR:** Despite its name, buckwheat flour doesn't contain any wheat. Rather, buckwheat is a grain-like fruit that's ground into flour. It has an earthy, nutty flavor.
**SHELF LIFE:** Store in an airtight container in refrigerator up to six months or in freezer up to one year.
**BEST FOR:** breakfast cereals, breads, pancakes, and waffles

**19. AMARANTH FLOUR:** This flour is made from amaranth seeds, which are ground into a dense flour.
**SHELF LIFE:** Store in an airtight container in refrigerator or freezer up to six months.
**BEST FOR:** pancakes, crepes, muffins, breads, crackers, and cookies

**20. SOY FLOUR:** This flour is made from finely ground roasted soybeans. It has a strong, nutty flavor and should be blended with other flours.
**SHELF LIFE:** Store in an airtight container in refrigerator up to six months or in freezer up to one year.
**BEST FOR:** quick breads, pancakes, muffins, and cakes

**21. SWEET RICE FLOUR:** This is a high-starch flour made from short-grain rice. Sweet rice flour is used in baked goods or as a thickening agent for gluten-free sauces. It's not interchangeable with white rice flour.
**SHELF LIFE:** Store in an airtight container in a cool, dry place up to three months or in refrigerator up to six months.
**BEST FOR:** pancakes, biscuits, cookies, and breads

**22. BEAN FLOURS:** Bean flours—made from garbanzo, fava, and navy beans—tend to be slightly bitter. Use them in small amounts blended with other gluten-free flours to minimize their flavor.
**SHELF LIFE:** Store in airtight containers in refrigerator up to six months or in freezer up to one year.
**BEST FOR:** cookies, cakes, and muffins

**23. BROWN RICE FLOUR:** This flour is a staple in gluten-free baking. It's dense, with a grainy texture and nutty flavor, and works best when blended with other gluten-free flours.
**SHELF LIFE:** Store in an airtight container in refrigerator up to six months.
**BEST FOR:** pancakes, waffles, crepes, piecrusts, biscuits, muffins, cookies, cakes, and pastries

**24. MILLET FLOUR:** This highly nutritious flour is ground from millet grains. It imparts a sweet and nutty flavor to baked goods and also gives them a crumbly texture.
**SHELF LIFE:** Store in an airtight container in refrigerator up to six months.
**BEST FOR:** breads and muffins

# HOMEMADE FLOUR BLENDS

While many recipes in this book share a variety of flour blends, I've included this primer so you can experiment with your own.

Blending successful gluten-free flour mixes is both an art and a science. In order to have a baked good that has the absolute best taste, texture, and color, you need the proper ratio of flours, sugars, fats, and liquid ingredients. Many people are looking to create their own perfect flour blend that they can go to in a pinch and that will meet all their baking needs. Unfortunately, it's just not that easy.

When baking with traditional wheat flour, the choice is pretty straightforward: Most people just grab a bag of all-purpose flour. In gluten-free baking, the right flour blend created for pancakes and biscuits won't work well when baking a hearty bread or pizza crust. The flours all have very different flavor profiles, protein levels, and starch levels, which affects their ability to give baked goods structure and tenderness.

A good method for learning to blend gluten-free flours starts with a 60/40 ratio, and then making desired adjustments as you go along. For those who prefer the taste of neutral flours and starches, such as white rice flour, tapioca flour, and potato starch, start by blending together 60 percent neutral flours and starches with 40 percent higher-protein or whole-grain flours, such as garbanzo, sorghum, almond meal, millet, and quinoa. For those desiring a denser, higher-protein, stronger-tasting baked good, begin by blending 60 percent whole-grain or higher-protein flours with 40 percent neutral flours and starches.

Gluten-free flours that are higher in protein, such as quinoa, oat, and amaranth, work best for breads that have a crispy outside and chewy inside, whereas the low-protein flours and starches are best for lighter fare, such as cookies and cupcakes. Depending upon the recipe, a combination of the high-protein, stronger-tasting flours blended with the lighter flours or starches may be in order. There are exceptions to the 60/40 and ratios, depending on the specific recipe. For example, the Brazilian Cheese Bread (page 82) and Whipped Cream Puffs (page 271) are made with all neutral flours and starches, so they're very light and airy.

Also, keep in mind that some gluten-free flours tend to add a touch of bitterness when used in excess, so choose and blend flours wisely. And most importantly, never leave out a gum ingredient such as xanthan gum or guar gum when it is specifically called for in a recipe. These gums are vital ingredients that give baked items structure and body. On the following page is a reference list to assist you in choosing and using the proper amounts of flours when creating blends or substituting flours that will work best in your kitchen.

**THE RIGHT RATIO OF INGREDIENTS IS KEY TO ENSURING THE BEST BAKED GOODS.**

# HIGHER-PROTEIN, WHOLE-GRAIN FLOURS

## USE UP TO 60% IN A FLOUR BLEND

- **BROWN RICE FLOUR:** Too much can result in a dry, crumbly product with a chalky, gritty aftertaste.

## USE UP TO 40% IN A FLOUR BLEND

- **ALMOND MEAL FLOUR:** Too much results in a heavy, dense baked good.

- **BUCKWHEAT FLOUR:** Too much can add an overpowering, robust flavor and dark color to baked goods.

- **OAT FLOUR:** Too much yields a heavy, dense baked good.

- **SORGHUM FLOUR:** Too much can cause baked goods to darken quickly in the oven and result in a slightly bitter aftertaste.

- **SWEET POTATO FLOUR:** Use no more than 40% in a flour blend for cakes, breads, or biscuits. However, more can be used in crepes and pancakes. Too much can add a rubbery texture to baked goods.

## USE UP TO 30% IN A FLOUR BLEND

- **CORN FLOUR:** Too much can cause baked items to be dry and crumbly.

- **GARBANZO BEAN FLOUR:** Too much can add a strong, bitter taste to baked goods.

- **MILLET FLOUR:** Too much can result in a bitter taste.

- **QUINOA FLOUR:** Too much can result in an overpowering, pungent taste.

- **SOY FLOUR:** Too much can add a harsh, bitter taste.

## USE UP TO 20% IN A FLOUR BLEND

- **AMARANTH FLOUR:** Too much adds a strong, bitter taste and can result in baked goods browning too quickly in the oven.

- **COCONUT FLOUR:** Excess coconut flour and not enough eggs or moisture can result in heavy, dense baked goods.

- **FLAXSEED MEAL:** Too much can result in a gummy texture and dull, nutty flavor.

## USE UP TO 15% IN A FLOUR BLEND

- **TEFF FLOUR:** Too much will result in a dry, gritty, and sour-tasting baked good.

# NEUTRAL FLOURS & STARCHES

## USE UP TO 60% IN A FLOUR BLEND

- **WHITE RICE FLOUR:** This works best when blended with high-protein flours, such as soy, sorghum, garbanzo, and oat flour. Too much can result in a dry, crumbly product with a chalky, gritty aftertaste. Brown rice flour can be used as a substitute even though it's a whole-grain flour.

## USE UP TO 30% IN A FLOUR BLEND

- **ARROWROOT STARCH:** Too much can cause baked goods to have a moist, gummy texture.

- **CORNSTARCH:** Too much can cause baked goods to have a chalky taste and gummy texture.

- **POTATO STARCH:** Too much can result in a baked good that is heavy, dense, and gummy.

- **SWEET RICE FLOUR:** Too much causes gumminess.

- **TAPIOCA FLOUR (STARCH):** Too much can result in sticky, gummy baked goods.

# EGGS & EGG WHITES

Eggs are an important part of gluten-free baking, as they replace the gluten and give a baked good necessary structure.

**1. WHOLE EGGS:** Whole eggs added to baked goods make them chewy, rich, and moist. Some recipes call for eggs to be separated—adding the egg yolks to the batter, and then whipping the egg whites and folding them in. This yields cakes that are rich and moist with a light and airy texture.

**2. EGG YOLKS:** Using egg yolks in a dough or batter is a great way to add necessary fat and richness to your baked goods without using an excess of butter or shortening. Egg yolks also add color, allowing baked goods to brown well.

**3. EGG WHITES:** When egg whites are beaten or whipped and incorporated into cakes or breads, they act as a leavener, adding air to baked items, making their texture and overall structure lighter.

# LEAVENERS & GUMS

**4. XANTHAN GUM AND GUAR GUM:** These two baking gums are extremely important in gluten-free baking and a must-have for baking without gluten or wheat flour. Xanthan gum is a corn-based product that's made by fermenting corn sugar. Guar gum is the seed of a bean from a legume plant. These two gums take the place of the gluten in baked goods, giving them moisture, texture, stickiness, and the ability to hold together.

After extensive testing, I've found that xanthan gum is the better choice because it yields a superior structure, body, crumb, and chew in baked goods. Guar gum results in a denser product, often yielding a dryer, more crumbly texture. Most gluten-free recipes call for xanthan gum, but there are exceptions, like recipes for pancakes, cobblers, and crackers that do not require a gum. When adding xanthan gum to a recipe, it's *important* to use an accurate measure of the gum. Too much xanthan gum will result in a heavy, gummy product, and too little leaves it dry and crumbly.

The chart below lists proper amounts of xanthan gum to blend with gluten-free flours when making specific baked goods.

| | |
|---|---|
| **Cookies and sweet bars** | 1/4 to 1/2 teaspoon xanthan gum per 1 cup of gluten-free flour |
| **Pancakes and waffles** | Up to 1/4 teaspoon xanthan gum per 1 cup of gluten-free flour |
| **Cakes** | 1/2 teaspoon xanthan gum per 1 cup of gluten-free flour |
| **Muffins and quick breads** | 1/2 to 3/4 teaspoon xanthan gum per 1 cup of gluten-free flour |
| **Breads and pizza crusts** | 3/4 to 1 teaspoon xanthan gum per 1 cup of gluten-free flour |

**5. BAKING POWDER:** Baking powder is a dry leavening agent made up of sodium bicarbonate and cream of tartar. Once a liquid comes in contact with baking powder, it produces a carbon dioxide gas, which begins the leavening process. Double-acting baking powder has a second leavening period when it is placed in the oven and heated. Too little baking powder will result in a dense product, whereas too much will cause a slightly bitter taste. To check the strength of baking powder, stir 1 teaspoon into 1/4 cup of warm water. If it fizzes immediately, it's effective.

**6. ACTIVE DRY YEAST:** Active dry yeast is a living organism that helps dough rise and develop structure while instilling flavor and texture. Yeast is usually mixed with warm water and sugar to activate it. When yeast is added to dough, it releases tiny carbon dioxide gas bubbles that form air pockets in the bread, making it light and airy. Don't use yeast that's past its expiration date.

**7. BAKING SODA:** Baking soda is sodium bicarbonate, which helps baked goods rise properly. It's typically used in recipes that contain acidic ingredients, such as buttermilk or vinegar. Baking soda reacts with acids to release a carbon dioxide gas, which creates air bubbles that promote rising. To test the effectiveness of baking soda, stir 1 teaspoon baking soda into 1/4 cup vinegar or lemon juice. If the soda fizzes immediately, it's effective. If the fizzing is delayed, it should not be used for baking.

# DAIRY & NON-DAIRY SUBSTITUTES

**1. HALF-AND-HALF:** This dairy product contains half cream and half milk. When substituted for milk in recipes, half-and-half gives baked goods a more tender crumb but also results in a slightly more dense and caloric product.

**2. EVAPORATED MILK:** Evaporated milk is milk that has had about 60 percent of its water removed, but no extra sugar is added as in sweetened condensed milk.

**3. SWEETENED CONDENSED MILK:** This milk has had some of its water content removed and a good dose of sugar added. Sweetened condensed milk tends to be very thick and is used in baked goods such as flan, cookies, bars, and pies. Low-fat sweetened condensed milk is also available.

**4. COCONUT MILK:** This milk is extracted from the meat of the coconut and has a subtle coconut flavor. It can be substituted cup for cup in place of regular milk.

**5. FAT-FREE HALF-AND-HALF:** Using fat-free half-and-half in baked goods is a great alternative to whole milk or regular half-and-half as long as there is another source of fat in the recipe, such as butter or shortening. If there's no fat, you'll end up with a dry, crumbly product.

**6. BUTTERMILK (REDUCED-FAT AND NONFAT BUTTERMILK):** Buttermilk is milk that has been churned until the fat is separated and removed from the cream. It has fewer calories than whole milk or cream and adds a rich, hearty flavor to baked goods while also yielding a flaky texture. The tartness of buttermilk comes from the lactic acid bacteria culture that gives it its characteristic thickness and richness.

**7. LOW-FAT MILKS:** Labeled 1% or 2%, low-fat milks have some of the cream removed. While not as full-bodied as whole milk, they are richer than fat-free milk and serve as a great alternative to baking with whole milk in order to reduce overall fat and calories.

**8. ALMOND MILK:** Made by combining finely ground almonds with water, almond milk is low in calories and fat, contains zero cholesterol and lactose, and still provides a good source of calcium. This nutty-tasting milk can be substituted cup for cup in place of regular milk in baked goods. There are a variety of flavors available, including chocolate, vanilla, and original unsweetened almond milks.

**9. FAT-FREE MILK:** In this milk, all the cream (milk fat) has been removed from the milk. Fat-free milk tends to have a more watered-down consistency when compared to low-fat or whole milks.

**10. RICE MILK:** Rice milk is usually made from brown rice that's cooked in water and strained. Low in fat and cholesterol and lactose free, rice milk can be substituted cup for cup in place of fat-free milk or low-fat milk because of its thinner consistency. It has a very mild, neutral flavor.

**11. SOY MILK:** Soy milk is made from soybeans that have been soaked in water, ground, and then strained. It's high in protein, calcium, and vitamin D. Soy milk can be substituted cup for cup in place of regular milk, but it will add a slightly nutty and bitter taste to baked goods.

**12. YOGURT:** Made when specific "good" bacteria are added to milk in a controlled environment and allowed to ferment, yogurt works as a great substitute for oil, butter, or sour cream in recipes. If a recipe calls for 1 cup butter, you can try substituting ½ cup butter and ¼ cup yogurt.

**13. DRY MILK:** This milk has been dehydrated to remove the water and can be purchased in fat-free, low-fat, or full-fat forms. It's often used in breads, cakes, and pizza crusts.

# SUGARS & SWEETENERS

**1. MOLASSES:** Molasses is a dark, sweet substance made from reducing sugar cane or sugar beet juice. It can be purchased in three flavor profiles: light, dark, and black-strap. Blackstrap molasses is known for its robust flavor, and is a good source of calcium, magnesium, potassium, and iron. Molasses is used in breads, cakes, and cookies.

**2. HONEY:** Honey is a natural sweetener made by the honeybees that collect nectar from a variety of flowers and plants. It's sweeter and tends to cook faster than sugar.

**3. CORN SYRUP:** Corn syrup is a liquid sweetener produced from the starch of maize. It does add sweetness to baked goods, but it is not as sweet as sugar. Corn syrup also lacks a characteristic flavor profile like that found in honey or molasses. It can be purchased in light or dark varieties.

**4. DARK BROWN SUGAR:** This dark, brownish sugar is made from pure cane sugar blended with double the molasses found in light brown sugar. It has a much stronger flavor than light brown sugar, but the two can be substituted for each other as desired.

**5. MAPLE SYRUP:** Maple syrup is a natural sweetener made from the sap of maple trees that has been boiled down to a thick liquid consistency. It's much different than manufactured imitation syrups that often include high fructose corn syrup and added preservatives or artificial colors. Pure maple syrup is labeled based on a grading system that accounts for the syrup's color, strength, and flavor.

**6. LIGHT BROWN SUGAR:** Brown sugar is pure cane sugar blended with molasses; it has a delicate and nutty caramel flavor. It's interchangeable with dark brown sugar in recipes.

**7. SUPERFINE SUGAR:** This sugar is similar to granulated sugar, but it's ground into smaller crystals, allowing it to dissolve more easily in baked goods. Superfine sugar is used in cakes, meringues, and frostings.

**8. TURBINADO SUGAR:** This sugar is also referred to as "sugar in the raw." It is called turbinado sugar because a turbine spins the sugar and produces the blondish-brown pale crystals that carry a hint of molasses. The crystals are larger than granulated sugar. It is most often used as a finishing sugar sprinkled on cookies, scones, and muffins just before baking.

**9. CONFECTIONERS' OR POWDERED SUGAR:** Powdered sugar is also referred to as icing sugar since it's often used in that application. Cup for cup, it is the sweetest of all sugars. It's ground 10 times finer than granulated sugar and is blended with cornstarch to prevent it from absorbing moisture. Powdered sugar is used for frostings, icings, and sprinkling on prepared baked goods.

**10. GRANULATED SUGAR:** Granulated sugar is a highly refined sugar usually made from sugar cane and occasionally derived from sugar beets. It's processed to remove the natural molasses, and then dried into crystals. It is the most popular and versatile sugar used in baked goods.

**11. FRUIT JUICES AND PUREES:** Fruit juices and purees are another way of adding natural sweetness to baked goods, often increasing the flavor profiles and texture at the same time. They can be found in countless varieties including apple, cherry, prune, raspberry, lemon, blueberry, and boysenberry.

# SHORTENING, BUTTERS & OILS

**1. VEGETABLE OIL:** Vegetable oil is any oil derived from a plant or seed that, like canola oil, has a neutral flavor. The most commonly available ones are a mixture of soybean oil blended with corn, safflower, cottonseed, or palm oil.

**2. OLIVE OIL:** Olive oil is extracted when olives are pressed or crushed. It's low in saturated fats and high in healthy mono- and polyunsaturated fats. Olive oil has an assertive olive flavor that can be tasted in the final product. It works best in recipes that benefit from that extra punch of flavor, such as focaccia bread, pizza crusts, and calzones.

**3. CANOLA OIL:** Canola oil has a mellow, adaptable flavor that makes it ideal for a wide range of uses, such as cakes, muffins, quick breads, and piecrusts. It also has the lowest amount of saturated fat of any cooking oil.

**4. COCONUT OIL:** Coconut oil is the natural edible oil extracted from the meat of fresh coconuts.

**5. NON-DAIRY BUTTERY SPREAD (EARTH BALANCE):** This is a non-dairy spread made from palm fruit, soybean, canola, flaxseed, and olive oils that has zero trans fat. Substitute 1 cup non-dairy buttery spread for 1 cup butter in recipes.

**6. VEGETABLE SHORTENING:** While shortening doesn't contribute any flavor to baked goods, its advantage over butter is that it won't separate into oil and milk solids, which creates baked goods that have a softer, lighter, and flakier texture. One disadvantage: Traditional vegetable shortenings use a hydrogenation process that adds unhealthy trans fat. The good news: There are shortenings available, such as Earth Balance, that contain no trans fats. They're made from blends of palm fruit, canola, soybean, flaxseed, and olive oils. You can substitute ½ cup Earth Balance shortening plus 1 tablespoon liquid for every ½ cup shortening in baked goods.

**7. SALTED BUTTER:** Salt is added to butter to enhance its flavor and act as a natural preservative to increase its shelf life. To substitute salted butter for unsalted butter in a recipe, reduce the salt in the recipe by ¼ teaspoon salt per ½ cup butter.

**8. UNSALTED BUTTER:** Made from the churned fat of cow's milk, unsalted butter is about 80 percent fat and 20 percent milk solids plus water. It contains no salt and less water than salted butter and is the butter of choice for most bakers and pastry chefs.

# NUTS & SEEDS

**1. POPPY SEEDS:** These tiny, blackish-blue seeds have a nutty aroma and flavor and add texture to cookies, muffins, breads, and cakes. Store them in an airtight container in the refrigerator up to three months or in the freezer up to six months.

**2. PUMPKINSEED KERNELS:** Pumpkinseed kernels can be purchased shelled or unshelled, raw or roasted, salted or unsalted. Add them to breads, muffins, and granola bars. Store them in an airtight container in the refrigerator up to three months.

**3. CASHEWS:** Cashews have a unique flavor. They blend nicely in the food processor to make a creamy paste, which can be used in numerous baked goods, soups, and sauces. Store in an airtight container in the refrigerator up to six months.

**4. HAZELNUTS:** These nuts are a great addition to cakes, quick breads, muffins, or cookies. Store them in an airtight container in the freezer up to one year.

**5. MACADAMIA NUTS:** These nuts can be purchased raw or roasted and are wonderful additions to muffins and cookies. Store them in an airtight container in the refrigerator for up to six months or in the freezer for up to one year.

**6. WALNUTS:** High in omega-3 fatty acids, walnuts are purchased raw or roasted, and have a rich flavor that complements any baked good. Store them in an airtight container in the refrigerator up to three months or in the freezer up to one year.

**7. FLAXSEEDS:** Called the "tiny, but mighty seed" because they are so high in omega-3 fatty acids, flaxseeds add a mildly nutty flavor to breads, muffins, cookies, and cakes. Store them in an airtight container in the refrigerator up to one year.

**8. PECANS:** With their buttery, rich flavor, pecans are ideal additions to pies, cakes, muffins, crisps, and pastries. Pecans can be stored in the refrigerator up to six months.

**9. ALMONDS:** Almonds can be purchased raw or roasted, salted or unsalted. If you're allergic to peanuts or peanut butter and not to tree nuts, try substituting almonds or almond butter in recipes. Store them in the freezer up to one year.

**10. PINE NUTS:** These are the sweet, crunchy seeds from pine trees and often are added to cookies, breads, and pastries. Store them in the refrigerator up to six months.

**11. SESAME SEEDS:** These small white seeds add a nutty crunch to breads and cookies. Store them in an airtight container up to three months, in the refrigerator up to six months, and in the freezer up to one year.

**12. PISTACHIOS:** Pistachios are sweet-flavored nuts that are often added to muffins, cookies, breads, or pastries or used as a garnish for a variety of baked goods. Unshelled pistachios can be stored in an airtight container in a cool, dry place up to three months. Shelled pistachios should be stored in the refrigerator up to six months.

**13. CHIA SEEDS:** These tiny black and white seeds impart a mild, nutty flavor that can be incorporated into breads, muffins, and puddings. Chia seeds are an unprocessed, whole-grain seed that can be absorbed by the body when they're whole (unlike flaxseeds, which must be ground). They make a great substitute for flaxseeds or poppy seeds. Store them in an airtight container in a cool, dry place up to one year.

**14. PEANUTS:** Peanuts are from the legume or bean family, which is why a person can be allergic to peanuts but not tree nuts and vice versa. They can be purchased raw, roasted, boiled, salted, or unsalted. Shelled peanuts can be stored in an airtight container in a cool, dry place up to three months or in the refrigerator up to six months.

**15. SUNFLOWER SEEDS:** Sunflower seeds are sold shelled or unshelled, raw or roasted, salted or unsalted. Add them to breads, muffins, and granola bars. Store sunflower seeds in an airtight container in the refrigerator up to three months or in the freezer up to six months.

# MEASURING DRY AND WET INGREDIENTS

I was in culinary school when I first learned that cooking and baking were two very different activities. When chefs cook, they tend to taste and adjust the ingredients and seasonings as they create and prepare a dish. However, with baking, there is an exact science involved. When the ingredients in baked items interact with each other, there are chemical reactions taking place causing them to rise, spread, or brown properly. If the right proportions aren't used, those reactions can go awry, and the cake or bread you're making may not taste or look right. That's why in baking, accurately measuring ingredients and using them in the right proportions are absolutely critical to creating a tasty finished product.

Over the years, I have found that weighing dry ingredients is much more accurate than using volume measurements with measuring cups, so I strongly suggest that you purchase a good scale. If a scale is not available, try using the guidelines below for the most accurate volume measurements.

**ACCURATELY MEASURING INGREDIENTS IS CRITICAL.**

**DRY INGREDIENTS:** When measuring flours, starches, and seeds, it is important to stir the ingredient with a spoon to aerate it before placing it into a measuring cup. When spooning the flour into the cup, don't press down or compact it into the cup. Rather, allow the flour to gradually fill the cup until it reaches just over the top of the rim. Then, using the flat edge of a knife or spatula, level the flour off evenly with the edge of the measuring cup. Don't use a measuring cup to directly scoop flour out of a bag or canister—you'll end up with much more than actually needed and the extra flour will be evident in dry baked goods. This same procedure can be followed for sugars, baking powder, baking soda, and xanthan gum.

When brown sugar is listed in a recipe, it is sometimes specifically called for as "packed." This requires applying pressure to the brown sugar in the measuring cup until it is level with the top. Brown sugar should actually retain the shape of the measuring cup when released into the mixing bowl.

**SEMI-LIQUID INGREDIENTS:** Ingredients such as sour cream, yogurt, shortenings, nut butters, butter, or non-dairy butter alternatives should be measured in dry measuring cups. Spoon the ingredients into a measuring cup, and then, using the back of a spoon or spatula, press down to remove any air pockets. Then, using a knife or spatula, level it off evenly. Some butters and shortenings are packaged in stick form with handy measurements on the side of the package, which makes measuring easy.

**LIQUID INGREDIENTS:** When measuring liquid ingredients, such as water, oil, and juices, it's important to use a liquid measuring cup to prevent messy overflow and spills. Place the cup on a flat, level surface, and then, while viewing at eye level, slowly pour the liquid ingredients into the cup until it reaches the desired measurement mark. Don't try holding the cup in your hand and bringing it to your eyes to read, which will likely result in an inaccurate measurement.

Measuring small amounts of liquid ingredients, such as vanilla extract, honey, or syrup, should be done with measuring spoons. Hold the measuring spoon over a clean, empty bowl or mug, and pour the liquid into a spoon until it reaches the top of the spoon. To prevent liquid ingredients from spilling into the mixture, never measure over the mixing bowl.

# SUBSTITUTIONS

For those of you who are avoiding other allergens or are looking for alternative ingredients to use as substitutions, try some of the suggestions below:

## BUTTER:

**1 tablespoon butter =**
- 1 tablespoon olive oil
- 1 tablespoon canola or vegetable oil
- 1 tablespoon Earth Balance non-dairy buttery spread

**1 cup butter =**
- ½ cup butter and ⅓ cup canola oil
- ¾ cup canola oil
- ¾ cup coconut oil
- ¾ cup vegetable oil

## YOGURT:

**1 cup yogurt =**
- 1 cup coconut or soy yogurt
- 1 cup applesauce
- 1 cup sour cream
- 1 cup buttermilk

## BUTTERMILK:

**1 cup buttermilk =**
- 1 cup yogurt
- 1 cup milk plus 1 tablespoon lemon juice or white vinegar
- 1 cup soy or coconut milk with 1 tablespoon lemon juice or white vinegar

## MILK:

**1 cup milk =**
- 1 cup almond milk
- 1 cup soy milk
- 1 cup rice milk
- ⅔ cup evaporated milk plus ⅓ cup water
- 1 cup coconut milk

## SHORTENING:

**1 cup shortening =**
- 1 cup butter
- 1 cup Earth Balance shortening

## SUGAR:

**1 cup sugar =**
- ¾ cup honey (reduce other liquids in recipe by 2 tablespoons)
- ¾ cup maple syrup (reduce other liquids in recipe by 3 tablespoons)
- ⅔ cup agave nectar (reduce other liquids in recipe by 2 tablespoons)
- 1⅓ cups molasses plus ½ teaspoon baking soda (reduce other liquids in recipe by 5 tablespoons)

## EGG:

**1 egg =**
- 1 tablespoon ground flaxseeds plus 3 tablespoons liquid (allow to rest 15 minutes before use)
- 1 tablespoon ground chia seeds plus 3 tablespoons liquid (allow to rest 15 minutes before use)
- 1 banana, pureed, plus 1 teaspoon baking powder
- 3 tablespoons applesauce plus 1 teaspoon baking powder

## XANTHAN GUM:

**1 teaspoon xanthan gum =**
- 1¼ teaspoons guar gum

chapter 2

# PANCAKES, WAFFLES, CREPES, AND QUICHE

**W**henever I make pancakes, I think of Eric Carle's book, *Pancakes, Pancakes!* It's the story of a young boy who wakes up in simpler times, wanting a giant pancake for breakfast. His mother uses the request to teach life lessons about hard work and not taking things for granted. The boy has to thresh his own grain, bring it to a miller, milk a cow, gather eggs from the hens, and churn his own butter before the griddle is even hot. His mother tops his pancake with pure strawberry jam—and it's probably the best pancake he's ever tried.

You certainly won't have to go to those lengths to create the pancakes, waffles, crepes, or quiche found in this chapter. All the heavy lifting has already been done for you. You'll find recipes that result in a range of spectacular breakfasts.

# FLAXSEED BUTTERMILK PANCAKES

Hands-on time: 16 min. Total time: 16 min.

*These pancakes are the perfect disguise for a breakfast with some nutritional heft thanks to the flaxseed meal, which also adds a nutty flavor. The tapioca flour and potato starch keep the texture light while the brown rice flour adds some whole grains and fiber.*

3.06 ounces brown rice flour (about ²/₃ cup)
1.05 ounces tapioca flour (about ¼ cup)
1.3 ounces potato starch (about ¼ cup)
0.9 ounce flaxseed meal (about ¼ cup)
2 teaspoons sugar
2 teaspoons baking powder
1 teaspoon baking soda
⅛ teaspoon salt
1 cup low-fat buttermilk
1 teaspoon vanilla extract
2 large eggs
¾ cup maple syrup
¾ cup fresh blueberries

1. Weigh or lightly spoon flours, potato starch, and flaxseed meal into dry measuring cups; level with a knife. Combine flours, potato starch, flaxseed meal, sugar, baking powder, baking soda, and salt in a large bowl, stirring with a whisk. Combine buttermilk, vanilla, and eggs; stir with a whisk. Add to flour mixture, stirring until smooth.

2. Heat a nonstick griddle or large nonstick skillet over medium heat. Pour 2 tablespoons batter per pancake onto pan; cook 1 minute or until tops are covered with bubbles and edges look cooked. Carefully turn pancakes over; cook 1 minute or until bottoms are lightly browned. Serve with maple syrup and blueberries. Serves 6 (serving size: 3 pancakes, 2 tablespoons syrup, and 2 tablespoons blueberries)

CALORIES 164; FAT 4.2g (sat 0.9g, mono 1.1g, poly 1.7g); PROTEIN 5.6g; CARB 26g; FIBER 1.9g; CHOL 65mg; IRON 0.6mg; SODIUM 476mg; CALC 163mg

## a mighty little seed

Flaxseeds may be tiny, but they are fiercely nutritious. While they contain a variety of healthy components, they get their stellar reputation from three in particular. They contain omega-3s, which have benefits for your heart; fiber, both soluble (good for your cholesterol) and insoluble (good for your digestive system); and lignans, which have antioxidant properties linked to lower rates of cancer. In fact, you'd have to eat about 35 cups of broccoli to get the same amount of lignans found in just 2 tablespoons of flaxseed meal.

# BLUEBERRY PANCAKES

Hands-on time: 14 min. Total time: 14 min.

*Flapjacks, griddlecakes, pancakes—call them what you will—they're an American favorite, and with good reason. The settlers on the American frontier made their breakfast cakes with handy ingredients, gathering fresh blueberries from the wild bushes and adding them to their thick cake batter. I added almond meal flour to boost the protein, and it tastes wonderful with the blueberries. Don't forget to serve them on January 28, National Blueberry Pancake Day.*

2.6 ounces potato starch (about ½ cup)
2.3 ounces brown rice flour (about ½ cup)
1.8 ounces almond meal flour (about ½ cup)
1 tablespoon sugar
2 teaspoons baking powder
½ teaspoon baking soda
¼ teaspoon salt
1 cup low-fat buttermilk
¼ cup water
2 tablespoons butter, melted
1 tablespoon canola oil
1 teaspoon vanilla extract
2 large eggs
¾ cup fresh blueberries

1. Weigh or lightly spoon potato starch and flours into dry measuring cups; level with a knife. Combine potato starch, flours, sugar, baking powder, baking soda, and salt in a medium bowl; stir with a whisk. Combine buttermilk and next 5 ingredients (through eggs) in a medium bowl; stir with a whisk. Add to flour mixture, stirring until smooth. Fold in blueberries.

2. Heat a nonstick griddle or large nonstick skillet over medium heat. Pour ¼ cup batter per pancake onto pan; cook 1 to 2 minutes or until tops are covered with bubbles and edges look cooked. Carefully turn pancakes over; cook 1 to 2 minutes or until bottoms are lightly browned. Serves 8 (serving size: 2 pancakes)

CALORIES 187; FAT 9.6g (sat 2.8g, mono 2.4g, poly 0.9g); PROTEIN 4.8g; CARB 21g; FIBER 1.4g; CHOL 56mg; IRON 0.7mg; SODIUM 342mg; CALC 137mg

## the best blue

t
i
p

Blueberries have a striking deep-blue color that means they're packed with antioxidants. Look for plump berries with a white bloom on them—the white dusty coating. If there's no bloom, it means they're probably past their prime. Wash the berries just before you use them.

# OATMEAL-CRANBERRY PANCAKES

Hands-on time: 20 min. Total time: 20 min.

*I have always been intrigued with the cuisine of local diners. When I was visiting Colorado, I found a hole-in-the-wall breakfast joint that had a menu with an amazing variety of pancakes. This granola-like oatmeal-cranberry pancake was a favorite of the local ski bums. This is my gluten-free version of that diner favorite.*

2.3 ounces brown rice flour (about ½ cup)
1.05 ounces tapioca flour (about ¼ cup)
1.3 ounces potato starch (about ¼ cup)
0.9 ounce flaxseed meal (about ¼ cup)
⅔ cup certified gluten-free quick-cooking oats
1 tablespoon granulated sugar
1 teaspoon baking powder
½ teaspoon baking soda
¼ teaspoon ground cinnamon
⅛ teaspoon salt
1 cup low-fat buttermilk
½ teaspoon vanilla extract
2 large eggs
⅓ cup sweetened dried cranberries
5 teaspoons powdered sugar

1. Weigh or lightly spoon flours, potato starch, and flaxseed meal into dry measuring cups; level with a knife. Combine flours, potato starch, flaxseed meal, oats, and next 5 ingredients (through salt) in a medium bowl; stir with a whisk. Combine buttermilk, vanilla, and eggs in a medium bowl; stir with a whisk until blended. Add to flour mixture, stirring until smooth. Fold in cranberries.

2. Heat a nonstick griddle or large nonstick skillet over medium heat. Pour 2 tablespoons batter per pancake onto pan; cook 2 to 3 minutes or until tops are covered with bubbles and edges look cooked. Carefully turn pancakes over; cook 2 to 3 minutes or until bottoms are lightly browned. Sprinkle with powdered sugar. Serves 5 (serving size: 3 pancakes and 1 teaspoon powdered sugar)

CALORIES 250; FAT 5.6g (sat 1.1g, mono 1.5g, poly 2.2g); PROTEIN 8.2g; CARB 43g; FIBER 3.6g; CHOL 77mg; IRON 1.2mg; SODIUM 357mg; CALC 130mg

# TOASTED COCONUT-STRAWBERRY PANCAKES

*This strange but delightful variation of an otherwise simple pancake is partially my fault. One morning, when my sons were yelling for pancakes, I challenged them to walk around the kitchen and pick whatever they wanted to put into their special pancakes. Thinking I would get the usual chocolate chips or blueberries and whipped cream, I was surprised by what I saw. Turns out that the toasted coconut adds a nutty, caramel flavor to these happily strawberry-dotted pancakes.*

2 cups sliced strawberries
1/4 cup sugar, divided
3.06 ounces brown rice flour (about 2/3 cup)
1.05 ounces tapioca flour (about 1/4 cup)
0.95 ounce coconut flour (about 1/4 cup)
1.3 ounces potato starch (about 1/4 cup)
1 tablespoon baking powder
1/2 teaspoon salt
1 1/4 cups light coconut milk
1/4 teaspoon vanilla extract
2 large eggs
1/3 cup diced strawberries
8 teaspoons flaked unsweetened coconut, toasted

1. Combine sliced strawberries and 3 tablespoons sugar in a small bowl; stir well. Let stand 15 minutes.

2. While strawberries stand, weigh or lightly spoon flours and potato starch into dry measuring cups; level with a knife. Combine flours, potato starch, 1 tablespoon sugar, baking powder, and salt in a medium bowl; stir with a whisk. Combine coconut milk, vanilla, and eggs; stir with a whisk. Add to flour mixture, stirring with a whisk until smooth. Fold in diced strawberries.

3. Heat a nonstick griddle or large nonstick skillet over medium heat. Pour 2½ tablespoons batter per pancake onto pan; cook 1 to 2 minutes or until tops are covered with bubbles and edges look cooked. Carefully turn pancakes over; cook 1 to 2 minutes or until bottoms are lightly browned. Spoon sliced strawberry mixture over pancakes, and sprinkle with toasted coconut. Serves 8 (serving size: 2 pancakes, about ¼ cup sliced strawberry mixture, and 1 teaspoon coconut)

---

CALORIES 172; FAT 5.1g (sat 3.7g, mono 0.9g, poly 0.5g); PROTEIN 4g; CARB 30g; FIBER 3.2g; CHOL 47mg; IRON 2.3mg; SODIUM 344mg; CALC 140mg

## lactose-free swap

Light coconut milk is a creamy alternative to dairy that is rich in medium-chain fatty acids, which have been shown to help lower the risk of heart disease.

# PUMPKIN-ALMOND PANCAKES

Hands-on time: 15 min. Total time: 15 min.

*On October 31, in our house, we celebrate All Hallow's Eve. After the kids dress up as their favorite saints and before we go out to meet our friends, we have this favorite breakfast for dinner, topped with butter and drenched in maple syrup. Whole-grain corn flour gives these pancakes a cakier texture and adds some fiber, too.*

2.1 ounces tapioca flour (about 1/2 cup)
1.3 ounces white rice flour (about 1/4 cup)
1 ounce stone-ground whole-grain corn flour
    (about 1/4 cup)
2 tablespoons brown sugar
1 teaspoon baking powder
1/2 teaspoon ground ginger

1/4 teaspoon ground cinnamon
1/4 teaspoon ground allspice
1/2 cup canned pumpkin
1/4 cup vanilla almond milk
1 tablespoon canola oil
1 teaspoon vanilla extract
2 large eggs
1/2 cup maple syrup

1. Weigh or lightly spoon flours into dry measuring cups; level with a knife. Combine flours, brown sugar, and next 4 ingredients (through allspice) in a medium bowl; stir with a whisk. Combine pumpkin, almond milk, oil, vanilla, and eggs; stir with a whisk. Add to flour mixture, stirring until smooth.

2. Heat a nonstick griddle or large nonstick skillet over medium heat. Pour 2 tablespoons batter per pancake onto pan; cook 1 to 2 minutes or until tops are covered with bubbles and edges look cooked. Carefully turn pancakes over; cook 1 to 2 minutes or until bottoms are lightly browned. Serve with maple syrup. Serves 4 (serving size: 4 pancakes and 2 tablespoons syrup)

CALORIES 324; FAT 6.6g (sat 1.3g, mono 2g, poly 2.6g); PROTEIN 5g; CARB 63.3g; FIBER 2.1g; CHOL 93mg; IRON 1.6mg; SODIUM 176mg; CALC 175mg

# CINNAMON-RAISIN FRENCH TOAST

Hands-on time: 26 min. Total time: 26 min.

*The Gala apples blended with the Calvados brandy in the topping give this dish a deep, sweet flavor. You can substitute apple cider or apple juice for the Calvados, if you like.*

**Topping:**
4 cups chopped peeled Gala apple (about 2 pounds)
1½ teaspoons cornstarch
1½ cups water
¼ cup packed brown sugar
3 tablespoons Calvados (apple brandy)
½ teaspoon vanilla extract
½ teaspoon ground cinnamon
¼ teaspoon ground nutmeg
¼ teaspoon salt
¼ cup maple syrup

**French Toast:**
1 cup 1% low-fat milk
1 tablespoon granulated sugar
¼ teaspoon salt
¼ teaspoon ground cinnamon
3 large eggs
1 tablespoon butter
12 slices Cinnamon Raisin Bread (pg. 231)

1. Preheat oven to 250°.

2. To prepare topping, combine apple and cornstarch in a medium bowl, tossing to combine.

3. Place 1½ cups water and next 6 ingredients (through salt) in a medium saucepan over medium heat. Bring to a simmer; cook 5 minutes. Add apple; cook 10 minutes or until apple begins to soften and release juices. Stir in maple syrup; remove from heat.

4. To prepare French toast, combine milk and next 4 ingredients (through eggs) in a medium bowl, stirring with a whisk.

5. Melt 1 teaspoon butter on a nonstick griddle or large nonstick skillet over medium-high heat. Dip 4 bread slices into milk mixture, turning to coat both sides and allowing excess milk mixture to drip off. Place bread on pan, and cook 2 to 3 minutes or until bottom of bread is lightly browned. Turn bread over, and cook 2 minutes until lightly browned. Place French toast on a baking sheet; place in oven to keep warm. Repeat procedure with remaining butter and bread slices. Serve apple mixture over French toast. Serves 6 (serving size: 2 slices French toast and ⅔ cup topping)

CALORIES 223; FAT 10g (sat 4.3g, mono 3.8g, poly 1.3g); PROTEIN 2.8g; CARB 32g; FIBER 1.1g; CHOL 39mg; IRON 0.5mg; SODIUM 248mg; CALC 73mg

# BUCKWHEAT BELGIAN WAFFLES

Hands-on time: 24 min. Total time: 24 min.

*The buckwheat flour adds an earthy, nutty flavor to these waffles, but it's also a flour that's heavy and dense. Here, it's blended with lighter tapioca flour and white rice flour to balance it. Beating the egg whites and folding them into the batter is also key to keeping the texture light. Top the waffles with slightly warm maple syrup and fresh fruit. They're so dreamy you could serve them for breakfast or dessert.*

2.2 ounces buckwheat flour (about ½ cup)
2.1 ounces tapioca flour (about ½ cup)
1.3 ounces white rice flour (about ¼ cup)
2 tablespoons flaxseed meal
2 tablespoons brown sugar
1 teaspoon baking soda
½ teaspoon baking powder
½ teaspoon xanthan gum
½ teaspoon ground cinnamon
¼ teaspoon salt
1 cup low-fat buttermilk
3 tablespoons unsalted butter, melted
1 teaspoon vanilla extract
3 large egg yolks
3 large egg whites
Cooking spray
½ cup maple syrup

1. Weigh or lightly spoon flours into dry measuring cups; level with a knife. Combine flours, flaxseed meal, and next 6 ingredients (through salt) in a large bowl; stir with a whisk. Combine buttermilk, melted butter, vanilla, and egg yolks; stir with a whisk. Add to flour mixture, stirring until smooth.

2. Beat egg whites with a mixer at high speed until soft peaks form. Fold egg whites into batter.

3. Coat a Belgian waffle iron with cooking spray; preheat. Spoon about ⅓ cup batter per 4-inch waffle onto hot waffle iron, spreading batter to edges. Cook 3 to 4 minutes or until steaming stops; repeat procedure with remaining batter. Serve with maple syrup. Serves 8 (serving size: 1 waffle and 1 table-spoon syrup)

CALORIES 225; FAT 7.7g (sat 3.6g, mono 2.2g, poly 1.1g); PROTEIN 5.2g; CARB 35.1g; FIBER 1.6g; CHOL 83mg; IRON 0.8mg; SODIUM 322mg; CALC 87mg

# STRAWBERRY-BANANA CREPES

Hands-on time: 41 min. Total time: 41 min.

*My stepmother, Mimie, was born and raised in France. She is a master crepe maker and a genius at mixing ingredients and flavor profiles that always seem to work. These crepes often landed on our plates on Sunday mornings. You can substitute orange juice for the Grand Marnier.*

2.6 ounces white rice flour (about ½ cup)
1.05 ounces tapioca flour (about ¼ cup)
1.15 ounces cornstarch (about ¼ cup)
1 tablespoon sugar, divided
¼ teaspoon salt
1½ cups 1% low-fat milk
3 tablespoons butter, melted
1 teaspoon vanilla extract
3 large eggs
Cooking spray
2 cups thinly sliced strawberries
1 large banana, thinly sliced (about 1 cup)
1 tablespoon Grand Marnier (orange-flavored liqueur)
9 tablespoons vanilla fat-free Greek yogurt

1. Weigh or lightly spoon flours and cornstarch into dry measuring cups; level with a knife. Combine flours, cornstarch, 2 teaspoons sugar, and salt in a medium bowl; stir with a whisk. Place milk, melted butter, vanilla, and eggs in a blender; process 15 seconds. Add flour mixture; process 1 minute or until smooth.

2. Heat a 10-inch crepe pan or nonstick skillet over medium heat. Coat pan with cooking spray. Remove pan from heat. Pour a heaping 2 tablespoons batter into pan; quickly tilt pan in all directions so batter covers pan with a thin film. Cook 45 to 50 seconds.

3. Carefully lift edge of crepe with a spatula to test for doneness. Turn crepe over when it can be shaken loose from the pan and the underside is lightly browned; cook 25 to 30 seconds.

4. Place crepe on a towel; cool. Repeat procedure with remaining batter, stirring batter before making each crepe. Stack crepes between single layers of wax paper or paper towels to prevent sticking.

5. Combine strawberries, banana, Grand Marnier, and 1 teaspoon sugar in a medium bowl; toss gently to coat.

6. Fold each crepe in half, then in half again to form a triangle. Spoon fruit mixture over crepes; top with a dollop of yogurt. Serves 9 (serving size: 2 crepes, ⅓ cup fruit mixture, and 1 tablespoon yogurt)

CALORIES 176; FAT 6.1g (sat 3.3g, mono 1.8g, poly 0.6g); PROTEIN 5.5g; CARB 25g; FIBER 1.4g; CHOL 75mg; IRON 0.6mg; SODIUM 146mg; CALC 81mg

## the best batter

I prefer using a blender or food processor over hand mixing. This ensures that your crepe batter will be silky smooth with no lumps.

# SWEET POTATO CREPES
## WITH CARAMELIZED PEACHES AND PECANS

Hands-on time: 37 min. Total time: 37 min.

*Some crepes are cooked once, and then filled with sweet or savory fillings. In this recipe, the crepes are filled with a sweetened cream cheese mixture, cooked a second time until the cheese warms and the crepes are golden brown on the edges, and then topped with caramelized peaches and toasted pecans. Use fresh peaches when they're in season.*

2.6 ounces white rice flour (about ½ cup)
1.4 ounces sweet potato flour (about ¼ cup)
1.05 ounces tapioca flour (about ¼ cup)
1 teaspoon granulated sugar
¼ teaspoon salt
¾ cup fat-free milk
½ cup water
2 large eggs
Cooking spray
6 ounces ⅓-less-fat cream cheese (about ¾ cup)
¼ cup packed brown sugar, divided
¾ teaspoon ground cinnamon, divided
⅛ teaspoon nutmeg
1 tablespoon butter
1 (16-ounce) package frozen sliced peaches, thawed
⅓ cup chopped pecans, toasted

1. Weigh or lightly spoon flours into dry measuring cups; level with a knife. Combine flours, granulated sugar, and salt in a medium bowl; stir with a whisk. Place milk, ½ cup water, and eggs in a blender; process 20 seconds. Add flour mixture; process 30 seconds or until smooth.

2. Heat a 9-inch crepe pan or nonstick skillet over medium heat. Coat pan with cooking spray. Remove pan from heat. Pour a scant ¼ cup batter into pan; quickly tilt pan in all directions so batter covers pan with a thin film. Cook about 1 minute.

3. Carefully lift edge of crepe with a spatula to test for doneness. Turn crepe over when it can be shaken loose from the pan and the underside is lightly browned; cook 30 seconds.

4. Place crepe on a towel; cool. Repeat procedure with remaining batter. Stack crepes between single layers of wax paper or paper towels to prevent sticking.

5. Place cream cheese, 2 tablespoon brown sugar, ½ teaspoon cinnamon, and nutmeg in a medium bowl; beat with a mixer at medium speed until smooth and creamy.

6. Working with 1 crepe at a time, spread about 2½ teaspoons cream cheese mixture on half of crepe; fold crepe in half to cover filling. Fold in half again to form a triangle; place on a platter (cover to keep from drying). Repeat procedure with remaining crepes and cream cheese mixture.

7. Melt butter in large skillet over medium heat. Add 2 tablespoons brown sugar, ¼ teaspoon cinnamon, and peaches; cook 5 minutes or until peaches are tender.

8. Heat a medium skillet over medium heat; coat pan with cooking spray. Add half of crepes; cook 1 to 2 minutes or until lightly browned on edges. Carefully turn crepes over, and cook 1 minute. Spoon peach mixture over crepes; sprinkle with toasted pecans. Serves 9 (serving size: 1 crepe, about ¼ cup peach mixture, and about 1½ teaspoons pecans)

---

CALORIES 213; FAT 9.9g (sat 3.9g, mono 3.7g, poly 1.4g); PROTEIN 5.2g; CARB 27g; FIBER 1.4g; CHOL 59mg; IRON 0.7mg; SODIUM 166mg; CALC 67mg

Crepes can be made ahead, placed between sheets of wax paper, sealed in a zip-top plastic freezer bag, and frozen for up to two months.

# SPINACH, BACON, AND CHEESE QUICHE

Hands-on time: 20 min. Total time: 1 hr. 30 min.

*Taste testing by family and friends is an integral part of the cookbook-writing process. When I served this quiche with its buttery crust, fluffy egg center with smoky and salty bacon, and blend of two cheeses, I thought I had a hit. When my brother-in-law, Kevin, went back for thirds and asked for more, I knew I was right.*

**Crust:**
1.5 ounces brown rice flour (about 1/3 cup)
1.4 ounces sweet white sorghum flour (about 1/3 cup)
1.4 ounces tapioca flour (about 1/3 cup)
1.3 ounces potato starch (about 1/4 cup)
1/4 teaspoon xanthan gum
1/4 teaspoon salt
3 tablespoons unsalted butter
1 tablespoon fat-free milk
1 large egg
Cooking spray

**Filling:**
9 center-cut bacon slices (4 ounces)
2 1/2 cups bagged baby spinach leaves (3 ounces)
2 ounces reduced-fat cheddar cheese, shredded (about 1 1/2 cups)
2 ounces Swiss cheese, shredded (about 1 1/2 cups)
1 1/4 cups fat-free milk
1/4 teaspoon freshly ground black pepper
1/8 teaspoon salt
5 large eggs
2 large egg whites

1. Preheat oven to 350°.

2. To prepare crust, weigh or lightly spoon flours and potato starch into dry measuring cups; level with a knife. Place flours, potato starch, xanthan gum, and salt in a food processor; pulse 2 times or until blended. Add butter; process 30 seconds or until mixture resembles coarse meal. With processor on, slowly add milk and egg through food chute; process until dough forms a ball.

3. Press mixture gently into a 4-inch circle on plastic wrap; cover. Chill 30 minutes. Slightly overlap 2 sheets of plastic wrap on work surface. Unwrap and place chilled dough on plastic wrap. Cover dough with 2 additional sheets of overlapping plastic wrap. Roll dough, still covered, into a 12-inch circle. Remove top sheets of plastic wrap; fit dough, plastic wrap side up, into a 9-inch pie plate coated with cooking spray. Remove remaining plastic wrap. Fold edges under; flute. Pierce bottom and sides of dough with a fork. Bake at 350° for 10 minutes. Cool on a wire rack.

4. To prepare filling, cook bacon in a large nonstick skillet over medium heat 8 minutes or until crisp. Remove bacon from pan; crumble. Add spinach to drippings in pan; sauté 1 minute or until spinach wilts.

5. Layer spinach, bacon, and cheeses in crust. Combine milk, pepper, salt, eggs, and egg whites in a medium bowl; stir well with a whisk. Pour over layered ingredients in crust.

6. Bake at 350° for 35 minutes or until crust is golden brown and eggs are set. Let stand 5 minutes before slicing. Serves 8 (serving size: 1 slice)

CALORIES 231; FAT 12.4g (sat 6.1g, mono 2.5g, poly 0.8g); PROTEIN 14g; CARB 16g; FIBER 0.9g; CHOL 142mg; IRON 1.1mg; SODIUM 451mg; CALC 148mg

# LEEK AND SMOKED GRUYÈRE MINI QUICHES

Hands-on time: 34 min. Total time: 61 min.

**Crust:**
1.5 ounces brown rice flour (about ⅓ cup)
1.4 ounces sweet white sorghum flour (about ⅓ cup)
1.4 ounces tapioca flour (about ⅓ cup)
1.3 ounces potato starch (about ¼ cup)
¼ teaspoon xanthan gum
¼ teaspoon salt
3 tablespoons unsalted butter
1 tablespoon 1% low-fat milk
1 large egg
Brown rice flour, for dusting
Cooking spray

**Filling:**
1 small leek
1 teaspoon thyme leaves
½ cup 1% low-fat milk
½ teaspoon Dijon mustard
¼ teaspoon salt
⅛ teaspoon freshly ground black pepper
2 large eggs
2 ounces applewood smoked Gruyère cheese,
  shredded (about ½ cup)
Freshly ground black pepper (optional)

1. Preheat oven to 350°.

2. To prepare crust, weigh or lightly spoon flours and potato starch into dry measuring cups; level with a knife. Place flours, potato starch, xanthan gum, and salt in a food processor; pulse 2 times or until blended. Add butter; process 30 seconds or until mixture resembles coarse meal. With processor on, slowly add milk and egg through food chute; process until dough forms a ball.

3. Divide dough into 24 equal portions, shaping each into a ball. Working with 1 portion at a time (cover remaining dough to prevent drying), roll each portion into a 2½-inch circle on a lightly floured surface, using brown rice flour. Gently press dough circles into miniature muffin cups coated with cooking spray. Bake at 350° for 7 minutes or until very lightly browned. Remove from oven; cool on a wire rack.

4. To prepare filling, remove roots, outer leaves, and tops from leek, leaving 2 inches of dark leaves. Cut leek in half lengthwise; rinse with cold water. Cut each half crosswise into ¼-inch-thick slices to measure ½ cup.

5. Heat a medium skillet over medium heat. Coat pan with cooking spray. Add leek and thyme; sauté 8 minutes or until tender and lightly browned. Cool.

6. Combine milk and next 4 ingredients (through eggs) in a medium bowl; stir with a whisk. Divide leek mixture and cheese among crusts; spoon egg mixture into crusts, covering leeks and cheese. Sprinkle with freshly ground black pepper, if desired.

7. Place muffin pans on a baking sheet. Bake at 350° for 20 minutes or until egg is set and crusts are lightly browned on edges. Cool 5 minutes in pan on a wire rack; remove from pan. Serve warm. Serves 24 (serving size: 1 quiche)

CALORIES 59; FAT 3g (sat 1.7g, mono 0.7g, poly 0.2g); PROTEIN 1.9g; CARB 6.2g; FIBER 0.3g; CHOL 29mg; IRON 0.4mg; SODIUM 95mg; CALC 35mg

chapter 3

BISCUITS
AND
SCONES

**B**iscuits and scones are longtime favorites. The buttery bite of a biscuit or the unique crumb of a scone are part of what makes them memorable.

When working with these in their gluten-free form, the key to creating those same unique characteristics is in handling them properly. You'll notice the doughs are much softer than when a wheat-based flour is used, and they're impossible to knead. A key phrase in these recipes: "mix just until moist." Make it your mantra. Overmixing breaks down the dough, leaving you with a sticky wet mess that's almost unworkable.

Both biscuits and scones start with similar ingredients: flour, butter, shortening, sugar, and typically either baking powder or baking soda to help them rise adequately. In some cases, you'll see scones that include an egg, which gives them a more tender bite and a less crumbly texture. No matter which you prefer, you'll find a variety of biscuits and scones in this chapter that will brighten your table.

# BUTTERMILK DROP BISCUITS

Hands-on time: 15 min. Total time: 27 min.

*Tapioca flour, white rice flour, and potato starch are lighter, starchier flours that produce a lighter, airier baked good, which is ideal for biscuits. They're also neutral-tasting, which allows the flavor of the other ingredients to shine through. These flaky, buttery biscuits are a great addition to the breakfast or dinner table. You can even serve them for dessert: Just slice them in half and fill them with fresh berries and whipped cream.*

3.15 ounces tapioca flour (about ¾ cup)
2.6 ounces white rice flour (about ½ cup)
2.6 ounces potato starch (about ½ cup)
1 tablespoon baking powder
1½ teaspoons xanthan gum
1 teaspoon baking soda
1 teaspoon sugar
¼ teaspoon salt
2 tablespoons vegetable shortening
2 tablespoons chilled unsalted butter, cut into
  small pieces
1 cup low-fat buttermilk

1. Preheat oven to 425°.

2. Weigh or lightly spoon flours and potato starch into dry measuring cups; level with a knife. Combine flours, potato starch, baking powder, and next 4 ingredients (through salt) in a medium bowl, stirring with a whisk; cut in shortening and butter with a pastry blender or 2 knives until mixture resembles coarse meal. Add buttermilk; stir just until moist.

3. Drop dough by ¼ cupfuls 2 inches apart onto a baking sheet lined with parchment paper. Bake at 425° for 12 minutes or until golden brown. Remove biscuits from baking sheet to a wire rack; cool slightly. Serves 12 (serving size: 1 biscuit)

CALORIES 114; FAT 4.2g (sat 1.9g, mono 1.2g, poly 0.6g); PROTEIN 1.1g; CARB 18g; FIBER 0.5g; CHOL 6mg; IRON 0.3mg; SODIUM 298mg; CALC 92mg

## don't get stuck

Reusable silicone mats are a great substitute for baking on parchment paper. These mats have a nonstick surface that doesn't require the addition of any oil or butter to prevent them from sticking, which helps keep calories in check.

# CHEDDAR-GARLIC BISCUITS

Hands-on time: 10 min. Total time: 22 min.

*These biscuits are a staple at our annual family gathering down at the shore at Fourth Cliff, Massachusetts, in October. With the cold wind whipping off the choppy waters, these warm and garlicky biscuits are just right served with a steaming bowl of gluten-free New England clam chowder.*

**Biscuits:**

3.15 ounces tapioca flour (about ¾ cup)

2.6 ounces white rice flour (about ½ cup)

2.6 ounces potato starch (about ½ cup)

2 teaspoons baking powder

1½ teaspoons xanthan gum

1 teaspoon baking soda

1 teaspoon sugar

½ teaspoon onion powder

½ teaspoon garlic powder

⅛ teaspoon salt

2 tablespoons vegetable shortening

2 tablespoons chilled unsalted butter, cut into small pieces

3 ounces reduced-fat sharp cheddar cheese, shredded (about ¾ cup)

1 tablespoon chopped fresh parsley

1 cup low-fat buttermilk

**Garlic Butter:**

1½ teaspoons unsalted butter, melted

⅛ teaspoon garlic powder

1. Preheat oven to 425°.

2. To prepare biscuits, weigh or lightly spoon flours and potato starch into dry measuring cups; level with a knife. Combine flours, potato starch, baking powder, and next 6 ingredients (through salt) in a medium bowl, stirring with a whisk; cut in shortening and butter with a pastry blender or 2 knives until mixture resembles coarse meal. Stir in cheese and parsley. Add buttermilk; stir just until moist.

3. Drop dough by ¼ cupfuls 2 inches apart onto a baking sheet lined with parchment paper. Bake at 425° for 12 minutes or until golden brown.

4. While biscuits bake, combine melted butter and garlic powder in a small bowl; stir with a whisk.

5. Remove biscuits from baking sheet to a wire rack; brush with garlic butter. Cool slightly. Serves 12 (serving size: 1 biscuit)

CALORIES 139; FAT 6g (sat 3g, mono 1.7g, poly 0.7g); PROTEIN 3g; CARB 19g; FIBER 0.5g; CHOL 11mg; IRON 0.3mg; SODIUM 285mg; CALC 158mg

# ORANGE-POPPY BISCUITS

*The buttermilk and orange add a tangy citrusy flavor to these lightly sweetened biscuits. Served warm, they are a favorite of mine for breakfast.*

3.15 ounces tapioca flour (about ¾ cup)
2.6 ounces white rice flour (about ½ cup)
1.7 ounces potato starch (about ⅓ cup)
1.4 ounces cornstarch (about ⅓ cup)
1 tablespoon granulated sugar
1 tablespoon baking powder
1 tablespoon poppy seeds
1 tablespoon grated orange rind

1½ teaspoons xanthan gum
1 teaspoon baking soda
¼ teaspoon salt
2 tablespoons vegetable shortening
2 tablespoons chilled unsalted butter, cut into
   small pieces
1 cup low-fat buttermilk
½ cup powdered sugar
1 tablespoon fresh orange juice

1. Preheat oven to 425°.

2. Weigh or lightly spoon flours, potato starch, and cornstarch into dry measuring cups; level with a knife. Combine flours, potato starch, cornstarch, granulated sugar, and next 6 ingredients (through salt) in a medium bowl, stirring with a whisk; cut in shortening and butter with a pastry blender or 2 knives until mixture resembles coarse meal. Add buttermilk; stir just until moist.

3. Drop dough by ¼ cupfuls 2 inches apart onto a baking sheet lined with parchment paper. Bake at 425° for 10 minutes or until lightly browned. Remove biscuits from baking sheet to a wire rack; cool.

4. Combine powdered sugar and orange juice in a small bowl. Drizzle over biscuits. Serves 12 (serving size: 1 biscuit)

CALORIES 146; FAT 4.5g (sat 1.9g, mono 1.3g, poly 0.8g); PROTEIN 1.2g; CARB 26g; FIBER 0.7g; CHOL 6mg; IRON 0.3mg; SODIUM 299mg; CALC 104mg

# STRAWBERRY-ALMOND BISCUITS

Hands-on time: 10 min. Total time: 50 min.

*Brown rice flour is mixed with neutral-tasting white rice flour and tapioca flour to give these biscuits a slightly nutty flavor that complements the almonds and strawberries. The end result is biscuits that have the flavor of strawberry shortcake with almonds stirred in for crunch. Delicious.*

**Biscuits:**

5.2 ounces white rice flour (about 1 cup)
2.3 ounces brown rice flour (about ½ cup)
2.1 ounces tapioca flour (about ½ cup)
¼ cup granulated sugar
1½ teaspoons baking powder
1 teaspoon xanthan gum
1 teaspoon salt
5 tablespoons chilled unsalted butter, cut into small pieces
1 cup fat-free half-and-half, plus extra for brushing
1 cup dried strawberries, sliced
¼ cup sliced almonds

**Glaze:**

½ cup powdered sugar
1 tablespoon fat-free half-and-half
¼ teaspoon almond extract

1. Preheat oven to 375°.

2. To prepare biscuits, weigh or lightly spoon flours into dry measuring cups; level with a knife. Combine flours, granulated sugar, baking powder, xanthan gum, and salt in a large bowl, stirring with a whisk; cut in butter with a pastry blender or 2 knives until mixture resembles coarse meal. Add 1 cup half-and-half; toss with a fork until moist. Stir in strawberries and almonds.

3. Drop dough by tablespoons 2 inches apart onto baking sheets lined with parchment paper. Brush tops of dough with extra half-and-half. Bake at 375° for 20 minutes or until edges are golden brown. Remove biscuits from baking sheet to a wire rack; cool 20 minutes.

4. To prepare glaze, combine powdered sugar, 1 table-spoon half-and-half, and almond extract in a small bowl, stirring until smooth. Drizzle glaze evenly over cooled biscuits. Serves 14 (serving size: 1 biscuit)

CALORIES 181; FAT 5.2g (sat 2.7g, mono 1.7g, poly 0.4g); PROTEIN 2.1g; CARB 31.1g; FIBER 1.3g; CHOL 11mg; IRON 0.3mg; SODIUM 232mg; CALC 70mg

# CINNAMON, APPLE, AND OAT SCONES

Hands-on time: 20 min. Total time: 34 min.

*I often use sorghum flour and brown rice flour in scone recipes because it gives them a heartier texture that mimics the wheat-based variety. The oats add some chew and also gives these scones a rustic appearance. Serve them with a mug of hot chocolate or mulled cider for a delicious breakfast or as an afternoon snack.*

4.2 ounces sweet white sorghum flour (about 1 cup)
1.3 ounces white rice flour (about ¼ cup)
1.15 ounces brown rice flour (about ¼ cup)
1.3 ounces potato starch (about ¼ cup)
1 cup certified gluten-free quick-cooking oats
¼ cup packed brown sugar
2 teaspoons baking powder
1 teaspoon xanthan gum
1 teaspoon baking soda
½ teaspoon salt
½ teaspoon ground cinnamon
¼ teaspoon ground nutmeg
5 tablespoons chilled unsalted butter, cut into small pieces
1 cup finely diced peeled Granny Smith apple
¼ cup cinnamon-flavored baking chips
½ cup low-fat buttermilk
¼ cup applesauce
White rice flour, for dusting
1 egg white, lightly beaten
2 teaspoons turbinado sugar or granulated sugar

1. Preheat oven to 400°.

2. Weigh or lightly spoon flours and potato starch into dry measuring cups; level with knife. Combine flours, potato starch, oats, and next 7 ingredients (through nutmeg) in a large bowl, stirring with a whisk; cut in butter with a pastry blender or 2 knives until mixture resembles coarse meal. Stir in apple and baking chips. Add buttermilk and applesauce; stir just until moist.

3. Turn dough out onto a surface lightly dusted with white rice flour. Pat dough into an 8-inch circle; cut into 14 wedges. Place wedges on a baking sheet lined with parchment paper. Brush egg white over surface of dough; sprinkle with turbinado sugar. Bake at 400° for 14 minutes or until golden brown. Remove scones from baking sheet to a wire rack. Serve warm. Serves 14 (serving size: 1 scone)

CALORIES 169; FAT 6.1g (sat 3.3g, mono 1.3g, poly 0.3g); PROTEIN 3.3g; CARB 26g; FIBER 1.9g; CHOL 11mg; IRON 0.8mg; SODIUM 269mg; CALC 67mg

## add some sparkle

Turbinado sugar has a coarser texture than granulated sugar and a subtle molasses flavor. Sprinkle it on top of baked goods to add a lovely crunch and a beautiful sparkling finish.

If you can't find fresh blueberries, or they're out of season, feel free to substitute frozen blueberries, but don't thaw them. Toss them into the batter frozen to keep them from making the batter too wet.

# GLAZED BLUEBERRY SCONES

Hands-on time: 15 min. Total time: 48 min.

*Back in the late '90s, I owned a bakery called the Sugar Shack, which was located on the edge of the University of Connecticut campus. One of my regular customers, Joseph Giannelli (UConn's Golf Coach), came in every day and purchased a blueberry scone and a cup of hot tea. This eventually led to a barter of blueberry scones for golf lessons. Thanks for the lessons, Coach— you will always be remembered, especially when I get those birdies!*

2.6 ounces white rice flour (about ¹/₂ cup)
2.3 ounces brown rice flour (about ¹/₂ cup)
2.1 ounces sweet white sorghum flour (about ¹/₂ cup)
¹/₃ cup granulated sugar
1¹/₂ teaspoons baking powder
1 teaspoon xanthan gum
1 teaspoon baking soda
¹/₈ teaspoon salt
3 tablespoons chilled unsalted butter, cut into small pieces
¹/₂ cup plus 1 tablespoon nonfat buttermilk, divided
1 large egg
1 cup fresh blueberries
White rice flour, for dusting
¹/₂ cup powdered sugar
1¹/₂ teaspoons grated lemon rind

1. Preheat oven to 400°.

2. Weigh or lightly spoon flours into dry measuring cups; level with a knife. Combine flours, granulated sugar, and next 4 ingredients (through salt) in a medium bowl; stir with a whisk. Cut in butter with a pastry blender or 2 knives until mixture resembles coarse meal.

3. Combine ¹/₂ cup buttermilk and egg in a small bowl; stir with a whisk. Add to flour mixture; stir just until moist. Fold in blueberries (do not overmix dough).

4. Turn dough out onto a surface lightly dusted with white rice flour. Pat dough into an 8-inch circle on a baking sheet lined with parchment paper; cut dough into 10 wedges, cutting into but not through dough.

5. Bake at 400° for 18 minutes or until edges are golden and center is firm. Remove scones from baking sheet to a wire rack; cool 10 minutes.

6. Combine powdered sugar, lemon rind, and 1 table-spoon buttermilk in a small bowl; stir with a whisk until smooth. Drizzle glaze over scones; let stand 5 minutes. Serve warm. Serves 10 (serving size: 1 scone)

CALORIES 173; FAT 4.4g (sat 2.4g, mono 1.2g, poly 0.3g); PROTEIN 2.9g; CARB 31g; FIBER 1.7g; CHOL 28mg; IRON 0.6mg; SODIUM 250mg; CALC 64mg

# BITTERSWEET CHOCOLATE SCONES

Hands-on time: 13 min. Total time: 31 min.

*I knew that these whimsical and bittersweet chocolate scones were a hit when I found my three boys wrestling under the kitchen table for the one that rolled away.*

2.6 ounces white rice flour (about ½ cup)
2.3 ounces brown rice flour (about ½ cup)
2.1 ounces sweet white sorghum flour (about ½ cup)
½ cup plus 1 teaspoon sugar, divided
1½ teaspoons baking powder
1 teaspoon xanthan gum
1 teaspoon baking soda
⅛ teaspoon salt
3 tablespoons chilled unsalted butter, cut into small pieces
2 ounces bittersweet chocolate, finely chopped
½ cup plus 1 tablespoon nonfat buttermilk, divided
1 large egg
White rice flour, for dusting

1. Preheat oven to 400°.

2. Weigh or lightly spoon flours into dry measuring cups; level with a knife. Combine flours, ½ cup sugar, and next 4 ingredients (through salt) in a medium bowl, stirring with a whisk; cut in butter with a pastry blender or 2 knives until mixture resembles coarse meal. Stir in chocolate.

3. Combine ½ cup buttermilk and egg in a small bowl; stir with a whisk. Add to flour mixture; stir just until moist.

4. Turn dough out onto a surface lightly dusted with white rice flour. Pat dough into an 8-inch circle; cut into 10 wedges. Place wedges on a baking sheet lined with parchment paper. Brush 1 tablespoon buttermilk over surface of dough; sprinkle with 1 teaspoon sugar.

5. Bake at 400° for 18 minutes or until golden brown. Remove scones from baking sheet to a wire rack. Serve warm. Serves 10 (serving size: 1 scone)

CALORIES 184; FAT 6.8g (sat 3.6g, mono 1.9g, poly 0.4g); PROTEIN 3.2g; CARB 30g; FIBER 1.7g; CHOL 28mg; IRON 0.7mg; SODIUM 249mg; CALC 63mg

## keep it neat

tip

Here's an easy way to chop chocolate so that it doesn't crumble into tiny pieces: Place the chocolate on a cutting board. Place the tines of a two- or three-tined roasting fork on top of the chocolate. Keeping the fork straight up, apply pressure downward. The chocolate will break neatly into pieces.

# PIZZA SCONES

Hands-on time: 9 min. Total time: 27 min.

2.1 ounces tapioca flour (about ½ cup)
1.3 ounces white rice flour (about ¼ cup)
1.15 ounces brown rice flour (about ¼ cup)
1.15 ounces cornstarch (about ¼ cup)
1 tablespoon baking powder
½ teaspoon xanthan gum
½ teaspoon dried Italian seasoning
¼ teaspoon garlic powder
¼ teaspoon salt
¼ cup chilled unsalted butter, cut into small
   pieces
1 ounce turkey pepperoni, chopped (¼ cup)
0.5 ounce part-skim mozzarella cheese, shredded
   (about 2 tablespoons)
0.5 ounce reduced-fat sharp cheddar cheese,
   shredded (about 2 tablespoons)
2 teaspoons grated fresh Parmesan cheese
¼ cup 2% reduced-fat milk
1 large egg
White rice flour, for dusting
Cooking spray

1. Preheat oven to 400°.

2. Weigh or lightly spoon flours and cornstarch into
   dry measuring cups; level with a knife. Combine
   flours, cornstarch, baking powder, and next 4 ingredients (through salt) in a medium bowl, stirring
   with a whisk; cut in butter with a pastry blender
   or 2 knives until mixture resembles coarse meal.
   Stir in pepperoni and cheeses.

3. Combine milk and egg in a small bowl; stir with
   a whisk until combined. Add to flour mixture; stir
   just until moist.

4. Turn dough out onto a surface lightly dusted with
   white rice flour. Pat dough into a 6½-inch circle
   on a baking sheet lined with parchment paper;
   cut dough into 10 wedges, cutting into but not
   through dough. Lightly coat top of dough with
   cooking spray.

5. Bake at 400° for 18 minutes or until edges are
   golden and center is firm. Remove scones from
   baking sheet to a wire rack. Serve warm. Serves 10
   (serving size: 1 scone)

CALORIES 128; FAT 6.5g (sat 3.6g, mono 1.9g, poly 0.5g);
PROTEIN 3.1g; CARB 15g; FIBER 0.4g; CHOL 37mg;
IRON 0.5mg; SODIUM 294mg; CALC 122mg

## a trimmer pepperoni

Turkey pepperoni is an excellent alternative to
the pork or beef variety. It has the same great
flavor kick, but with 70% less fat per serving.

chapter 4

MUFFINS
AND
QUICK
BREADS

When baking powder was invented in 1854, it changed the way society baked its breads. It gave bakers a non-yeast leavening option that required no rising time and yielded quick and easy-to-make baked items that were lighter and flakier than ever before. It does the same in gluten-free baking, only it has a more illustrious status since it's one of the ingredients, in the absence of gluten, that helps these muffins and quick breads rise properly.

These batters also rely on the air that's incorporated when mixing to give them a sufficient boost. Overmixing them beats the air right out of them, turning your muffins and loaves into dense bricks.

Whether you enjoy sweet or savory, this chapter will provide you with a cache of delectable recipes to be enjoyed at breakfast, brunch, snack time, or dinner.

# FRUIT OF THE FOREST MUFFINS

Hands-on time: 10 min. Total time: 45 min.

*My neighbors, the Rices, have an abundant supply of wild blueberries, raspberries, and blackberries growing on their property. Every season we barter: fresh berries for a steady supply of Fruit of the Forest Muffins. When berries are not in season, I substitute frozen berries for fresh.*

3.45 ounces brown rice flour (about ³/₄ cup)
2.6 ounces potato starch (about ¹/₂ cup)
1.8 ounces oat flour (about ¹/₂ cup)
¹/₃ cup granulated sugar
¹/₄ cup packed brown sugar
1¹/₂ teaspoons baking powder
1 teaspoon xanthan gum
¹/₂ teaspoon salt
¹/₂ cup 1% low-fat milk
¹/₄ cup butter, melted
2 large eggs
1¹/₂ cups mixed fresh berries (such as blueberries, raspberries, and blackberries)
Cooking spray
1 tablespoon turbinado sugar or granulated sugar

1. Preheat oven to 350°.

2. Weigh or lightly spoon brown rice flour, potato starch, and oat flour into dry measuring cups; level with a knife. Combine brown rice flour, potato starch, oat flour, granulated sugar, and next 4 ingredients (through salt) in a medium bowl; stir with a whisk. Make a well in center of mixture. Combine milk, butter, and eggs; stir with a whisk. Add to flour mixture, stirring just until moist. Fold in berries.

3. Place 12 paper muffin cup liners in muffin cups; coat liners with cooking spray. Spoon batter into prepared cups, and sprinkle with turbinado sugar.

Bake at 350° for 25 minutes or until lightly browned and muffins spring back when lightly touched. Cool 10 minutes in pan on a wire rack; remove from pan. Serves 12 (serving size: 1 muffin)

**Note:** If you're planning to freeze all or some of the muffins, leave off the turbinado sugar.

CALORIES 172; FAT 5.6g (sat 3g, mono 1.7g, poly 0.6g); PROTEIN 2.8g; CARB 28g; FIBER 1.7g; CHOL 42mg; IRON 0.6mg; SODIUM 206mg; CALC 70mg

## d.i.y. oat flour

If you can't find oat flour, make your own. Just place oats into a food processor, and grind into a powdery consistency. The oats add a hearty flavor to these muffins. They owe some of their distinctive taste to the roasting process that happens after the oats are harvested and cleaned. Beyond the benefits for your taste buds, they're also high in fiber and help control cholesterol levels.

# TOP OF THE MORNING MUFFINS

Hands-on time: 20 min. Total time: 55 min.

*On a visit home to Indiana, our friend Carrie Ellis's rambunctious 4-year-old, Eileen, went on a morning muffin-baking spree with her grandmother every day of their two-week stay. These muffins were a big hit and made it into the muffin rotation several times. This flour blend works wonders. Brown rice flour and sorghum flour give muffins a great texture and crumb. Packed with flavorful spices, such as cinnamon, ginger, and nutmeg, they make getting out of bed so much easier.*

2.6 ounces white rice flour (about ½ cup)
2.3 ounces brown rice flour (about ½ cup)
2.1 ounces sweet white sorghum flour (about ½ cup)
1.05 ounces tapioca flour (about ¼ cup)
1 teaspoon xanthan gum
1 teaspoon baking soda
1 teaspoon ground cinnamon
½ teaspoon salt
¼ teaspoon ground ginger
¼ teaspoon ground nutmeg
½ cup non-dairy buttery spread
½ cup granulated sugar
½ cup packed brown sugar
2 large eggs, lightly beaten
½ cup applesauce
1 cup shredded carrot
⅓ cup flaked sweetened coconut
¼ cup raisins
Cooking spray
¼ cup chopped walnuts

1. Preheat oven to 350°.

2. Weigh or lightly spoon flours into dry measuring cups; level with a knife. Combine flours, xanthan gum, and next 5 ingredients (through nutmeg) in a medium bowl; stir with a whisk.

3. Place buttery spread and sugars in a medium bowl; beat with a mixer at medium speed until light and fluffy. Add eggs, 1 at a time, beating well after each addition. Beat in applesauce. Add flour mixture; beat at low speed just until combined. Stir in carrot, coconut, and raisins.

4. Place 16 paper muffin cup liners in muffin cups; coat liners with cooking spray. Spoon batter into prepared cups, and sprinkle with walnuts. Bake at 350° for 25 minutes or until a wooden pick inserted in center comes out clean. Cool 10 minutes in pan on a wire rack; remove from pan. Serves 16 (serving size: 1 muffin)

CALORIES 186; FAT 8.3g (sat 2.3g, mono 3.1g, poly 2.6g); PROTEIN 2.2g; CARB 28g; FIBER 1.5g; CHOL 23mg; IRON 0.6mg; SODIUM 224mg; CALC 17mg

## toothpick test

t i p

To see if muffins and quick breads are done, insert a wooden pick into the center of the baked good, and remove it. If the wooden pick has moist batter attached, you need to bake it longer.

# RASPBERRY-YOGURT MUFFINS

Hands-on time: 13 min. Total time: 45 min.

*Muffins have always been a breakfast staple, but they can be laden with fat and calories. These delightful muffins contain fat-free yogurt, which allows you to decrease the oil, omit the butter, and keep calories in check while adding a dose of calcium and protein. This blend of flours produces a milder muffin that allows the flavor of the raspberries and vanilla to come through. They'll satisfy your sweet tooth without weighing you down.*

4.6 ounces brown rice flour (about 1 cup)
2.6 ounces white rice flour (about ½ cup)
⅓ cup plus 1 teaspoon sugar, divided
2 tablespoons potato starch
2 tablespoons cornstarch
1 teaspoon baking powder
1 teaspoon baking soda
½ teaspoon xanthan gum
¼ teaspoon salt
1 cup vanilla fat-free yogurt
¼ cup fat-free milk
2 tablespoons canola oil
¼ teaspoon almond extract
1 large egg
1 cup fresh raspberries
1 tablespoon brown rice flour
Cooking spray

1. Preheat oven to 375°.

2. Weigh or lightly spoon 4.6 ounces brown rice flour (about 1 cup) and white rice flour into dry measuring cups; level with a knife. Combine flours, ⅓ cup sugar, and next 6 ingredients (through salt) in a medium bowl; stir with a whisk. Make a well in center of mixture. Combine yogurt and next 4 ingredients (through egg); stir with a whisk. Add to flour mixture, stirring just until moist.

3. Toss raspberries with 1 tablespoon brown rice flour in a small bowl; gently fold into batter.

4. Place 12 paper muffin cup liners in muffin cups; coat liners with cooking spray. Spoon batter into prepared cups, and sprinkle with 1 teaspoon sugar. Bake at 375° for 22 minutes or until lightly browned and muffins spring back when lightly touched. Cool 10 minutes in pan on a wire rack; remove from pan. Serves 12 (serving size: 1 muffin)

CALORIES 145; FAT 3.4g (sat 0.5g, mono 1.9g, poly 0.9g); PROTEIN 2.8g; CARB 26g; FIBER 1.5g; CHOL 16mg; IRON 0.4mg; SODIUM 212mg; CALC 70mg

## keep it clean

**tip**

When making muffins, I always recommend spraying muffin tins with cooking spray or using muffin cup liners—or both—to line the muffin tins. This ensures that your muffins won't stick and makes for easy cleanup. If you use a loaf pan, always coat it with cooking spray to ensure that the bread won't cling.

# PUMPKIN-SPICE MUFFINS

Hands-on time: 18 min. Total time: 49 min.

*Every Columbus Day weekend my cousin Gary holds our annual family reunion at his house, which overlooks his apple orchards, in upstate New York. He makes a huge batch of mulled cider and serves it with these spiced pumpkin muffins. The pumpkin adds gorgeous color, flavor, and moisture as well as fiber, vitamin A, and potassium.*

2.6 ounces potato starch (about ½ cup)
2.6 ounces white rice flour (about ½ cup)
2.3 ounces brown rice flour (about ½ cup)
2.1 ounces sweet white sorghum flour (about ½ cup)
1 teaspoon baking soda
1 teaspoon ground cinnamon
½ teaspoon xanthan gum
½ teaspoon salt
½ teaspoon ground ginger
¼ teaspoon ground cloves
¼ teaspoon ground nutmeg
1 cup canned pumpkin
¾ cup low-fat buttermilk
½ cup packed brown sugar
3 tablespoons canola oil
2 tablespoons honey
1 teaspoon vanilla extract
2 large eggs
Cooking spray
2 tablespoons unsalted pumpkinseed kernels
2 teaspoons turbinado sugar or granulated sugar

1. Preheat oven to 375°.

2. Weigh or lightly spoon potato starch and flours into dry measuring cups; level with a knife. Combine potato starch, flours, baking soda, and next 6 ingredients (through nutmeg) in a medium bowl; stir with a whisk. Make a well in center of mixture. Combine pumpkin and next 6 ingredients (through eggs); stir with a whisk. Add to flour mixture, stirring just until moist.

3. Place 16 paper muffin cup liners in muffin cups; coat liners with cooking spray. Spoon batter into prepared cups, and sprinkle with pumpkinseed kernels and turbinado sugar. Bake at 375° for 21 to 23 minutes or until muffins spring back when lightly touched. Cool 10 minutes in pan on a wire rack; remove from pan. Cool completely on wire rack. Serves 16 (serving size: 1 muffin)

CALORIES 186; FAT 8.7g (sat 0.9g, mono 4.9g, poly 2.4g); PROTEIN 2.8g; CARB 25g; FIBER 1.5g; CHOL 24mg; IRON 0.6mg; SODIUM 177mg; CALC 27mg

# ALMOND COFFEE CAKE MUFFINS

Hands-on time: 18 min. Total time: 53 min.

*As a child and before she was diagnosed with celiac disease, my wife and her siblings loved Drake's coffee cakes. After some experimenting in the kitchen, I allowed her to relive that experience with a healthier, more flavorful version. These sweet muffins are an ideal dessert or an indulgent breakfast. Whichever you choose, you'll love them.*

### Topping:
1.05 ounces sweet white sorghum flour (about ¼ cup)
2 tablespoons packed brown sugar
½ teaspoon ground cinnamon
⅛ teaspoon ground allspice
⅛ teaspoon salt
1 tablespoon chilled butter, cut into small pieces

### Muffins:
3.15 ounces sweet white sorghum flour (about ¾ cup)
1.8 ounces almond meal flour (about ½ cup)
2.6 ounces potato starch (about ½ cup)
2 teaspoons baking powder
1 teaspoon xanthan gum
1 teaspoon baking soda
½ teaspoon salt
⅓ cup granulated sugar
⅓ cup packed brown sugar
2 tablespoons butter, softened
2 large eggs
¾ cup reduced-fat sour cream
2 tablespoons canola oil
½ teaspoon almond extract
½ cup cinnamon-flavored baking chips
Cooking spray

1. Preheat oven to 350°.

2. To prepare topping, weigh or lightly spoon 1.05 ounces sweet white sorghum flour (about ¼ cup) into a dry measuring cup; level with a knife. Combine flour, 2 tablespoons brown sugar, cinnamon, allspice, and salt in a small bowl; cut in butter with a pastry blender or 2 knives until mixture resembles coarse meal. Cover and chill.

3. To prepare muffins, weigh or lightly spoon 3.15 ounces sweet white sorghum flour (about ¾ cup), almond meal flour, and potato starch into dry measuring cups; level with a knife. Combine flours, potato starch, baking powder, and next 3 ingredients (through salt) in a medium bowl; stir with a whisk.

4. Place sugars and butter in a medium bowl; beat with a mixer at medium speed until well blended. Add eggs, 1 at a time, beating well after each addition. Beat in sour cream, canola oil, and almond extract. Add flour mixture; beat at low speed just until blended. Stir in baking chips.

5. Place 12 paper muffin cup liners in muffin cups; coat liners with cooking spray. Spoon batter into prepared cups, and sprinkle with topping. Bake at 350° for 25 minutes or until a wooden pick inserted in center comes out clean. Cool 10 minutes in pan on a wire rack; remove from pan. Serves 12 (serving size: 1 muffin)

CALORIES 277; FAT 13.5g (sat 5.1g, mono 4.7g, poly 1.6g); PROTEIN 4.8g; CARB 35g; FIBER 1.6g; CHOL 44mg; IRON 0.8mg; SODIUM 376mg; CALC 127mg

After muffins cool completely, you can wrap them in plastic wrap and store them at room temperature for three days. If they're made with perishable ingredients like cheese or fresh fruits, store them in the refrigerator.

# CHOCOLATE CHIP-HAZELNUT MUFFINS

Hands-on time: 14 min. Total time: 49 min.

*Hazelnuts and chocolate make the perfect pair. This muffin uses non-dairy buttery spread and coconut milk to create a dairy-free muffin layered with flavors. It's sure to be a winner at your house, too.*

3.6 ounces oat flour (about 1 cup)
2.6 ounces white rice flour (about ½ cup)
1.05 ounces tapioca flour (about ¼ cup)
½ cup packed brown sugar
1 teaspoon baking powder
1 teaspoon baking soda
½ teaspoon xanthan gum
¼ teaspoon salt
1 cup unsweetened coconut milk
¼ cup non-dairy buttery spread (such as Earth
   Balance), melted
1 teaspoon vanilla extract
2 large eggs
¼ cup semisweet chocolate minichips
¼ cup finely chopped hazelnuts
Cooking spray

1. Preheat oven to 375°.

2. Weigh or lightly spoon flours into dry measuring cups; level with a knife. Combine flours, brown sugar, and next 4 ingredients (through salt) in a medium bowl; stir with a whisk. Make a well in center of mixture. Combine coconut milk and next 3 ingredients (through eggs); stir with a whisk. Add to flour mixture, stirring just until moist. Fold in chocolate minichips and hazelnuts.

3. Place 15 paper muffin cup liners in muffin cups; coat liners with cooking spray. Spoon batter into prepared cups. Bake at 375° for 25 minutes or until lightly browned and muffins spring back when lightly touched. Cool 10 minutes in pan on a wire rack; remove from pan. Serves 15 (serving size: 1 muffin)

CALORIES 156; FAT 6.9g (sat 2.2g, mono 2.8g, poly 1.3g); PROTEIN 2.7g; CARB 21g; FIBER 0.8g; CHOL 25mg; IRON 0.6mg; SODIUM 195mg; CALC 40mg

## how to skin hazelnuts

**tip**

If you can't find hazelnuts that have already been skinned, use this procedure: Place the nuts on a baking pan, and bake them at 350° for 5 to 10 minutes. Pour the toasty hazelnuts into a clean dishtowel, and fold it up so none of the nuts are exposed. Let them sit for 5 minutes—this allows the heat from the warm nuts to create steam that will loosen the skins—and then rub the nuts together in the dishtowel. The skins will flake right off.

# CHOCOLATE MUFFINS

Hands-on time: 10 min. Total time: 45 min.

*"Do you know the muffin man, the muffin man, the muffin man, yes we know the muffin man, and he lives right in our house!" My son always sings this when I make these muffins, and it always makes me laugh. Chocolate chips in any muffins are always a hit with the kids.*

2.3 ounces brown rice flour (about ½ cup)
2.1 ounces tapioca flour (about ½ cup)
1.8 ounces almond meal flour (about ½ cup)
1.05 ounces sweet white sorghum flour
    (about ¼ cup)
¾ cup granulated sugar
⅓ cup unsweetened cocoa
1 teaspoon xanthan gum
1 teaspoon baking powder
½ teaspoon baking soda
¼ teaspoon salt
¾ cup low-fat buttermilk
4 tablespoons unsalted butter, melted
2 tablespoons canola oil
2 large eggs
⅓ cup semisweet chocolate minichips
Cooking spray

1. Preheat oven to 350°.

2. Weigh or lightly spoon flours into dry measuring cups; level with a knife. Combine flours, granulated sugar, and next 5 ingredients (through salt) in a medium bowl; stir with a whisk. Make a well in center of mixture. Combine buttermilk, melted butter, oil, and eggs; stir with a whisk. Add to flour mixture, stirring just until moist. Fold in chocolate minichips.

3. Place 15 paper muffin cup liners in muffin cups; coat liners with cooking spray. Spoon batter into prepared cups. Bake at 350° for 25 minutes or until a wooden pick inserted in center comes out clean. Cool 10 minutes in pan on a wire rack; remove from pan. Serves 15 (serving size: 1 muffin)

CALORIES 177; FAT 9.0g (sat 3.3g, mono 2.7g, poly 0.9g); PROTEIN 3.1g; CARB 24g; FIBER 1.8g; CHOL 36mg; IRON 0.9mg; SODIUM 137mg; CALC 51mg

You can also use fresh
shucked corn kernels in
place of the frozen corn
in this recipe.

# JALAPEÑO-CHEDDAR-CORN MUFFINS

Hands-on time: 20 min. Total time: 50 min.

*These hot and spicy cheddar–pepper muffins are sure to give you a little taste of fire. Seed the jalapeño for a muffin with less heat.*

7.6 ounces certified gluten-free stone-ground cornmeal (about 1¼ cups)
1.7 ounces white rice flour (about ⅓ cup)
1.5 ounces brown rice flour (about ⅓ cup)
2 tablespoons tapioca flour
2 tablespoons potato starch
2 tablespoons sugar
1 tablespoon baking powder
½ teaspoon baking soda
½ teaspoon xanthan gum
⅛ teaspoon salt
⅛ teaspoon ground chipotle chile pepper
1½ cups nonfat buttermilk
¼ cup reduced-fat sour cream
2 tablespoons unsalted butter, melted
2 tablespoons canola oil
2 large eggs
4 ounces reduced-fat sharp cheddar cheese, shredded (about ½ cup)
¼ cup frozen whole-kernel corn, thawed
2 tablespoons minced jalapeño pepper
Cooking spray

1. Preheat oven to 375°.

2. Weigh or lightly spoon cornmeal, white rice flour, and brown rice flour into dry measuring cups; level with a knife. Combine cornmeal, white rice flour, brown rice flour, tapioca flour, and next 7 ingredients (through chipotle chile pepper) in a medium bowl; stir with a whisk. Make a well in center of mixture. Combine buttermilk and next 4 ingredients (through eggs); stir with a whisk. Add to flour mixture, stirring just until moist. Stir in cheese, corn, and jalapeño pepper.

3. Place 15 paper muffin cup liners in muffin cups; coat liners heavily with cooking spray. Spoon batter into prepared cups. Bake at 375° for 20 minutes or until muffins spring back when lightly touched. Cool 10 minutes in pan on a wire rack; remove from pan. Serves 15 (serving size: 1 muffin)

CALORIES 161; FAT 6.9g (sat 2.7g, mono 2.1g, poly 0.8g); PROTEIN 5.1g; CARB 20g; FIBER 2.2g; CHOL 36mg; IRON 0.6mg; SODIUM 250mg; CALC 218mg

# BRAZILIAN CHEESE BREAD

Hands-on time: 12 min. Total time: 57 min.

*This bread is dedicated to Pope Francis, who on a journey to Brazil, reportedly took a special side trip to the small fishing village of Aparecida. There he spoke to the bishops of Brazil, sharing his reflections on the importance of humility, the beauty of life, the creativity of love, and the power that can germinate from simplicity. With its six simple ingredients, this Brazilian cheese bread delivers abundant and powerful flavor in every single bite. Tapioca flour plays a key role. It's light and starchy, producing a bread that is crisp on the outside with airy pockets in the middle.*

8.4 ounces tapioca flour (about 2 cups)
1 cup 1% low-fat milk
6 tablespoons canola oil
2 large eggs, lightly beaten
2 ounces reduced-fat sharp cheddar cheese, shredded (about ½ cup)
1.3 ounces grated fresh Parmesan cheese (about ⅓ cup)
Tapioca flour, for dusting

1. Preheat oven to 400°. Cover 2 metal baking pans with parchment paper.

2. Weigh or lightly spoon flour into dry measuring cups; level with a knife. Place flour in a large bowl.

3. Combine milk and oil in a small saucepan over medium heat; bring to a boil. Slowly pour milk mixture into flour, stirring until blended. Let cool 5 minutes. Add eggs and cheeses, stirring until blended. Place dough in refrigerator, and chill 20 minutes.

4. Turn dough out onto a well-floured surface. With floured hands, shape dough into 15 balls, about 3 tablespoons each. Place 2 inches apart on prepared baking pans. Bake at 400° for 20 minutes or until puffed and golden. Serves 15 (serving size: 1 piece)

CALORIES 140; FAT 7.8g (sat 1.6g, mono 4.2g, poly 1.8g); PROTEIN 3.4g; CARB 15g; FIBER 0g; CHOL 30mg; IRON 0.3mg; SODIUM 82mg; CALC 86mg

This delectable cheese bread is best when served hot directly from the oven.

# APPLE-FLAX-PECAN BREAD

Hands-on time: 20 min. Total time: 2 hr. 20 min.

*This flavorful bread is teeming with antioxidants, vitamins, and omega-3 fatty acids from the hearty combination of fruit, nuts, and flaxseed.*

3.45 ounces brown rice flour (about ¾ cup)
2.6 ounces white rice flour (about ½ cup)
1.05 ounces tapioca flour (about ¼ cup)
0.9 ounce flaxseed meal (about ¼ cup)
2 teaspoons baking powder
1 teaspoon xanthan gum
½ teaspoon baking soda
½ teaspoon ground cinnamon
½ teaspoon salt
1 cup granulated sugar
¾ cup light sour cream
1 tablespoon vanilla extract
2 large eggs
1½ cups finely chopped peeled Granny Smith apple (about 1 pound)
¼ cup chopped pecans
Cooking spray
2 tablespoons butter
2 tablespoons packed brown sugar

1. Preheat oven to 350°.

2. Weigh or lightly spoon flours and flaxseed meal into dry measuring cups; level with a knife. Combine flours, flaxseed meal, baking powder, and next 4 ingredients (through salt) in a bowl.

3. Place granulated sugar and sour cream in a large bowl; beat with a mixer at medium speed until blended. Beat in vanilla and eggs. Gradually add flour mixture, beating at low speed until smooth. Stir in apple and pecans.

4. Pour batter into a 9 x 5–inch loaf pan coated with cooking spray. Bake at 350° for 50 minutes or until a wooden pick inserted in center comes out clean. Cool 15 minutes in pan on a wire rack; remove from pan.

5. Combine butter and brown sugar in a small saucepan; bring to a boil over medium heat, stirring constantly. Boil 1 minute. Spoon mixture over warm bread. Cool completely on wire rack. Serves 15 (serving size: 1 slice)

CALORIES 187; FAT 5.8g (sat 2.2g, mono 2g, poly 1.2g); PROTEIN 2.7g; CARB 32g; FIBER 1.7g; CHOL 33mg; IRON 0.4mg; SODIUM 213mg; CALC 72mg

## sour cream savings

When added to baked goods, sour cream has the wonderful effect of making them moister and also keeping them that way for longer. And you don't need the full-fat variety to achieve this result. The light version works the same and lets you use less oil and butter.

# MAPLE-WALNUT-BANANA BREAD

Hands-on time: 11 min. Total time: 2 hr. 26 min.

*This quick bread is a favorite for our whole family. A harmonious blend of bananas and walnuts wrapped in the sweetness of pure maple syrup, it makes for an easy breakfast treat or after-school snack.*

4.6 ounces brown rice flour (about 1 cup)
1.3 ounces white rice flour (about 1/4 cup)
1.05 ounces sweet white sorghum flour
    (about 1/4 cup)
1 1/2 teaspoons xanthan gum
1 teaspoon baking soda
1 teaspoon baking powder
1/2 teaspoon ground cinnamon
1/4 teaspoon salt
1 cup mashed ripe banana (about 2 medium)
1/2 cup sugar
1/3 cup maple syrup
1/4 cup butter, melted
1/4 cup plain fat-free yogurt
1 teaspoon vanilla extract
2 large eggs, lightly beaten
Cooking spray
1/4 cup finely chopped walnuts

1. Preheat oven to 350°.

2. Weigh or lightly spoon flours into dry measuring cups; level with a knife. Combine flours, xanthan gum, and next 4 ingredients (through salt) in a medium bowl; stir with a whisk.

3. Place banana and next 6 ingredients (through eggs) in a medium bowl; beat with a mixer at medium speed until blended. Gradually add flour mixture, beating at low speed until smooth.

4. Pour batter into a 9 x 5–inch loaf pan coated with cooking spray, and sprinkle with walnuts. Bake at 350° for 1 hour or until a wooden pick inserted in center comes out clean. Cool 15 minutes in pan on a wire rack; remove from pan. Cool completely on wire rack. Serves 14 (serving size: 1 slice)

CALORIES 172; FAT 5.9g (sat 2.5g, mono 1.5g, poly 1.4g); PROTEIN 2.7g; CARB 28g; FIBER 1.5g; CHOL 35mg; IRON 0.5mg; SODIUM 209mg; CALC 49mg

## freeze it: bananas

**tip**

If you have an overabundance of ripe bananas, it is perfectly OK to freeze them. If you plan on using the frozen bananas for banana bread or a recipe that calls for mashed banana, freeze them in their peels. You'll need to thaw the bananas before removing the peel. If you plan to use the bananas for something that calls for pieces, remove the peels, slice the fruit to the desired size, and place on a baking sheet in the freezer. After the banana pieces are frozen, transfer them to a zip-top plastic bag, and store for 3 to 4 months.

# CRANBERRY-ORANGE-NUT BREAD

*This zesty and festive nut bread wrapped up with a bow makes for a welcome holiday gift.*

2.6 ounces potato starch (about ½ cup)
2.3 ounces brown rice flour (about ½ cup)
2.1 ounces sweet white sorghum flour (about ½ cup)
1.05 ounces tapioca flour (about ¼ cup)
½ cup granulated sugar
1 teaspoon xanthan gum
1 teaspoon baking soda
½ teaspoon baking powder
½ teaspoon salt
¾ cup fresh orange juice (about 3 oranges)
¼ cup canola oil
2 large eggs
1 cup fresh or frozen cranberries, chopped
⅓ cup chopped walnuts
Cooking spray
1 tablespoon turbinado sugar or granulated sugar

1. Preheat oven to 350°.

2. Weigh or lightly spoon potato starch and flours into dry measuring cups; level with a knife. Combine potato starch, flours, granulated sugar, and next 4 ingredients (through salt) in a medium bowl; stir with a whisk. Make a well in center of mixture. Combine orange juice, oil, and eggs; stir with a whisk. Add to flour mixture, stirring just until moist. Fold in cranberries and walnuts.

3. Pour batter into a 9 x 5–inch loaf pan coated with cooking spray, and sprinkle with turbinado sugar. Bake at 350° for 50 minutes or until a wooden pick inserted in center comes out clean. Cool 15 minutes in pan on a wire rack; remove from pan. Cool completely on wire rack. Serves 16 (serving size: 1 slice)

Note: If you're planning to freeze this loaf, leave off the turbinado sugar.

CALORIES 143; FAT 6.1g (sat 0.7g, mono 2.8g, poly 2.4g); PROTEIN 1.9g; CARB 21g; FIBER 1.1g; CHOL 23mg; IRON 0.4mg; SODIUM 176mg; CALC 19mg

# LEMON-POPPY SEED BREAD

Hands-on time: 15 min. Total time: 2 hr. 20 min.

*Our friend, Bryce, said he would nearly give up his life for this bread. It's great with yogurt and a little honey for breakfast.*

3.15 ounces sweet white sorghum flour
   (about ¾ cup)
2.3 ounces brown rice flour (about ½ cup)
2.1 ounces tapioca flour (about ½ cup)
1 teaspoon xanthan gum
1 teaspoon baking powder
1 teaspoon baking soda
½ teaspoon salt
⅔ cup granulated sugar

¼ cup unsalted butter, softened
2 large egg yolks
¾ cup buttermilk
1 tablespoon grated lemon rind
3 tablespoons fresh lemon juice
1 tablespoon canola oil
2 large egg whites
2 tablespoons poppy seeds
Cooking spray
1 tablespoon turbinado sugar or granulated sugar

1. Preheat oven to 350°.

2. Weigh or lightly spoon flours into dry measuring cups; level with a knife. Combine flours, xanthan gum, and next 3 ingredients; stir with a whisk.

3. Place granulated sugar and butter in a bowl; beat with a mixer at medium speed until blended. Beat in egg yolks. Beat in buttermilk, lemon rind, lemon juice, and canola oil until well blended. Gradually add flour mixture, beating at low speed until smooth.

4. Place egg whites in a small bowl; beat with a whisk until foamy. Add poppy seeds and egg whites to batter; beat at low speed just until blended.

5. Pour batter into a 9 x 5–inch loaf pan coated with cooking spray, and sprinkle with turbinado sugar. Bake at 350° for 50 minutes or until a wooden pick inserted in center comes out clean. Cool 15 minutes in pan on a wire rack; remove from pan. Cool completely on wire rack. Serves 12 (serving size: 1 slice)

CALORIES 186; FAT 7.3g (sat 3.1g, mono 2.5g, poly 1.2g); PROTEIN 3g; CARB 29g; FIBER 1.3g; CHOL 42mg; IRON 0.7mg; SODIUM 267mg; CALC 78mg

# PUMPKIN-OAT BREAD

Hands-on time: 8 min. Total time: 2 hr. 23 min.

*Oat flour is used in this recipe because it absorbs a lot of liquid and maintains the moisture of baked goods for longer. Serve with butter and warm cider for a satisfying autumn treat.*

5.4 ounces oat flour (about 1½ cups)
1.3 ounces white rice flour (about ¼ cup)
1.05 ounces tapioca starch (about ¼ cup)
1½ teaspoons baking powder
1 teaspoon baking soda
1 teaspoon ground cinnamon
½ teaspoon xanthan gum
½ teaspoon salt
¼ teaspoon ground ginger
¼ teaspoon ground nutmeg
1 cup fresh or canned pumpkin puree
½ cup canola oil
⅓ cup honey
¼ cup sugar
2 large eggs
Cooking spray
1 tablespoon unsalted pumpkinseed kernels
1 tablespoon certified gluten-free quick-cooking oats

1. Preheat oven to 350°.

2. Weigh or lightly spoon flours and tapioca starch into dry measuring cups; level with a knife. Combine flours, tapioca starch, baking powder, and next 6 ingredients (through nutmeg) in a large bowl; stir with a whisk. Make a well in center of mixture. Combine pumpkin and next 4 ingredients (through eggs); stir with a whisk. Add to flour mixture, stirring just until moist.

3. Pour batter into a 9 x 5–inch loaf pan coated with cooking spray. Sprinkle with pumpkinseed kernels and oats. Bake at 350° for 1 hour or until a wooden pick inserted in center comes out clean. Cool 15 minutes in pan on a wire rack; remove from pan. Cool completely on wire rack. Serves 16 (serving size: 1 slice)

CALORIES 169; FAT 9g (sat 1g, mono 5.1g, poly 2.6g); PROTEIN 2.8g; CARB 20g; FIBER 1.5g; CHOL 23mg; IRON 0.7mg; SODIUM 205mg; CALC 45mg

# ZUCCHINI-SPICE BREAD

Hands-on time: 9 min. Total time: 2 hr. 29 min.

*This scrumptious bread is a tasty way to get your kids to eat more veggies. Serve it alongside some hot cocoa, and watch them devour their zucchini.*

5.2 ounces white rice flour (about 1 cup)
4.6 ounces brown rice flour (about 1 cup)
1.05 ounces tapioca flour (about 1/4 cup)
1 1/4 teaspoons ground cinnamon
1 teaspoon xanthan gum
1 teaspoon baking soda
1/2 teaspoon baking powder
1/2 teaspoon salt
1/2 teaspoon ground ginger
1/4 teaspoon ground nutmeg
3/4 cup sugar
2 cups shredded zucchini (1 large)
1/2 cup canola oil
1/2 teaspoon vanilla extract
2 large eggs
Cooking spray

1. Preheat oven to 350°.

2. Weigh or lightly spoon flours into dry measuring cups; level with a knife. Combine flours, cinnamon, and next 6 ingredients (through nutmeg) in a large bowl; stir with a whisk. Make a well in center of mixture. Combine sugar and next 4 ingredients (through eggs); stir with a whisk. Add to flour mixture, stirring just until moist.

3. Pour batter into an 8 x 4–inch loaf pan coated with cooking spray, and smooth top with a spatula. Bake at 350° for 1 hour and 5 minutes or until very firm to the touch. Cool 15 minutes in pan on a wire rack; remove from pan. Cool completely on wire rack. Serves 16 (serving size: 1 slice)

CALORIES 183; FAT 8.2g (sat 0.8g, mono 4.9g, poly 2.2g); PROTEIN 2.2g; CARB 26g; FIBER 1.1g; CHOL 23mg; IRON 0.4mg; SODIUM 178mg; CALC 21mg

## extra zucchini

t
i
p

If you're like me and find yourself with more fresh zucchini from the garden than you know what to do with, freeze it. Grate the zucchini on a box grater, and place it in a colander. Using your hands, squeeze as much water from the zucchini as possible, and then place it in a zip-top plastic freezer bag. Store the zucchini in the freezer for up to 3 months.

Currants are a sweet dried berry that are slightly smaller than raisins and come in red, black, or white. If you like, raisins can be substituted for the currants in this recipe.

# IRISH SODA BREAD

Hands-on time: 15 min. Total time: 2 hr. 5 min.

*When I baked this for my friend, Joe McLaughlin, he paused and reminisced, "There is just something about Irish Soda Bread that always reminds me of the warmth in my Aunt Peggy's welcoming smile when we would visit her in the village of Clonbern in County Galway. The tea is steeping on the turf stove in the kitchen, and the smell of that heavenly bread is in the air." That's when Irish eyes are smiling.*

3.9 ounces potato starch (about ¾ cup)
3.45 ounces brown rice flour (about ¾ cup)
2.1 ounces sweet white sorghum flour (about ½ cup)
1.05 ounces tapioca flour (about ¼ cup)
⅓ cup sugar
1 teaspoon xanthan gum
1 teaspoon baking powder
½ teaspoon baking soda
½ teaspoon salt
¼ cup chilled butter, cut into small pieces
1⅓ cups low-fat buttermilk
1 teaspoon grated orange rind
1 large egg
½ cup dried currants
Cooking spray

1. Preheat oven to 350°.

2. Weigh or lightly spoon potato starch and flours into dry measuring cups; level with knife. Combine potato starch, flours, sugar, and next 4 ingredients (through salt) in a large bowl, stirring with a whisk. Cut in butter with a pastry blender or 2 knives until mixture resembles coarse meal.

3. Combine buttermilk, orange rind, and egg in a medium bowl, stirring with a whisk. Add egg mixture to flour mixture; stir just until moist. Gently fold in currants.

4. Pour batter into a 9 x 5–inch loaf pan coated with cooking spray. Bake at 350° for 55 minutes or until a wooden pick inserted in center comes out clean. Cool 10 minutes in pan on a wire rack; remove from pan. Cool completely on wire rack. Serves 16 (serving size: 1 slice)

CALORIES 134; FAT 3.8g (sat 2.1g, mono 1g, poly 0.2g); PROTEIN 2.2g; CARB 24g; FIBER 1g; CHOL 21mg; IRON 0.5mg; SODIUM 193mg; CALC 50mg

# FETA AND DILL QUICK BREAD

Hands-on time: 6 min. Total time: 2 hr. 6 min.

*Years ago I had an opportunity to work with a chef from Greece whom we referred to as "Nick the Greek." He taught me how to prepare some amazing cuisine, which included this tangy bread.*

3.45 ounces brown rice flour (about 3/4 cup)
2.6 ounces white rice flour (about 1/2 cup)
1.05 ounces tapioca flour (about 1/4 cup)
2 teaspoons baking powder
1 teaspoon xanthan gum
3/4 teaspoon salt
4 ounces feta cheese, crumbled (about 1 cup)
1 tablespoon chopped fresh dill
3/4 cup fat-free half-and-half
1/4 cup olive oil
2 large eggs
Cooking spray

1. Preheat oven to 350°.

2. Weigh or lightly spoon flours into dry measuring cups; level with a knife. Combine flours, baking powder, xanthan gum, and salt; stir with a whisk. Stir in feta cheese and dill; make a well in center of mixture. Combine half-and-half, olive oil, and eggs; stir with a whisk. Add to flour mixture, stirring just until moist.

3. Pour batter into an 8 x 4–inch loaf pan coated with cooking spray. Bake at 350° for 45 minutes or until a wooden pick inserted in center comes out clean. Cool 15 minutes in pan on a wire rack; remove from pan. Cool completely on wire rack. Serves 16 (serving size: 1 slice)

CALORIES 113; FAT 5.9g (sat 1.8g, mono 3.2g, poly 0.6g); PROTEIN 2.9g; CARB 12g; FIBER 0.6g; CHOL 30mg; IRON 0.3mg; SODIUM 263mg; CALC 96mg

## fresh vs. dry

tip

If you have only dried dill, feel free to substitute that in this recipe. Because fresh herbs are not as strong or concentrated as the dried versions, use 1 teaspoon of dried dill for every tablespoon of fresh.

# MEDITERRANEAN OLIVE QUICK BREAD

Hands-on time: 7 min. Total time: 1 hr. 52 min.

*If you're a big fan of kalamata olives and fresh rosemary, then you are going to love this slightly salty bread. Serve it with platters of roasted vegetables, fresh mozzarella, and extra-virgin olive oil.*

2.6 ounces white rice flour (about ½ cup)
2.3 ounces brown rice flour (about ½ cup)
1.05 ounces tapioca flour (about ¼ cup)
1.3 ounces potato starch (about ¼ cup)
0.9 ounce flaxseed meal (about ¼ cup)
1 teaspoon xanthan gum
1 teaspoon baking soda

½ teaspoon baking powder
½ teaspoon salt
½ cup pitted kalamata olives, chopped
1½ tablespoons chopped fresh rosemary
½ cup nonfat buttermilk
¼ cup olive oil
2 tablespoons honey
2 large eggs
Cooking spray

1. Preheat oven to 350°.

2. Weigh or lightly spoon flours, potato starch, and flaxseed meal into dry measuring cups; level with a knife. Combine flours, potato starch, flaxseed meal, xanthan gum, and next 3 ingredients (through salt) in a medium bowl; stir with a whisk. Stir in olives and rosemary; make a well in center of mixture. Combine buttermilk and next 3 ingredients (through eggs); stir with a whisk. Add to flour mixture, stirring just until moist.

3. Pour batter into an 8 x 4–inch loaf pan coated with cooking spray. Bake at 350° for 30 to 40 minutes or until a wooden pick inserted in center comes out clean. Cool 15 minutes in pan on a wire rack; remove from pan. Cool completely on wire rack. Serves 16 (serving size: 1 slice)

CALORIES 120; FAT 6.3g (sat 0.9g, mono 4g, poly 1.2g); PROTEIN 2.1g; CARB 14g; FIBER 1g; CHOL 23mg; IRON 0.3mg; SODIUM 267mg; CALC 27mg

# BUTTERMILK CORN BREAD

Hands-on time: 15 min. Total time: 50 min.

*This rich and buttery corn bread is an ideal pairing alongside a big steaming pot of chili.*

9.1 ounces certified gluten-free stone-ground cornmeal (about 1½ cups)
2.6 ounces white rice flour (about ½ cup)
1.05 ounces tapioca flour (about ¼ cup)
1.3 ounces potato starch (about ¼ cup)
2 tablespoons sugar
1 teaspoon xanthan gum
1 teaspoon baking powder
1 teaspoon salt
½ teaspoon baking soda
1½ cups low-fat buttermilk
⅓ cup canola oil
1 large egg
Cooking spray

1. Preheat oven to 400°.

2. Weigh or lightly spoon cornmeal, flours, and potato starch into dry measuring cups; level with a knife. Combine cornmeal, flours, potato starch, sugar, and next 4 ingredients (through baking soda) in a medium bowl; stir with a whisk. Make a well in center of mixture. Combine buttermilk, oil, and egg; stir with a whisk. Add to flour mixture, stirring just until moist.

3. Pour batter into a 9-inch square metal baking pan coated with cooking spray. Bake at 400° for 25 minutes or until edges are lightly browned. Cool 10 minutes in pan on a wire rack. Serve warm, or cool completely on wire rack. Serves 16 (serving size: 1 square)

CALORIES 139; FAT 5.8g (sat 0.8g, mono 2.2g, poly 2.1g); PROTEIN 2.3g; CARB 20g; FIBER 2.3g; CHOL 13mg; IRON 0.5mg; SODIUM 248mg; CALC 50mg

## cornmeal check

Stone-ground cornmeal adds a delightful corn flavor and crunchy texture to corn bread. And although cornmeal is naturally gluten-free, it's still necessary to buy a brand marked as certified gluten-free to ensure it's produced in a facility that follows the necessary protocols to prevent cross-contamination.

chapter 5

# COOKIES, BROWNIES, ☒AND☒ SWEET BARS

"**D**addy, where do cookies come from?" asked my son, Andrew. "Phew!" I thought, "I can answer that one!" Food historians believe the earliest cookie-style cakes date all the way back to 7th-century Persia, but it was the Dutch who popularized cookies for Americans, and they did so accidentally.

Dutch cake bakers would test oven temperatures by putting dollops of cake batter on baking pans to watch how fast they "set up." The bakers, thoroughly enjoying these test items, started calling them "koekje," or little cakes, which quickly became very popular. The Dutch settlers of North America changed the word "koekje" to "cookie."

Gluten-free cookies, brownies, and sweet bars employ a handful of helpful techniques to mimic the bites that brought them to prominence: chilling the batter; not spraying the baking sheet to prevent them from spreading; and leaning heavily on eggs, which help hold them together. The results are gluten-free versions of favorite cookies, brownies, and sweet bars, all guaranteed to succeed.

# OATMEAL-RAISIN COOKIES

Hands-on time: 16 min. Total time: 64 min.

*Just like grandma used to make—and Gramma Fitz still does! These cookies are chewy and not too sweet, with plenty of ground cinnamon, nutmeg, ginger, and allspice folded into a batter that's packed with juicy raisins. Serve with a tall glass of milk for lots of smiles.*

½ cup raisins
1.05 ounces garbanzo bean flour (about ¼ cup)
1.05 ounces sweet white sorghum flour
   (about ¼ cup)
1.3 ounces potato starch (about ¼ cup)
½ teaspoon xanthan gum
½ teaspoon baking powder
½ teaspoon ground cinnamon
½ teaspoon ground ginger
¼ teaspoon ground nutmeg
¼ teaspoon ground allspice
¼ teaspoon salt
½ cup packed brown sugar
½ cup granulated sugar
⅓ cup unsalted butter, softened
1 teaspoon vanilla extract
1 large egg
1 cup certified gluten-free quick-cooking oats

1. Preheat oven to 350°.

2. Place raisins in a small bowl; cover with warm water. Let stand 5 minutes. Drain.

3. Weigh or lightly spoon flours and potato starch into dry measuring cups; level with a knife. Combine flours, potato starch, and next 7 ingredients (through salt) in a medium bowl; stir with a whisk.

4. Place sugars and butter in a large bowl; beat with a mixer at high speed until well blended. Add vanilla and egg; beat until blended. Gradually add flour mixture, beating at low speed until blended. Add raisins and oats; beat until blended.

5. Drop dough by tablespoonfuls 2 inches apart onto baking sheets lined with parchment paper. Bake at 350° for 12 to 14 minutes or until edges of cookies are lightly browned. Cool 2 minutes on pans. Remove cookies from pans; cool on wire racks. Serves 38 (serving size: 1 cookie)

CALORIES 62; FAT 2g (sat 1.1g, mono 0.5g, poly 0.1g); PROTEIN 0.9g; CARB 11g; FIBER 0.6g; CHOL 9mg; IRON 0.3mg; SODIUM 25mg; CALC 11mg

## raisin transformation

Since raisins are dried fruit, they can sometimes be quite dry. Soaking the raisins in warm water rehydrates them, allowing them to absorb some of the liquid and plump up, leaving you with a softer texture that can be a nice change of pace from their typically chewy state. It also adds moisture to your baked goods.

# PB, BANANA, AND OAT COOKIES

Hands-on time: 15 min. Total time: 59 min.

*When my wife's sister, Kathleen, visits from the Boston area, she inevitably brings along her beloved Chow mix, Desilu. We have heard many times that Desi can't have chocolate or raisins or onions (and believe it or not, this dog is on a gluten-free diet), as a dog's delicate digestive system can't handle those foods. It turns out, however, that peanut butter, bananas, and oatmeal are OK, as I found out when I walked down the stairs one Sunday morning and found Kathleen and Desi sitting on the couch together, thoroughly enjoying a whole plate of these breakfast cookies. "One for Desi, and one for me. One for Desi…"*

1.8 ounces flaxseed meal (about 1/2 cup)
1.8 ounces oat flour (about 1/2 cup)
2 3/4 cups certified gluten-free old-fashioned rolled oats
1 teaspoon baking soda
3/4 cup peanut butter
2 tablespoons non-dairy buttery spread (such as Earth Balance)
1/3 cup granulated sugar
1/3 cup packed brown sugar
1/2 cup mashed ripe banana
1/2 teaspoon vanilla extract
2 large eggs, lightly beaten
1/3 cup semisweet chocolate minichips
1/4 cup unsalted, roasted sunflower seeds

1. Preheat oven to 350°.

2. Weigh or lightly spoon flaxseed meal and flour into dry measuring cups; level with a knife. Combine flaxseed meal, flour, oats, and baking soda in a medium bowl; stir with a whisk.

3. Place peanut butter, buttery spread, and sugars in a large bowl; beat with a mixer at medium speed until blended. Add banana, vanilla, and eggs, beating until blended. Add flour mixture, minichips, and sunflower seeds, beating until incorporated.

4. Drop by tablespoonfuls 2 inches apart onto baking sheets lined with parchment paper. Bake at 350° for 12 minutes or until edges of cookies are lightly browned. Cool completely on pans before serving. Serves 47 (serving size: 1 cookie)

CALORIES 82; FAT 4.2g (sat 1g, mono 1.6g, poly 1.2g); PROTEIN 2.7g; CARB 9g; FIBER 1.3g; CHOL 8mg; IRON 0.5mg; SODIUM 54mg; CALC 6mg

## better with banana

Using bananas in baked goods is an easy and flavorful way to decrease the amount of eggs in a recipe while retaining moisture and achieving the proper texture. Plus, they add potassium, fiber, and vitamin B6.

# OATMEAL, CHOCOLATE, AND WALNUT COOKIES

Hands-on time: 25 min. Total time: 55 min.

*Chewy oatmeal and crunchy walnuts can completely transform the typical lunch box chocolate chip cookie, adding new flavors and texture while subtly increasing the cookie's nutritional value.*

2.3 ounces brown rice flour (about ½ cup)
1.3 ounces white rice flour (about ¼ cup)
1.3 ounces potato starch (about ¼ cup)
1.15 ounces cornstarch (about ¼ cup)
1 cup certified gluten-free quick-cooking oats
1 teaspoon xanthan gum
1 teaspoon baking powder
½ teaspoon baking soda
¼ teaspoon salt
¾ cup granulated sugar
½ cup packed brown sugar
⅓ cup butter, softened
2 teaspoons vanilla extract

1 large egg
¼ cup chopped walnuts
¼ cup semisweet chocolate minichips

1. Preheat oven to 375°.

2. Weigh or lightly spoon flours, potato starch, and cornstarch into dry measuring cups; level with a knife. Combine flours, potato starch, cornstarch, and next 5 ingredients in a bowl; stir with a whisk.

3. Place granulated sugar, brown sugar, and butter in a large bowl; beat with a mixer at medium speed until well blended. Beat in vanilla and egg. Gradually add flour mixture, beating at low speed until blended. Fold in walnuts and chocolate minichips.

4. Drop dough by level tablespoonfuls 2 inches apart onto baking sheets lined with parchment paper. Bake at 375° for 10 minutes or until edges of cookies begin to brown. Cool 5 minutes on pans. Remove from pans; cool completely on wire racks. Serves 39 (serving size: 1 cookie)

CALORIES 77; FAT 2.7g (sat 1.3g, mono 0.8g, poly 0.5g); PROTEIN 1g; CARB 12.6g; FIBER 0.5g; CHOL 9mg; IRON 0.2mg; SODIUM 62mg; CALC 7mg

## smart selection
**t i p**

Most oats on the market today are cross-contaminated with wheat, barley, or rye, so make sure you select a brand that is certified gluten-free. That labeling ensures that precautions were taken to avoid cross-contamination.

# DOUBLE-CHOCOLATE COOKIES

Hands-on time: 20 min. Total time: 3 hr.

*With a hint of coffee, these are the cookie version of chocolate-covered coffee beans! Send them to your children who are off at college in the next care package. They will be the best thing going in the dorm during those long "all-nighters."*

1.3 ounces white rice flour (about 1/4 cup)
1.15 ounces brown rice flour (about 1/4 cup)
1 tablespoon unsweetened cocoa
1 teaspoon xanthan gum
1/2 teaspoon baking powder
1/8 teaspoon salt
3/4 cup semisweet chocolate minichips, divided
1/4 cup non-dairy buttery spread (such as Earth Balance)
2 ounces unsweetened chocolate
1/2 teaspoon instant coffee granules
1 teaspoon vanilla extract
1/2 cup sugar
2 large eggs
Cooking spray

1. Weigh or lightly spoon flours into dry measuring cups; level with a knife. Combine flours, cocoa, xanthan gum, baking powder, and salt in a small bowl; stir well with a whisk.

2. Combine 1/2 cup chocolate minichips, buttery spread, unsweetened chocolate, and coffee granules in a small saucepan; cook over medium-low heat 4 minutes or until chocolate melts, stirring until mixture is smooth and creamy. Remove from heat; cool 10 minutes. Stir in vanilla.

3. Place sugar and eggs in a medium bowl; beat with a mixer at medium speed 2 minutes or until light and fluffy. Add chocolate mixture; beat until blended. Add flour mixture; beat just until blended. Fold in 1/4 cup chocolate minichips. Cover and chill 2 hours.

4. Preheat oven to 350°.

5. Lightly coat hands with cooking spray; shape dough into 30 (1-inch) balls. Place balls 2 inches apart on baking sheets lined with parchment paper. Flatten cookies slightly with hand. Bake at 350° for 8 to 10 minutes or until edges look cooked. Cool 2 minutes on pans. Remove cookies from pans; cool on wire racks. Serves 30 (serving size: 1 cookie)

CALORIES 71; FAT 4.1g (sat 1.9g, mono 1.6g, poly 0.6g); PROTEIN 1g; CARB 9g; FIBER 0.8g; CHOL 12mg; IRON 0.6mg; SODIUM 36mg; CALC 11mg

# CHEWY ALMOND-COCOA COOKIES

*These classic Italian cookies, also referred to as amaretti, are crispy on the outside and chewy on the inside. We were first introduced to these while sipping espresso in a café in Florence on an incredible trip to Italy with our dear friends, the McLaughlins…even the Irish love to eat Italian!*

5.4 ounces almond meal flour (about 1½ cups)
⅔ cup sugar, divided
1 tablespoon unsweetened cocoa
2 large egg whites
¼ teaspoon cream of tartar
¼ teaspoon almond extract
2 tablespoons sliced almonds

1. Preheat oven to 325°.

2. Combine almond flour, ⅓ cup sugar, and cocoa in a medium bowl; stir well with a whisk.

3. Place egg whites in a large bowl; beat with a mixer at high speed until foamy. Add cream of tartar; beat until soft peaks form. Add ⅓ cup sugar, 1 tablespoon at a time, beating until stiff peaks form. Fold in almond extract. Sprinkle flour mixture over egg white mixture; fold in.

4. Spoon mixture into a pastry bag fitted with a ¼-inch round tip. Pipe 53 (1½-inch-round) mounds 1 inch apart onto baking sheets lined with parchment paper. Gently press an almond slice into top of each cookie. Bake at 325° for 12 to 15 minutes or until edges of cookies are crisp. Cool 10 minutes on pans. Remove cookies from pans; cool on wire racks. Serves 53 (serving size: 1 cookie)

---

CALORIES 29; FAT 1.6g (sat 0.1g, mono 0.1g, poly 0g); PROTEIN 0.8g; CARB 3.3g; FIBER 0.4g; CHOL 0mg; IRON 0.1mg; SODIUM 3mg; CALC 7mg

## making meringue

t
i
p

Cream of tartar is often added when beating egg whites to make meringue. It keeps the whites stable and adds volume.

# CHOCOLATE-FROSTED COOKIES

Hands-on time: 15 min. Total time: 55 min.

*My sister, Dana, has always gone out of her way to provide gluten-free options for our family when she has a party or dinner at her home. This recipe—reminiscent of the classic black and white cookie—was one I shared for her to make, as it is quick, easy, and loved by all. In addition to adding whole grains, sorghum flour adds a nutty flavor that pairs well with bittersweet chocolate.*

3.15 ounces sweet white sorghum flour
    (about ³/₄ cup)
2.6 ounces white rice flour (about ¹/₂ cup)
2.3 ounces cornstarch (about ¹/₂ cup)
1 teaspoon xanthan gum
³/₄ cup sugar
10 tablespoons butter, softened
1¹/₂ teaspoons vanilla extract
2 large eggs
1 large egg white
¹/₂ cup bittersweet chocolate chips

1. Preheat oven to 375°.

2. Weigh or lightly spoon flours into dry measuring cups; level with a knife. In a medium bowl, sift together flours, cornstarch, and xanthan gum.

3. Combine sugar and butter in a large bowl; beat with a mixer at medium speed until light and fluffy. Add vanilla, eggs, and egg white, beating until blended. Add flour mixture, beating at low speed until blended.

4. Drop dough by tablespoonfuls 2 inches apart onto baking sheets lined with parchment paper. Bake at 375° for 13 to 15 minutes or until cookies are lightly browned on edges. Cool completely on pans.

5. Place chips in microwave-safe bowl; microwave at HIGH 1 minute. Remove and stir. If needed, microwave 15 seconds and stir; repeat until chocolate is melted and smooth. Spoon melted chocolate on top of each cookie; place on parchment paper until set. Serves 44 (serving size: 1 cookie)

CALORIES 63; FAT 3.2g (sat 1.9g, mono 0.8g, poly 0.2g); PROTEIN 0.8g; CARB 8.1g; FIBER 0.3g; CHOL 15mg; IRON 0.2mg; SODIUM 28mg; CALC 2mg

# LEMON SUGAR COOKIES

*The stark contrast between the sweet sugars and the tart lemon rind give these cookies personality and bite. They're a great afternoon treat with coffee or tea.*

2.3 ounces brown rice flour (about 1/2 cup)
1.8 ounces almond meal flour (about 1/2 cup)
1.05 ounces tapioca flour (about 1/4 cup)
1.3 ounces potato starch (about 1/4 cup)
1 teaspoon xanthan gum
1 teaspoon baking powder
1/4 teaspoon salt
1/2 cup packed brown sugar
1/2 cup granulated sugar
4 tablespoons butter, softened
1 tablespoon fresh lemon juice
1 teaspoon vanilla extract
1/2 teaspoon grated lemon rind
2 large egg yolks

1. Preheat oven to 350°.

2. Weigh or lightly spoon flours into dry measuring cups; level with a knife. Combine flours, potato starch, xanthan gum, baking powder, and salt in a medium bowl, stirring with a whisk.

3. Place sugars and butter in a large bowl; beat with a mixer at medium speed until well blended. Add lemon juice, vanilla, rind, and egg yolks; beat until blended. Add flour mixture, 1/4 cup at a time, beating after each addition.

4. Cover a large baking sheet with parchment paper. Shape dough into 20 balls. Place 2 inches apart on baking sheet. Bake at 350° for 15 to 20 minutes or until lightly browned. Cool 5 minutes on pan. Remove cookies from pan; cool completely on wire racks. Serves 20 (serving size: 1 cookie)

CALORIES 105; FAT 4.1g (sat 1.7g, mono 0.8g, poly 0.2g); PROTEIN 1.1g; CARB 16.7g; FIBER 0.6g; CHOL 25mg; IRON 0.3mg; SODIUM 75mg; CALC 30mg

*Almond meal flour has a sweet, buttery flavor and smooth texture when baked.*

# SNICKERDOODLES

Hands-on time: 8 min. Total time: 36 min.

*These cinnamon-spiced cookies are an absolute favorite of my boys, Joseph, Andrew, and Stephen, when they spend a day filled with hiking and swimming at Grampa Landolphi's house. Lots of good-hearted sparring begins when hungry cousins Luke, Brooke, and Gus are there, too. The Snickerdoodles fuel their fun and quickly run low.*

4.2 ounces garbanzo bean flour (about 1 cup)
1.3 ounces potato starch (about 1/4 cup)
1 teaspoon baking soda
3/4 teaspoon xanthan gum
1/2 teaspoon cream of tartar
1/4 teaspoon salt
1/4 cup butter, softened
1/4 cup packed brown sugar
1/4 cup granulated sugar
1 tablespoon corn syrup
1 teaspoon vanilla extract
2 large egg yolks
3 tablespoons turbinado sugar
1 teaspoon ground cinnamon

1. Preheat oven to 350°.

2. Weigh or lightly spoon flour and potato starch into dry measuring cups; level with a knife. Combine flour, potato starch, and next 4 ingredients (through salt) in a medium bowl, stirring with a whisk.

3. Place butter, brown sugar, and granulated sugar in a large bowl; beat with a mixer at medium speed until blended. Add corn syrup, vanilla, and egg yolks beating at low speed. Add flour mixture; beat at low speed until blended.

4. Combine turbinado sugar and cinnamon in a small bowl. Shape dough with moist hands into 1-inch balls. Roll balls in sugar mixture. Place 2 inches apart on a baking sheet lined with parchment paper; flatten cookies with the bottom of a glass. Bake at 350° for 8 to 10 minutes or until edges of cookies are golden brown. Cool completely on pan. Serves 16 (serving size: 1 cookie)

---

CALORIES 106; FAT 3.9g (sat 2g, mono 1g, poly 0.2g); PROTEIN 1.9g; CARB 16.7g; FIBER 1.5g; CHOL 31mg; IRON 0.6mg; SODIUM 145mg; CALC 18mg

# MEXICAN WEDDING COOKIES

*Also known as Russian teacakes or snowball cookies, these dense, crumbly, bite-sized cookies are just soooo good. Enjoy them with a frothy cappuccino.*

2.6 ounces potato starch (about ½ cup)
2.3 ounces cornstarch (about ½ cup)
2.1 ounces garbanzo bean flour (about ½ cup)
2.1 ounces sweet white sorghum flour (about ½ cup)
1 teaspoon xanthan gum
¼ teaspoon salt
½ cup sifted powdered sugar
5 tablespoons butter, softened
2 teaspoons vanilla extract
2 tablespoons canola oil
1 tablespoon 1% low-fat milk

2 large egg yolks
½ cup pecans, finely chopped
⅓ cup powdered sugar

1. Preheat oven to 350°.

2. Weigh or lightly spoon potato starch, cornstarch, and flours into dry measuring cups; level with a knife. Combine potato starch, cornstarch, flours, xanthan gum, and salt in a medium bowl, stirring with a whisk.

3. Place ½ cup powdered sugar, butter, and vanilla in a large bowl; beat with a mixer at medium speed until well blended. Add canola oil, milk, and egg yolks, beating until blended. Gradually add flour mixture, beating until blended. Stir in pecans.

4. Shape dough into 38 (1-inch) balls, and place 2 inches apart on baking sheets lined with parchment paper. Flatten tops of cookies slightly with fingers. Bake at 350° for 10 to 12 minutes or until bottoms of cookies are lightly browned.

5. Immediately roll warm cookies in ⅓ cup powdered sugar; cool completely on a wire rack, reserving powdered sugar. Reroll cooled cookies in remaining powdered sugar. Serves 38 (serving size: 1 cookie)

**Note:** These cookies can be stored in an airtight container up to 2 weeks.

CALORIES 68; FAT 3.7g (sat 1.2g, mono 1.6g, poly 0.6g); PROTEIN 0.8g; CARB 8.2g; FIBER 0.6g; CHOL 14mg; IRON 0.2mg; SODIUM 30mg; CALC 5mg

# LADYFINGERS

*These light and dainty sponge cake cookies of English descent are quite versatile. You can dip them in tea as they are, top them with cocoa for an extra-special treat, or use them for layering in a scrumptious tiramisu (see page 257).*

1.15 ounces brown rice flour (about ¼ cup)
2 tablespoons tapioca flour
1 tablespoon white rice flour
1 tablespoon potato starch
1 tablespoon cornstarch
½ teaspoon xanthan gum
½ teaspoon baking powder
¼ cup granulated sugar
3 large egg yolks
½ teaspoon vanilla extract
⅛ teaspoon cream of tartar
3 large egg whites
3 tablespoons powdered sugar

1. Preheat oven to 350°.

2. Weigh or lightly spoon brown rice flour into a dry measuring cup; level with a knife. Combine flours, potato starch, cornstarch, xanthan gum, and baking powder in a medium bowl; stir with a whisk.

3. Place granulated sugar and egg yolks in a large bowl; beat with a mixer at medium speed 3 minutes or until mixture becomes pale yellow. Add vanilla; beat until blended.

4. Place cream of tartar and egg whites in a medium bowl; beat with a mixer at medium speed until soft peaks form using clean, dry beaters. Slowly add powdered sugar; beat until stiff peaks form. Fold egg white mixture and flour mixture into egg yolk mixture, stirring just until blended.

5. Spoon batter into a pastry bag fitted with a ½-inch round tip; pipe 24 (2½ x 1–inch) cookies 1 inch apart on baking sheets lined with parchment paper. Bake at 350° for 12 minutes or until edges of cookies are golden brown. Cool 2 minutes on pan. Remove from pans, and cool completely on wire racks. Serves 24 (serving size: 1 ladyfinger)

CALORIES 33; FAT 0.6g (sat 0.2g, mono 0.3g, poly 0.1g); PROTEIN 0.9g; CARB 5.8g; FIBER 0.1g; CHOL 23mg; IRON 0.2mg; SODIUM 18mg; CALC 11mg

# GINGERBREAD COOKIES

Hands-on time: 30 min. Total time: 62 min.

*No Christmas season is complete without the mouthwatering ginger and spice cookies that we all loved as kids. Break out the cookie cutters to turn them into holiday gingerbread men. For an easy, make-ahead cookie, shape the dough into 1½-inch-diameter logs, wrap in plastic wrap, and freeze. When ready to bake, defrost the dough for 20 minutes, cut it into ½-inch-thick slices, and bake as directed.*

9.2 ounces brown rice flour (about 2 cups)
2.6 ounces white rice flour (about ½ cup)
1.05 ounces tapioca flour (about ¼ cup)
1.15 ounces cornstarch (about ¼ cup)
1½ teaspoons baking soda
1 teaspoon xanthan gum
1 teaspoon ground ginger
1 teaspoon ground cinnamon
¼ teaspoon salt
¼ teaspoon ground nutmeg
¼ teaspoon ground cloves
¼ teaspoon ground allspice
½ cup butter, softened
½ cup packed light brown sugar
¼ cup granulated sugar
½ cup light molasses
1 large egg
Cooking spray
1 teaspoon granulated sugar

1. Preheat oven to 375°.

2. Weigh or lightly spoon flours and cornstarch into dry measuring cups; level with a knife. Combine flours, cornstarch, baking soda, and next 7 ingredients (through allspice) in a medium bowl; stir with a whisk.

3. Place butter, brown sugar, and ¼ cup granulated sugar in a large bowl; beat with a mixer at low speed 1 to 2 minutes; increase speed to medium, and beat until well blended. Add molasses and egg; beat well. Gradually add flour mixture, beating until well blended.

4. Lightly coat hands with cooking spray; shape dough into 60 (1-inch) balls. Place 2 inches apart on baking sheets lined with parchment paper. Flatten cookies with the bottom of a glass. Sprinkle cookies with 1 teaspoon granulated sugar. Bake at 375° for 10 minutes or until golden brown. Cool 2 minutes on pans. Remove cookies from pans; cool on wire racks. Serves 60 (serving size: 1 cookie)

CALORIES 58; FAT 1.8g (sat 1g, mono 0.5g, poly 0.1g); PROTEIN 0.5g; CARB 10g; FIBER 0.3g; CHOL 7mg; IRON 0.3mg; SODIUM 58mg; CALC 9mg

*Lightly coating your hands with cooking spray will allow you to shape the dough into balls with the palms of your hands—no sticky mess!*

# ROLL-OUT HOLIDAY COOKIES

Hands-on time: 24 min. Total time: 2 hr. 39 min.

*This gluten-free recipe makes classic sugar cookies complete with frosting and sprinkles that are perfect for decorating to your liking—shape them into pretty hearts for St. Valentine's Day, egg-shaped ovals for Easter, four-leaf clovers for St. Patrick's Day, and trees or stars for Christmas.*

**Cookies:**
3.9 ounces white rice flour (about ³/₄ cup)
2.6 ounces potato starch (about ¹/₂ cup)
1.05 ounces tapioca flour (about ¹/₄ cup)
¹/₂ teaspoon baking powder
¹/₂ teaspoon xanthan gum
¹/₂ cup granulated sugar
6 tablespoons butter, softened
1¹/₂ teaspoons vanilla extract
1 teaspoon 1% low-fat milk
1 large egg
White rice flour, for dusting

**Frosting:**
1 cup powdered sugar
1¹/₂ tablespoons 1% low-fat milk
¹/₄ teaspoon vanilla extract
1 tablespoon sugar sprinkles

1. To prepare cookies, weigh or lightly spoon white rice flour, potato starch, and tapioca flour into dry measuring cups; level with a knife. Sift together white rice flour, potato starch, tapioca flour, baking powder, and xanthan gum.

2. Place granulated sugar and butter in a medium bowl; beat with a mixer at medium speed until light and fluffy. Add 1½ teaspoons vanilla, 1 teaspoon milk, and egg, beating until blended. Add flour mixture, stirring until blended. Shape dough into a ball; wrap in plastic wrap. Chill 1 hour.

3. Preheat oven to 375°.

4. Roll dough to a ⅛-inch thickness on a lightly floured surface. Cut with a 2-inch round cookie cutter into 30 cookies, rerolling scraps as necessary. Place cookies 1 inch apart on baking sheets lined with parchment paper. Bake at 375° for 10 minutes or until edges of cookies are lightly browned. Remove from pans; cool completely on a wire rack.

5. To prepare frosting, combine powdered sugar, 1½ tablespoons milk, and ¼ teaspoon vanilla in a small bowl, stirring with a whisk until smooth. Spread 1 teaspoon frosting on each cookie; top with sprinkles. Place cookies on wire rack until set. Serves 30 (serving size: 1 cookie)

CALORIES 78; FAT 2.5g (sat 1.5g, mono 0.7g, poly 0.1g); PROTEIN 0.5g; CARB 13.4g; FIBER 0.1g; CHOL 12mg; IRON 0.1mg; SODIUM 31mg; CALC 9mg

# COCONUT MACAROONS
## WITH BITTERSWEET CHOCOLATE AND PISTACHIOS

Hands-on time: 16 min. Total time: 1 hr. 33 min.

*Sweet and chewy coconut macaroons have always been an easy favorite for persons following a gluten-free diet, but these beauties are dipped in bittersweet chocolate and studded with salty pistachios to jazz them right up. When my stepsister, Heidi, made these for an annual birthday blowout, they were gone before I could even cut the cake!*

¼ teaspoon cream of tartar
2 large egg whites
3 tablespoons sugar
¼ teaspoon vanilla extract
Pinch of salt
2 cups flaked sweetened coconut
½ cup bittersweet chocolate chips
¼ cup finely chopped pistachios

1. Preheat oven to 325°.

2. Place cream of tartar and egg whites in a large bowl; beat with a mixer at high speed until foamy. Gradually add sugar, vanilla, and salt, beating at high speed until foamy and opaque, about 1 minute. Fold coconut into egg white mixture using a rubber spatula.

3. Spoon egg white mixture by tablespoonfuls 2 inches apart onto a baking sheet lined with parchment paper. Bake at 325° for 20 minutes or until edges are golden brown. Cool completely on pan on a wire rack.

4. Place chocolate chips in a small microwave-safe bowl; microwave at HIGH 45 seconds or until chips melt, stirring until smooth. Dip top of each macaroon into chocolate, and sprinkle with pistachios. Allow cookies to set 20 to 30 minutes. Serves 21 (serving size: 1 cookie)

CALORIES 62; FAT 3.5g (sat 2.6g, mono 0.5g, poly 0.2g); PROTEIN 1g; CARB 7.2g; FIBER 1g; CHOL 0mg; IRON 0.3mg; SODIUM 36mg; CALC 3mg

# VANILLA MERINGUES

*Here is the simplest version of the light, sweet, flourless Swiss cookie. The basic recipe can be used in countless variations, including mint, chocolate, cherry, cappuccino, or almond, with the quick addition of your favorite flavoring or extract.*

²/₃ cup granulated sugar
¹/₃ cup powdered sugar
4 large egg whites (at room temperature)
¹/₂ teaspoon cream of tartar
¹/₈ teaspoon salt
2 teaspoons vanilla extract
³/₄ cup semisweet chocolate minichips

1. Preheat oven to 250°.

2. Combine sugars in a small bowl; stir with a whisk. Beat egg whites with a mixer at high speed until foamy. Add cream of tartar and salt; beat until soft peaks form. Add sugars, 2 tablespoons at a time, beating until stiff peaks form. Beat in vanilla. Fold in minichips.

3. Spoon meringue into a pastry bag fitted with a ½-inch round tip. Pipe 48 (1½-inch) mounds 1 inch apart on baking sheets lined with parchment paper.

4. Bake at 250° for 1 hour or until dry. Turn oven off; cool meringues in closed oven at least 3 hours. Carefully remove meringues from paper. Serves 48 (serving size: 1 cookie)

**Note:** I use an Ateco #807 round tip to pipe the meringues.

CALORIES 29; FAT 0.8g (sat 0.5g, mono 0.3g, poly 0g); PROTEIN 0.4g; CARB 5.4g; FIBER 0.2g; CHOL 0mg; IRON 0.1mg; SODIUM 11mg; CALC 1mg

## no piping necessary

If you don't happen to have a pastry bag, you can scoop the batter with a spoon, using your finger to transfer the batter onto the baking sheets. The meringues won't be as picture-perfect, but they'll still taste amazing.

Toasting the oats, coconut, sunflower seeds, and flaxseed before baking enhances the flavors and adds a rich, nutty taste to these granola bars.

# CHEWY OAT AND FRUIT GRANOLA BARS

Hands-on time: 11 min. Total time: 3 hr. 41 min.

*A much healthier and gluten-free alternative to the store-bought granola bar, these homemade treats are a wonderful addition to any child's lunch box. They have an abundance of chewy oats and coconut; are flavored with honey, maple syrup, and vanilla; and are embellished with dried cherries or cranberries, apricots, and dates.*

Cooking spray
2 cups certified gluten-free quick-cooking oats
1 cup flaked sweetened coconut
½ cup sunflower seed kernels
½ cup flaxseed
½ cup sweetened dried cranberries or dried
   cherries, chopped
½ cup dried apricots, chopped
½ cup whole pitted dates (about 10 dates), chopped
½ cup honey
¼ cup maple syrup
3 tablespoons brown sugar
3 tablespoons butter
1 teaspoon vanilla extract
¼ teaspoon kosher salt

1. Preheat oven to 350°.

2. Line a 13 x 9–inch metal baking pan with foil, allowing foil to extend over edge of pan; coat foil with cooking spray.

3. Place oats, coconut, sunflower seed kernels, and flaxseed on a baking sheet, spreading evenly. Bake at 350° for 10 to 12 minutes or until toasted, stirring occasionally. Reduce oven temperature to 300°. Combine oat mixture, cranberries, apricots, and dates in a large bowl.

4. Combine honey and next 5 ingredients (through salt) in a small saucepan; bring to a boil over medium heat, stirring constantly with a whisk. Boil 1 minute, stirring constantly. Immediately pour honey mixture over oat mixture; toss gently to coat.

5. Firmly press mixture into prepared pan, using a rubber spatula or hands coated with cooking spray. Bake at 300° for 30 minutes or until slightly golden brown. Cool completely in pan on a wire rack. Lift bars from pan, using foil sides as handles. Place on a cutting board; cut into 18 bars. Remove from foil. Serves 18 (serving size: 1 bar)

CALORIES 197; FAT 7.1g (sat 2.9g, mono 1.1g, poly 1.7g); PROTEIN 3.5g; CARB 31.3g; FIBER 3.4g; CHOL 5mg; IRON 1.1mg; SODIUM 48mg; CALC 25mg

## foiling a mess

tip

Lining the inside of the baking pan with foil that's been coated with cooking spray makes removing these bars from the pan, cutting them, and cleanup a cinch. You can store these bars in an airtight container at room temperature or in the refrigerator.

# CHOCOLATE-WALNUT-GRAHAM CRACKER BARS

Hands-on time: 4 min. Total time: 1 hr. 29 min.

*These tasty treats are more like a candy bar than a cookie. Served with hot chocolate, they're a children's sticky-finger favorite!*

Cooking spray
1¼ cups gluten-free graham cracker crumbs
   (about 10 large cookie sheets)
1 cup semisweet chocolate chips
½ cup chopped walnuts
½ teaspoon vanilla extract
1 (14-ounce) can fat-free sweetened condensed milk

1. Preheat oven to 375°.

2. Coat a 13 x 9–inch metal baking pan with cooking spray; line bottom of pan with parchment paper.

3. Combine graham cracker crumbs, chocolate chips, and walnuts in a large bowl. Add vanilla and milk, stirring until well blended. Spread mixture into prepared pan. Bake at 375° for 20 to 25 minutes or until edges are golden brown. Cool completely in pan on a wire rack. Serves 20 (serving size: 1 bar)

CALORIES 146; FAT 4.8g (sat 1.7g, mono 1.3g, poly 1.2g); PROTEIN 2.9g; CARB 24.3g; FIBER 1.2g; CHOL 3mg; IRON 0.5mg; SODIUM 115mg; CALC 82mg

## a sweet addition

Fat-free sweetened condensed milk is simply a mixture of fat-free milk and sugar that's heated until about 60% of the water evaporates. The result is a milk that is sticky and delightfully sweet. Store opened milk in an airtight container in the refrigerator for no more than five days.

*Since these bars are moist and sticky, lining the pan with parchment paper is a crucial step—you'll be able to cleanly remove them from the pan before cutting them.*

# ALMOND-LEMON BARS

Hands-on time: 12 min. Total time: 1 hr. 37 min.

*These bars have a thin layer of tangy, sweet lemon atop a buttery crust made with almond meal flour. There is big citrus flavor in every little bite. A few years ago, I had the pleasure of demonstrating these popular dessert bars for an autism fundraiser chaired by Cheryl Sanderson. Through her tireless efforts to increase awareness of autism and raise funds for research, resources, and therapeutic options, Cheryl has had a profound impact on many lives in our community as well as on our family.*

Cooking spray
1.3 ounces potato starch (about ¼ cup)
1.15 ounces brown rice flour (about ¼ cup)
0.9 ounce almond meal flour (about ¼ cup)
¼ cup packed brown sugar
1 tablespoon butter, softened
½ teaspoon salt, divided
¼ teaspoon almond extract
1½ cups granulated sugar
2 tablespoons white rice flour
2 tablespoons grated lemon rind
6 tablespoons fresh lemon juice
1 teaspoon baking powder
4 large eggs
2 teaspoons powdered sugar

1. Preheat oven to 350°.

2. Line an 8-inch square metal baking pan with foil, allowing foil to extend over edge of pan; coat foil with cooking spray.

3. Weigh or lightly spoon potato starch, brown rice flour, and almond meal flour into dry measuring cups; level with a knife. Place potato starch, brown rice flour, almond meal flour, brown sugar, butter, ¼ teaspoon salt, and almond extract in a food processor; process until well blended. Press mixture into bottom of prepared pan. Bake at 350° for 10 minutes; cool 15 minutes on a wire rack.

4. Wipe crumbs from food processor bowl with a paper towel. Place ¼ teaspoon salt, granulated sugar, white rice flour, and next 4 ingredients (through eggs) in food processor; process until well blended. Pour into prepared crust.

5. Bake at 350° for 25 to 27 minutes or just until center is set. Cool completely in pan on a wire rack.

6. Lift lemon bars from pan, using foil sides as handles. Place on a cutting board; cut into 16 squares. Remove from foil; place on a platter. Dust with powdered sugar. Serves 16 (serving size: 1 bar)

CALORIES 142; FAT 2.8g (sat 0.9g, mono 0.7g, poly 0.3g); PROTEIN 2.2g; CARB 28.1g; FIBER 0.4g; CHOL 48mg; IRON 0.4mg; SODIUM 130mg; CALC 32mg

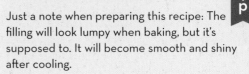

## a smooth finish

**tip**

Just a note when preparing this recipe: The filling will look lumpy when baking, but it's supposed to. It will become smooth and shiny after cooling.

# CHERRY-COCONUT BARS

Hands-on time: 12 min. Total time: 1 hr. 32 min.

*Chewy, sweet, and flavorful, these fanciful bars are a favorite for all ages and make for a bright and elegant display on the dessert table.*

Cooking spray
2.3 ounces brown rice flour (about ½ cup)
1.3 ounces potato starch (about ¼ cup)
1.05 ounces tapioca flour (about ¼ cup)
¾ cup flaked sweetened coconut, divided
¼ cup chopped walnuts
¼ cup packed brown sugar
2 tablespoons granulated sugar
½ teaspoon xanthan gum
¼ teaspoon salt
6 tablespoons chilled butter, cut into small pieces
¾ cup cherry preserves

1. Preheat oven to 375°.

2. Line an 8-inch square metal baking pan with foil, allowing foil to extend over edge of pan; coat foil with cooking spray.

3. Weigh or lightly spoon brown rice flour, potato starch, and tapioca flour into dry measuring cups; level with a knife. Place brown rice flour, potato starch, tapioca flour, ¼ cup coconut, walnuts, and next 4 ingredients (through salt) in a food processor; pulse 2 times or until blended. Add butter; process until mixture resembles fine meal.

4. Reserve ¼ cup flour mixture. Firmly press remaining flour mixture into bottom of prepared pan. Spoon cherry preserves over crust, spreading evenly. Combine reserved ¼ cup flour mixture and ½ cup coconut; sprinkle over cherry preserves. Bake at 375° for 20 minutes or until bubbly and top is lightly browned. Cool completely in pan on a wire rack.

5. Lift bars from pan, using foil sides as handles. Place on a cutting board; cut into 16 squares. Remove from foil. Serves 16 (serving size: 1 bar)

---

CALORIES 155; FAT 6.9g (sat 3.9g, mono 1.5g, poly 0.9g); PROTEIN 0.9g; CARB 23.7g; FIBER 0.8g; CHOL 11mg; IRON 0.3mg; SODIUM 88mg; CALC 6mg

It really is easiest to use your fingers to press the flour mixture into the bottom of the pan. You'll be able to evenly and firmly pack it in much better than with any utensil.

# MAPLE-PECAN BARS

Hands-on time: 9 min. Total time: 2 hr. 3 min.

*The Hurst Family Farm in Andover, Connecticut, has thrived for decades, despite dips in the economy, wild changes in the weather, and the competition posed by supermarkets. Their farm survives through the love, mutual respect, and hard work shared by all in this large family. I use the pure maple syrup produced in their sugarhouse to form the gooey and extra-sweet brown sugar and pecan mixture needed to make these heavenly bars.*

## Crust:
2.6 ounces white rice flour (about ½ cup)
2.3 ounces cornstarch (about ½ cup)
2.1 ounces sweet white sorghum flour (about ½ cup)
½ cup packed brown sugar
6 tablespoons butter
1 teaspoon xanthan gum
2 teaspoons vanilla extract
¼ teaspoon salt

## Filling:
½ cup maple syrup
⅓ cup packed brown sugar
¼ cup 1% low-fat milk
1 tablespoon butter
½ cup whole pecans
½ teaspoon vanilla extract

1. Preheat oven to 375°.

2. Line a 9-inch square metal baking pan with parchment paper.

3. To prepare crust, weigh or lightly spoon white rice flour, cornstarch, and sorghum flour into dry measuring cups; level with a knife. Place white rice flour, cornstarch, sorghum flour, ½ cup brown sugar, and next 4 ingredients (through salt) in a food processor; pulse until mixture resembles fine meal. Press flour mixture into bottom of prepared pan. Bake at 375° for 15 minutes or until edges of crust are slightly browned.

4. While crust bakes, combine syrup and next 3 ingredients (through 1 tablespoon butter) in a medium saucepan; bring to a boil over medium heat. Cook 2 minutes, stirring constantly with a whisk until sugar dissolves. Remove from heat; add pecans and ½ teaspoon vanilla, stirring with a whisk. Pour mixture into hot crust. Bake at 375° for 10 minutes or until filling is bubbly. Cool completely in pan. Cut into 20 bars. Serves 20 (serving size: 1 bar)

CALORIES 149; FAT 6.2g (sat 2.8g, mono 2.2g, poly 0.8g); PROTEIN 1g; CARB 23g; FIBER 0.8g; CHOL 11mg; IRON 0.3mg; SODIUM 70mg; CALC 23mg

# PECAN-PUMPKIN CHEESECAKE BARS

Hands-on time: 8 min. Total time: 4 hr. 53 min.

*The distinctive flavor of pumpkin pie spice folded into a creamy cheesecake and baked into chewy brown-sugar bars makes for an extra-special autumnal treat.*

4.6 ounces brown rice flour (about 1 cup)
2.6 ounces potato starch (about 1/2 cup)
2.1 ounces tapioca flour (about 1/2 cup)
2/3 cup packed brown sugar
1/4 teaspoon salt
1/4 teaspoon ground ginger
7 tablespoons chilled unsalted butter, cut into
    pieces
4 ounces 1/3-less-fat cream cheese (about 1/2 cup),
    softened
4 ounces fat-free cream cheese (about 1/2 cup),
    softened
3/4 cup packed brown sugar
1 cup canned unsweetened pumpkin
2 large eggs
2 tablespoons maple syrup
1 teaspoon pumpkin pie spice
1 teaspoon vanilla extract
1/4 teaspoon salt
1 (12-ounce) can evaporated fat-free milk
30 pecan halves

1. Preheat oven to 350°.

2. Line a 13 x 9–inch metal baking pan with parchment paper, allowing paper to extend over edge of pan.

3. Weigh or lightly spoon brown rice flour, potato starch, and tapioca flour into dry measuring cups; level with a knife. Place brown rice flour, potato starch, tapioca flour, 2/3 cup brown sugar, salt, and ginger in a food processor; pulse 2 times or until blended. Add butter; pulse 10 times or until blended. Firmly press flour mixture into bottom of prepared pan. Bake at 350° for 10 minutes or just until set and lightly browned.

4. Place cream cheeses and 3/4 cup brown sugar in a large bowl; beat with a mixer at high speed until creamy. Add pumpkin; beat until blended. Add eggs, 1 at a time, beating well after each addition. Add maple syrup, pumpkin pie spice, vanilla, salt, and milk; beat until blended (mixture will be thin).

5. Pour pumpkin mixture over prepared crust, and bake at 350° for 35 to 40 minutes or until center is set. Cool completely in pan on a wire rack. Cover and chill 2 hours or until ready to serve. Lift bars from pan, using parchment paper sides as handles. Place on a cutting board; cut into 30 bars. Press a pecan half into top of each bar. Serves 30 (serving size: 1 bar)

CALORIES 139; FAT 5.2g (sat 2.5g, mono 1.7g, poly 0.6g); PROTEIN 3g; CARB 21g; FIBER 0.7g; CHOL 23mg; IRON 0.4mg; SODIUM 102mg; CALC 71mg

*Using a combination of ⅓-less-fat and fat-free cream cheese helps keep the total fat low but still adds richness to these bars. Don't be tempted to use all fat-free cream cheese—the texture won't be nearly as luscious.*

# BLONDIES

*Blondies are like a second-generation brownie. They're cakey and comforting and awesome with milk, but teeming with vanilla, toffee, and brown sugar in place of all that chocolate. I've made these especially for the Wilkinson girls, Abigail and Catherine, two of our family's favorite little "blondies."*

2.3 ounces brown rice flour (about ½ cup)
2.1 ounces sweet white sorghum flour (about ½ cup)
1.3 ounces potato starch (about ¼ cup)
1 teaspoon baking powder
½ teaspoon xanthan gum
½ teaspoon salt
¾ cup packed brown sugar
¼ cup unsalted butter, melted
2 tablespoons canola oil
1 teaspoon vanilla extract
2 large eggs
½ cup semisweet chocolate minichips
¼ cup almond brickle chips (such as Heath)
¼ cup chopped pecans
Cooking spray

1. Preheat oven to 350°.

2. Weigh or lightly spoon flours and potato starch into dry measuring cups; level with a knife. Combine flours, potato starch, baking powder, xanthan gum, and salt in a medium bowl; stir with a whisk.

3. Combine brown sugar, melted butter, and oil in a medium bowl; stir with a whisk until blended. Add vanilla and eggs, stirring with whisk until blended. Gradually add flour mixture, stirring until blended. Fold in minichips, brickle chips, and pecans.

4. Pour batter into an 8-inch square metal baking pan coated with cooking spray. Bake at 350° for 20 minutes or until a wooden pick inserted in center comes out clean. Cool completely in pan on a wire rack. Serves 16 (serving size: 1 blondie)

---

CALORIES 185; FAT 9.6g (sat 3.7g, mono 3.4g, poly 1.2g); PROTEIN 2.2g; CARB 24.2g; FIBER 1.1g; CHOL 32mg; IRON 0.6mg; SODIUM 129mg; CALC 37mg

# CHOCOLATE-NUT BARS

Hands-on time: 13 min. Total time: 1 hr. 33 min.

*Flaxseed meal adds to the nuttiness of the walnuts and almonds in these delicious chocolate bar cookies. These bars are lovingly dedicated to the Duda family—with John and Lisa raising 10 children and now adding grandchildren into the mix, it's always a little nutty over there!*

2.3 ounces brown rice flour (about 1/2 cup)
1.15 ounces cornstarch (about 1/4 cup)
1/3 cup packed brown sugar
1 tablespoon flaxseed meal
2 tablespoons butter, softened
2 tablespoons canola oil
Cooking spray
1 cup semisweet chocolate chips
1 (14-ounce) can sweetened condensed milk
1 teaspoon vanilla extract
1/4 cup chopped walnuts
1/4 cup chopped almonds

1. Preheat oven to 350°.

2. Weigh or lightly spoon flour and cornstarch into dry measuring cups; level with a knife. Place flour, cornstarch, brown sugar, and flaxseed meal in a food processor; pulse 2 times or until blended. Add butter and oil; process until mixture resembles fine meal.

3. Firmly press flour mixture into bottom of an 8-inch square metal baking pan coated with cooking spray. Bake at 350° for 10 minutes or until crust is set.

4. Combine chocolate chips and milk in a small saucepan; cook over medium heat 2 minutes or until chocolate melts, stirring constantly. Remove from heat; stir in vanilla. Pour mixture over prepared crust; sprinkle with walnuts and almonds. Bake at 350° for 20 minutes or until center is set. Cool completely in pan on a wire rack. Serves 20 (serving size: 1 bar)

CALORIES 178; FAT 8.7g (sat 3.5g, mono 3.2g, poly 1.4g); PROTEIN 2.9g; CARB 24.3g; FIBER 1g; CHOL 10mg; IRON 0.5mg; SODIUM 38mg; CALC 67mg

# DECADENT FUDGE BROWNIES

Hands-on time: 6 min. Total time: 1 hr. 36 min.

*A recipe for decadent, thick, dark chocolate brownies is a must-have for any kitchen, including a gluten-free kitchen. This version is much lighter than the typical brownie (unless you serve them with a giant bowl of vanilla ice cream). You can also dust them with powdered sugar for an even sweeter finish. I made these brownies for a cooking demo at the Scotland Library during the summer of 2013. Mary (the librarian) and I had planned on about 8 to 10 people attending, and we were both surprised by the crowd of 30+ that filled up the room!*

2.3 ounces brown rice flour (about ½ cup)
1.3 ounces white rice flour (about ¼ cup)
2 tablespoons potato starch
2 tablespoons cornstarch
½ teaspoon xanthan gum
6 tablespoons butter
4 ounces unsweetened chocolate
6 tablespoons canola oil
1½ cups sugar
1 teaspoon vanilla extract
2 large eggs
Cooking spray

1. Preheat oven to 350°.

2. Weigh or lightly spoon flours into dry measuring cups; level with a knife. Combine flours, potato starch, cornstarch, and xanthan gum in a medium bowl; stir with a whisk.

3. Combine butter and chocolate in a large microwave-safe bowl. Microwave at HIGH 1 minute or until melted, stirring after 30 seconds. Add canola oil, stirring until smooth. Add sugar, vanilla, and eggs, and stir until well blended. Gradually add flour mixture, stirring until well blended. Spread batter into a 9-inch square metal baking pan coated with cooking spray. Bake at 350° for 30 minutes or until a wooden pick inserted in center comes out clean. Cool completely in pan on a wire rack. Serves 24 (serving size: 1 brownie)

CALORIES 158; FAT 9.5g (sat 3.8g, mono 3.9g, poly 1.3g); PROTEIN 1.5g; CARB 18.9g; FIBER 1g; CHOL 23mg; IRON 1mg; SODIUM 33mg; CALC 9mg

# FLOURLESS PEPPERMINT BROWNIES

Hands-on time: 10 min. Total time: 50 min.

*Decadent, minty, and fudgy, these brownies, made with black beans, will fool even the savviest sweet tooth. The hearty, wholesome beans, which are high in fiber and protein, completely take the place of any flour. For our friends the Buteras and their four active children who have multiple food sensitivities, these were the perfect dessert and party-food solution: no milk, gluten, yeast, nuts, corn, soy, or grains, and lots of chocolaty-minty fun.*

¾ cup granulated sugar
¼ cup unsweetened cocoa
3 tablespoons canola oil
1 teaspoon instant coffee granules
½ teaspoon baking powder
½ teaspoon peppermint extract
⅛ teaspoon salt
1 (15-ounce) can black beans, rinsed and drained
3 large eggs
½ cup bittersweet chocolate chips
2 tablespoons powdered sugar

1. Preheat oven to 350°.

2. Place first 9 ingredients in a food processor; process until completely smooth, scraping sides of bowl occasionally. Fold in chocolate chips; pour batter into a 9-inch square metal baking pan.

3. Bake at 350° for 20 minutes or until edge of brownies begin to pull away from sides of pan. Cool 20 minutes in pan on a wire rack. Sprinkle with powdered sugar. Serves 12 (serving size: 1 brownie)

CALORIES 145; FAT 6.1g (sat 1.5g, mono 2.8g, poly 1.2g); PROTEIN 3.6g; CARB 21g; FIBER 2g; CHOL 47mg; IRON 1mg; SODIUM 114mg; CALC 31mg

## a coffee boost

The instant coffee granules bring their own subtle flavor to these brownies, and also enhance the flavor of the cocoa, resulting in a richer chocolate taste. Store any remaining coffee granules in a sealed jar or airtight container in the freezer for up to a year.

# SALTED CARAMEL BROWNIES

Hands-on time: 19 min. Total time: 2 hr. 49 min.

*Made with rich, dark chocolate, these luscious layered brownies beautifully combine salty and sweet. It also comes with its very own story. While enlisting more taste testers for the recipes in this cookbook, we naturally thought of John Norton, a trusted friend who is notorious for his sweet tooth. After consuming half a pan of these brownies, he came up with the "system"—we now fly a red flag off the porch to signal when he is to stop and sample on his way home from work!*

**Caramel Sauce:**
¾ cup granulated sugar
2 tablespoons light-colored corn syrup
2 tablespoons water
¼ cup half-and-half
1 teaspoon sea salt

**Brownie Batter:**
2.1 ounces sweet white sorghum flour (about ½ cup)
1.3 ounces white rice flour (about ¼ cup)
½ cup unsweetened cocoa
2 tablespoons potato starch
2 tablespoons tapioca flour
½ teaspoon xanthan gum
½ teaspoon sea salt
⅓ cup butter
2 ounces bittersweet chocolate, chopped
½ cup granulated sugar
½ cup packed brown sugar
6 tablespoons 1% low-fat milk
1 teaspoon vanilla extract
2 large eggs
Cooking spray

1. To prepare caramel sauce, combine ¾ cup granulated sugar, corn syrup, and 2 tablespoons water in a small saucepan; cook over medium-high heat 7 to 8 minutes or until mixture is amber colored, stirring frequently. Remove from heat; add half-and-half, stirring with a whisk until blended (mixture will bubble). Stir in salt.

2. Preheat oven to 350°.

3. To prepare brownie batter, weigh or lightly spoon flours into dry measuring cups; level with a knife. Combine flours, cocoa, and next 4 ingredients (through ½ teaspoon sea salt) in a medium bowl; stir with a whisk.

4. Combine butter and bittersweet chocolate in a large microwave-safe bowl. Microwave at HIGH 1 minute or until melted, stirring every 30 seconds. Add ½ cup granulated sugar, brown sugar, milk, vanilla, and eggs, stirring until well blended. Gradually add flour mixture, stirring until moist.

5. Spread half of batter into an 8-inch square metal baking pan coated with cooking spray; pour caramel sauce over batter in pan. Drop remaining batter by tablespoonfuls onto caramel sauce; swirl gently with tip of a knife. Bake at 350° for 30 minutes or until brownies are set. Cool completely on a wire rack. Serves 16 (serving size: 1 brownie)

CALORIES 204; FAT 7g (sat 4g, mono 1.5g, poly 0.3g); PROTEIN 2.2g; CARB 35g; FIBER 1.5g; CHOL 35mg; IRON 1.1mg; SODIUM 278mg; CALC 25mg

"Biscotti" is an Italian word referring to hard, crunchy, twice-baked cookies. These biscotti can be kept for weeks in an airtight container, but are pretty enough to be wrapped in clear plastic with a ribbon and given as a gift.

# MOCHA-PISTACHIO BISCOTTI

Hands-on time: 11 min. Total time: 1 hr. 47 min.

4.6 ounces brown rice flour (about 1 cup)
2.1 ounces tapioca flour (about ½ cup)
0.9 ounce almond meal flour (about ¼ cup)
1.15 ounces cornstarch (about ¼ cup)
½ cup unsweetened cocoa
2 tablespoons flaxseed meal
1 teaspoon xanthan gum
½ teaspoon baking powder
½ teaspoon baking soda
½ teaspoon salt
⅓ cup packed brown sugar
⅓ cup granulated sugar
1 teaspoon instant coffee granules
1 teaspoon vanilla extract
3 large eggs
¾ cup shelled dry-roasted pistachios
Brown rice flour, for dusting

1. Preheat oven to 350°.

2. Weigh or lightly spoon flours and cornstarch into dry measuring cups; level with a knife. Combine flours, cornstarch, cocoa, and next 5 ingredients (through salt) in a medium bowl; stir with a whisk.

3. Beat brown sugar, granulated sugar, coffee granules, vanilla, and eggs with a stand mixer at medium speed until well blended. Gradually add flour mixture; beat until blended. Add pistachios; beat on low until blended.

4. Turn dough out onto a lightly floured surface; divide dough in half. Shape each half of dough into a 12-inch-long roll on a baking sheet lined with parchment paper; pat to a ¾-inch thickness. (Flour hands with brown rice flour if dough is sticky.)

5. Bake at 350° for 20 minutes or until firm to touch. Remove rolls from baking sheets; cool 30 minutes on a wire rack. Cut each roll diagonally into 20 (½-inch) slices. Place slices on baking sheets, and bake at 350° for 6 to 8 minutes. Turn slices over, and bake an additional 6 to 8 minutes (cookies will be slightly soft in center but will harden as they cool). Remove from baking sheets; cool completely on wire rack. Serves 40 (serving size: 1 cookie)

CALORIES 61; FAT 2.2g (sat 0.4g, mono 0.8g, poly 0.5g); PROTEIN 1.6g; CARB 9.7g; FIBER 1g; CHOL 14mg; IRON 0.4mg; SODIUM 58mg; CALC 13mg

## a time-saving biscotti tip

To shave six to eight minutes off your baking time, place the sliced biscotti straight up on the baking sheet with cut edges exposed for the second bake. This allows both sides to brown evenly without having to flip them.

chapter 6

CAKES
AND
CUPCAKES

**Y**ears ago, I owned a small bakery called the Sugar Shack on the outskirts of the University of Connecticut. We had cake baking down to a science, making hundreds of cakes a week for birthdays, christenings, weddings, and basketball games.

Customers began requesting gluten-free items, and the bakery business had to change. I had to re-learn how to make a cake. I bought rice flour and xanthan gum, and mistakenly broke out my usual recipes, thinking the substitutions would do the trick. I proceeded to make the heaviest, most brick-like, crumbly 9-inch cake rounds since the dawn of time. Once the second one landed on the floor with a thud, I knew that the easy, wheat-flour cake days were gone forever.

I spent countless hours in the kitchen experimenting, trying again and again and again until the cake came out just right. In this chapter, I happily share the closely held secrets and recipes needed to create superb coffee cakes, light and fluffy angel food cakes, rich and buttery-tasting pound cakes, sweet layer cakes, fanciful cupcakes, and the perfect cheesecakes for all your special occasions.

# LEMON CAKE

Hands-on time: 17 min. Total time: 2 hr. 2 min.

*This lemon layer cake has a bright flavor and a wonderfully rich frosting. Garnish it with thin lemon slices.*

**Cake:**
2.6 ounces white rice flour (about ½ cup)
2.3 ounces brown rice flour (about ½ cup)
2.1 ounces sweet white sorghum flour (about ½ cup)
2.1 ounces tapioca flour (about ½ cup)
1 teaspoon xanthan gum
1 teaspoon baking soda
½ teaspoon baking powder
½ teaspoon salt
1 cup granulated sugar
¼ cup unsalted butter, softened
3 large eggs
⅓ cup canola oil
2 tablespoons grated lemon rind
¼ cup fresh lemon juice (about 2 lemons)
1 cup low-fat buttermilk
Cooking spray

**Frosting:**
4 ounces ⅓-less-fat cream cheese
  (about ½ cup), softened
3 tablespoons unsalted butter, softened
3 cups powdered sugar
1 teaspoon grated lemon rind
2 teaspoons fresh lemon juice
½ teaspoon vanilla extract

1. Preheat oven to 350°.

2. To prepare cake, weigh or lightly spoon flours into dry measuring cups; level with a knife. Combine flours, xanthan gum, and next 3 ingredients (through salt) in a medium bowl; stir with a whisk.

3. Place granulated sugar and ¼ cup butter in a large bowl; beat with a mixer at medium speed until well blended. Add eggs, 1 at a time, beating well after each addition. Beat in canola oil, lemon rind, and lemon juice. Add flour mixture and buttermilk alternately to sugar mixture, beginning and ending with flour mixture.

4. Pour batter into 2 (8-inch) round cake pans coated with cooking spray; sharply tap pans once on counter to remove air bubbles.

5. Bake at 350° for 30 minutes or until a wooden pick inserted in center comes out clean. Cool 10 minutes in pans on a wire rack; remove from pans. Cool completely on wire rack.

6. To prepare frosting, place cream cheese and 3 tablespoons butter in a medium bowl; beat with a mixer at medium speed until light and fluffy. Add powdered sugar, 1 cup at a time, beating until well blended. Beat in 1 teaspoon lemon rind, 2 teaspoons lemon juice, and vanilla until smooth.

7. Place 1 cake layer on a plate; spread with ½ cup frosting. Top with second cake layer. Spread remaining frosting over top and sides of cake. Store cake loosely covered in refrigerator. Serves 16 (serving size: 1 slice)

---

CALORIES 321; FAT 12.8g (sat 4.9g, mono 5.2g, poly 1.8g); PROTEIN 3.5g; CARB 50g; FIBER 0.9g; CHOL 54mg; IRON 0.5mg; SODIUM 222mg; CALC 44mg

# COCONUT LAYER CAKE
## WITH MARSHMALLOW FROSTING

Hands-on time: 41 min. Total time: 3 hr. 41 min.

1/4 cup fresh orange juice (about 1 orange)
1 tablespoon sugar
3.9 ounces white rice flour (about 3/4 cup)
3.45 ounces brown rice flour (about 3/4 cup)
3.15 ounces sweet white sorghum flour (about 3/4 cup)
2.3 ounces cornstarch (about 1/2 cup)
1 tablespoon baking powder
2 teaspoons xanthan gum
1 teaspoon salt
1 1/4 cups sugar, divided
7 tablespoons canola oil
3 tablespoons unsalted butter, melted
2 teaspoons vanilla extract
2 cups 1% low-fat milk
6 large egg whites
Cooking spray
3 large egg whites
1/2 cup plus 1 tablespoon sugar
1 tablespoon plus 1 teaspoon corn syrup
1/2 teaspoon cream of tartar
1/8 teaspoon salt
1 teaspoon vanilla extract
1/3 cup flaked unsweetened coconut, toasted

1. Combine orange juice and 1 tablespoon sugar in a small saucepan. Bring mixture to a boil over medium heat; cook 1 minute, stirring until sugar dissolves. Remove from heat; cool.

2. Preheat oven to 350°.

3. Weigh or lightly spoon flours and cornstarch into dry measuring cups; level with a knife. Combine flours, cornstarch, baking powder, xanthan gum, and salt in a medium bowl; stir with a whisk.

4. Place 1 cup sugar, oil, and butter in a large bowl; beat with a mixer at medium speed until blended. Beat in 2 teaspoons vanilla. Add flour mixture and milk alternately to sugar mixture, beginning and ending with flour mixture.

5. Beat 6 egg whites with a mixer at high speed until foamy; gradually add 1/4 cup sugar, 1 tablespoon at a time, beating until stiff peaks form. Fold egg whites into batter. Pour batter into 2 (9-inch) round cake pans coated with cooking spray.

6. Bake at 350° for 35 minutes or until a wooden pick inserted in center comes out clean. Cool 10 minutes in pans on a wire rack; remove from pans. Cool completely on wire rack. Pierce entire surface of cake layers at 1/2-inch intervals with a wooden pick. Drizzle syrup over cakes. Let stand 20 minutes.

7. Combine 3 egg whites and next 4 ingredients (through 1/8 teaspoon salt) in the top of a double boiler. Cook over simmering water until a thermometer registers 160°, stirring constantly with a whisk. Pour egg white mixture into a large bowl; add 1 teaspoon vanilla. Beat at high speed until stiff peaks form and frosting is cool.

8. Place 1 cake layer on a plate; spread with 1/2 cup frosting. Top with second cake layer. Spread remaining frosting over top and sides of cake. Sprinkle coconut over top of cake. Chill 1 hour. Store cake loosely covered in refrigerator. Serves 16 (serving size: 1 slice)

CALORIES 294; FAT 10.3g (sat 3g, mono 4.7g, poly 1.9g); PROTEIN 4.7g; CARB 46g; FIBER 1.6g; CHOL 7mg; IRON 0.5mg; SODIUM 296mg; CALC 105mg

# SPICED CARROT CAKE
## WITH CREAM CHEESE FROSTING

Hands-on time: 17 min. Total time: 2 hr. 12 min.

*When I say this is a family favorite, I mean favorite! Spiced Carrot Cake with Cream Cheese Frosting was the flavor of our wedding cake, served on a picturesque and happy day in January 1996. Now, it is gluten free, so we can relive the memories with every delightful bite.*

**Cake:**
4.6 ounces brown rice flour (about 1 cup)
2.6 ounces white rice flour (about 1/2 cup)
1.05 ounces tapioca flour (about 1/4 cup)
1 teaspoon xanthan gum
1 teaspoon baking soda
1 teaspoon baking powder
1 teaspoon ground cinnamon
1/2 teaspoon salt
1/2 teaspoon ground ginger
1/4 teaspoon ground nutmeg
1/2 cup granulated sugar
1/2 cup packed brown sugar
1/4 cup canola oil
1/4 cup applesauce
1/2 teaspoon vanilla extract
2 large eggs
2 cups shredded carrot (about 8 ounces)
1/2 cup raisins
1/4 cup chopped pecans
Cooking spray

**Frosting:**
2 tablespoons butter, softened
1 teaspoon vanilla extract
1 (8-ounce) block 1/3-less-fat cream cheese
2 cups powdered sugar

1. Preheat oven to 350°.

2. To prepare cake, weigh or lightly spoon flours into dry measuring cups; level with a knife. Combine flours, xanthan gum, and next 6 ingredients (through nutmeg) in a medium bowl; stir with a whisk. Place sugars, oil, applesauce, vanilla, and eggs in a large bowl; beat with a mixer at medium speed until blended. Gradually add flour mixture, beating at low speed until smooth. Fold in carrot, raisins, and pecans.

3. Pour batter into an 11 x 7–inch metal baking pan coated with cooking spray. Bake at 350° for 35 minutes or until a wooden pick inserted in center comes out clean. Cool completely in pan on a wire rack.

4. To prepare frosting, combine butter, vanilla, and cream cheese in a medium bowl; beat with a mixer at medium speed until blended. Gradually add powdered sugar, beating until smooth. Spread frosting over top of cake. Store cake loosely covered in refrigerator. Serves 18 (serving size: 1 piece)

CALORIES 257; FAT 9.3g (sat 3g, mono 4g, poly 1.6g); PROTEIN 3.1g; CARB 41.6g; FIBER 1.4g; CHOL 33mg; IRON 0.5mg; SODIUM 233mg; CALC 52mg

# CHOCOLATE JAVA LAVA CAKES

*These sumptuous chocolate concoctions, with their molten interior, are a chocolate-lover's dream.*

1.2 ounces oat flour (about ⅓ cup)
2 tablespoons potato starch
¼ teaspoon xanthan gum
¾ cup bittersweet chocolate chips (about 4 ounces)
¼ cup canola oil
½ cup powdered sugar
½ teaspoon instant coffee granules
2 large eggs
2 large egg whites
Cooking spray
1 tablespoon powdered sugar
½ cup fresh raspberries

1. Preheat oven to 425°.

2. Weigh or lightly spoon oat flour into a dry measuring cup; level with a knife. Combine oat flour, potato starch, and xanthan gum in a small bowl; stir with a whisk.

3. Place chips and oil in a medium microwave-safe bowl; microwave at HIGH 1 minute or until melted, stirring after 30 seconds. Stir in ½ cup powdered sugar and coffee granules. Add eggs and egg whites; stir with a whisk until blended. Add flour mixture; stir just until blended.

4. Spoon batter into 6 (6-ounce) ramekins or custard cups coated with cooking spray. Place ramekins on a baking sheet. Bake at 425° for 10 minutes or until edges are puffed and set but center is soft. Cool 2 minutes in ramekins; remove from ramekins and place onto serving plates. Sprinkle with 1 tablespoon powdered sugar, and top with raspberries. Serves 6 (serving size: 1 cake)

CALORIES 241; FAT 14.8g (sat 3.4g, mono 6.9g, poly 3.2g); PROTEIN 4.8g; CARB 23.9g; FIBER 1.7g; CHOL 62mg; IRON 1.2mg; SODIUM 46mg; CALC 16mg

# POUND CAKE

Hands-on time: 8 min. Total time: 2 hr. 3 min.

*Serve this moist pound cake with fresh mixed berries and reduced-calorie whipped topping.*

5.2 ounces white rice flour (about 1 cup)
1.05 ounces tapioca flour (about ¼ cup)
1.3 ounces potato starch (about ¼ cup)
1 teaspoon xanthan gum
1 teaspoon baking powder
½ teaspoon salt
¼ teaspoon baking soda
1 cup sugar
¼ cup unsalted butter, softened
2 large eggs
2 tablespoons canola oil
1 teaspoon vanilla extract
¾ cup low-fat buttermilk
Cooking spray

1. Preheat oven to 350°.

2. Weigh or lightly spoon flours and potato starch into dry measuring cups; level with a knife. Combine flours, potato starch, xanthan gum, and next 3 ingredients (through baking soda) in a medium bowl; stir with a whisk.

3. Place sugar and butter in a medium bowl; beat with a mixer at medium speed until well blended. Add eggs, 1 at a time, beating well after each addition. Beat in oil and vanilla. Add flour mixture and buttermilk alternately to sugar mixture, beginning and ending with flour mixture.

4. Spoon batter into an 8 x 4–inch loaf pan coated with cooking spray. Bake at 350° for 55 minutes or until a wooden pick inserted in center comes out clean. Cool completely in pan on a wire rack. Serves 14 (serving size: 1 slice)

CALORIES 176; FAT 6.4g (sat 2.6g, mono 2.5g, poly 0.9g); PROTEIN 2g; CARB 28g; FIBER 0.4g; CHOL 36mg; IRON 0.2mg; SODIUM 164mg; CALC 43mg

## the perfect flour blend

The key to this picture-perfect pound cake is this tried-and-true blend of flours and starches. The white rice flour makes the pound cake light and tender, the tapioca flour helps increase the moisture content, and the potato starch adds structure and creates a tender bite.

# GOLDEN RUM CAKE

Hands-on time: 22 min. Total time: 1 hr. 32 min.

*This rich-tasting, liquor-laced cake will add warmth and comfort to any cold winter night… toasty!*

Cooking spray
1/3 cup finely chopped pecans
1 cup water
1 cup sugar, divided
1/4 cup dark rum
1/2 cup 2% reduced-fat milk
6 tablespoons unsalted butter
3.45 ounces brown rice flour (about 3/4 cup)
2.6 ounces white rice flour (about 1/2 cup)
2.1 ounces tapioca flour (about 1/2 cup)
1 tablespoon baking powder
3/4 teaspoon xanthan gum
1 teaspoon vanilla extract
3 large eggs, lightly beaten
1 cup frozen fat-free whipped topping, thawed

1. Preheat oven to 375°.

2. Coat a 10-inch tube pan with cooking spray; sprinkle pecans in bottom of pan.

3. Combine 1 cup water and 1/2 cup sugar in a small saucepan. Bring to a simmer over medium heat; cook 10 minutes or until mixture is reduced to 3/4 cup. Remove from heat; stir in rum.

4. Combine milk and butter in a small saucepan. Cook over medium heat 3 minutes or until butter melts. Remove from heat; cool 5 minutes.

5. Weigh or lightly spoon flours into dry measuring cups; level with a knife. Combine flours, 1/2 cup sugar, baking powder, and xanthan gum in a medium bowl; stir with a whisk. Add vanilla, eggs, and milk mixture; beat with a mixer at medium speed until well blended. Spoon batter over pecans in pan; sharply tap pan once on counter to remove air bubbles.

6. Bake at 375° for 30 minutes or until a wooden pick inserted in center comes out clean. Cool 10 minutes in pan on a wire rack. Remove from pan; place on a serving plate.

7. Brush rum syrup over cake; let stand 10 minutes. Repeat twice, reserving 1/3 cup rum syrup for serving. Spoon whipped topping and reserved rum syrup over slices of cake. Serves 16 (serving size: 1 slice cake, 1 tablespoon whipped topping, and 1 teaspoon rum syrup)

CALORIES 190; FAT 7.3g (sat 3.3g, mono 2.6g, poly 0.9g); PROTEIN 2.4g; CARB 27g; FIBER 0.7g; CHOL 47mg; IRON 0.4mg; SODIUM 103mg; CALC 80mg

## rum range

t i p

Dark rums are often aged in oak barrels for long periods of time and can range from light amber to black in color. They have a much more robust flavor than white rums and an underlying molasses flavor.

# SPICED CARAMEL BUNDT CAKE

Hands-on time: 13 min. Total time: 2 hr. 43 min.

4.6 ounces brown rice flour (about 1 cup)
3.15 ounces tapioca flour (about ¾ cup)
2.1 ounces sweet white sorghum flour (about ½ cup)
2 teaspoons baking soda
1¼ teaspoons ground cinnamon
1 teaspoon xanthan gum
1 teaspoon salt
½ teaspoon ground ginger
½ teaspoon ground nutmeg
1 cup granulated sugar
¼ cup unsalted butter, softened
¼ cup honey
2 large eggs
¼ cup canola oil
1½ cups applesauce
Cooking spray
¼ cup packed brown sugar
3 tablespoons half-and-half
2 tablespoons unsalted butter
½ teaspoon vanilla extract
¾ cup powdered sugar

1. Preheat oven to 350°.

2. Weigh or lightly spoon flours into dry measuring cups; level with a knife. Combine flours, baking soda, and next 5 ingredients (through nutmeg) in a medium bowl; stir with a whisk.

3. Place sugar, ¼ cup butter, and honey in a bowl; beat with a mixer at medium speed until well blended. Add eggs, 1 at a time, beating well after each addition. Beat in oil. Add flour mixture and applesauce alternately to sugar mixture, beginning and ending with flour mixture.

4. Spoon batter into a 12-cup Bundt pan coated with cooking spray, spreading evenly.

5. Bake at 350° for 55 minutes or until a wooden pick inserted in center comes out clean. Cool completely in pan on a wire rack. Remove from pan.

6. Combine brown sugar, half-and-half, and 2 tablespoons butter in a small saucepan. Bring to a boil over medium-low heat; cook 1 minute. Remove from heat; add vanilla. Cool 1 minute; add powdered sugar, stirring with a whisk until smooth. Spoon glaze over cake. Serves 16 (serving size: 1 slice)

CALORIES 255; FAT 9.2g (sat 3.5g, mono 3.8g, poly 1.4g); PROTEIN 2g; CARB 43g; FIBER 1.3g; CHOL 36mg; IRON 0.6mg; SODIUM 318mg; CALC 15mg

# SCANDINAVIAN ALMOND CAKE

Hands-on time: 8 min. Total time: 1 hr. 38 min.

*Claimed by both the Norwegians and Danes, this sugary almond-topped cake is a favorite for all. Our friend, Dr. Marianne Barton, lovingly shared this recipe when Angela was dealing with a prolonged and debilitating illness.*

2.1 ounces sweet white sorghum flour (about ½ cup)
1.15 ounces brown rice flour (about ¼ cup)
1.05 ounces tapioca flour (about ¼ cup)
1 teaspoon xanthan gum
½ teaspoon baking powder
¼ teaspoon salt
¾ cup plus 1 tablespoon sugar, divided

5 tablespoons butter, melted and divided
⅔ cup unsweetened coconut milk
1 teaspoon almond extract
1 large egg
Cooking spray
⅓ cup sliced almonds

1. Preheat oven to 350°.

2. Weigh or lightly spoon flours into dry measuring cups; level with a knife. Combine flours, xanthan gum, baking powder, and salt in a medium bowl; stir with a whisk. Make a well in center of mixture. Combine ¾ cup sugar, ¼ cup melted butter, and next 3 ingredients (through egg); add to flour mixture, stirring with a whisk until blended.

3. Pour batter into a 9-inch round cake pan coated with cooking spray. Combine 1 tablespoon sugar, 1 tablespoon melted butter, and almonds in a small bowl; sprinkle over batter. Bake at 350° for 30 minutes or until edges are lightly browned and a wooden pick inserted in center comes out clean. Cool completely in pan on a wire rack. Serves 10 (serving size: 1 slice)

CALORIES 189; FAT 8.5g (sat 4.2g, mono 2.8g, poly 0.7g); PROTEIN 2.3g; CARB 27g; FIBER 1.3g; CHOL 34mg; IRON 0.6mg; SODIUM 142mg; CALC 31mg

# LEMON, ALMOND, AND POLENTA CAKE

Hands-on time: 12 min. Total time: 2 hr. 32 min.

*This uniquely textured and flavor-packed lemon-almond cake has become a family favorite.*

**Cake:**
4.6 ounces certified gluten-free stone-ground cornmeal (about ¾ cup)
3.6 ounces almond meal flour (about 1 cup)
2.6 ounces white rice flour (about ½ cup)
1.15 ounces brown rice flour (about ¼ cup)
1.05 ounces tapioca flour (about ¼ cup)
2 teaspoons baking powder
½ teaspoon xanthan gum
1 cup granulated sugar
½ cup unsalted butter, softened
3 large eggs
2 tablespoons grated lemon rind
½ cup buttermilk
Cooking spray

**Glaze:**
¾ cup powdered sugar
⅓ cup fresh lemon juice

**Topping:**
2 tablespoons sliced almonds, toasted

1. Preheat oven to 350°.

2. To prepare cake, weigh or lightly spoon cornmeal and flours into dry measuring cups; level with a knife. Combine cornmeal, flours, baking powder, and xanthan gum in a medium bowl; stir with a whisk. Place sugar and butter in a large bowl; beat with a mixer at medium speed until light and fluffy. Add eggs, 1 at a time, beating well after each addition. Beat in lemon rind. Add flour mixture and buttermilk alternately to sugar mixture, beginning and ending with flour mixture.

3. Pour batter into a 9-inch springform pan coated with cooking spray. Bake at 350° for 40 minutes or until a wooden pick inserted in center comes out clean. Cool 10 minutes in pan on a wire rack.

4. To prepare glaze, combine powdered sugar and lemon juice in a small saucepan. Bring to a boil over medium heat, stirring constantly; cook 1 minute or until sugar dissolves. Remove from heat.

5. Pierce entire surface of cake with a wooden pick. Slowly pour warm glaze over cake, letting it soak into cake. Sprinkle with almonds. Cool cake completely in pan on wire rack. Serves 14 (serving size: 1 slice)

CALORIES 276; FAT 12.4g (sat 5.2g, mono 4.9g, poly 1.5g); PROTEIN 4.6g; CARB 38g; FIBER 2.7g; CHOL 58mg; IRON 0.9mg; SODIUM 92mg; CALC 91mg

# VANILLA ANGEL FOOD CAKE WITH BERRY COMPOTE

Hands-on time: 29 min. Total time: 3 hr.

*The lack of gluten in the angel food cakes in this book makes them taste better than the wheat-based variety—they're missing that tiny bit of chew. The white rice flour, cornstarch, and just a little brown rice flour along with the egg whites give the cake a light airy texture. The result is a cake that tastes simply heavenly.*

**Cake:**
3.9 ounces white rice flour (about ³/₄ cup)
1.15 ounces brown rice flour (about ¹/₄ cup)
1.15 ounces cornstarch (about ¹/₄ cup)
1¹/₂ cups sugar, divided
1¹/₂ teaspoons xanthan gum
12 large egg whites
1 teaspoon cream of tartar
¹/₄ teaspoon salt
1¹/₂ teaspoons vanilla extract

**Compote:**
1¹/₄ cups fresh raspberries
1¹/₄ cups fresh blackberries
1 cup quartered hulled strawberries
¹/₄ cup sugar
2 tablespoons water

**Topping:**
³/₄ cup frozen reduced-calorie whipped topping, thawed

1. Preheat oven to 375°.

2. To prepare cake, weigh or lightly spoon flours and cornstarch into dry measuring cups; level with a knife. Combine flours, cornstarch, ¾ cup sugar, and xanthan gum in a medium bowl; stir with a whisk.

3. Place egg whites in a large bowl; beat with a mixer at high speed until foamy. Add cream of tartar and salt; beat until soft peaks form. Gradually add ¾ cup sugar, 2 tablespoons at a time, beating until stiff peaks form. Add vanilla; beat well. Sift flour mixture over egg white mixture, ¼ cup at a time; fold in.

4. Spoon batter into an ungreased 10-inch tube pan. Break air pockets by cutting through batter with a knife. Bake at 375° for 45 minutes or until cake springs back when lightly touched and small cracks form on top of cake. Invert pan (but don't remove from pan); cool completely. Loosen cake from sides of pan using a narrow metal spatula. Invert cake onto a plate. Cut cake into 24 slices.

5. To prepare compote, combine berries, ¼ cup sugar, and 2 tablespoons water in a medium saucepan. Bring to a simmer over medium heat; cook 8 minutes or until berries soften and juices thicken slightly. Cool 10 minutes. Spoon compote and whipped topping over cake. Serves 12 (serving size: 2 slices cake, about 3 tablespoons compote, and 1 tablespoon whipped topping)

CALORIES 215; FAT 1g (sat 0.6g, mono 0.1g, poly 0.2g); PROTEIN 4.8g; CARB 48g; FIBER 2.5g; CHOL 0mg; IRON 0.4mg; SODIUM 106mg; CALC 14mg

If your angel
food cake pan
doesn't have
feet to set on for
cooling, invert
the pan on
the neck of
a wine bottle.

# CHOCOLATE-ALMOND ANGEL FOOD CAKE

Hands-on time: 18 min. Total time: 2 hr. 43 min.

*This is not your typical angel food cake. The texture is still light, but the chocolate and almond add a decadence that takes it a few steps beyond the classic.*

**Cake:**
1.3 ounces white rice flour (about 1/4 cup)
1.15 ounces cornstarch (about 1/4 cup)
1.05 ounces sweet white sorghum flour (about 1/4 cup)
0.9 ounce almond meal flour (about 1/4 cup)
1 1/2 cups granulated sugar, divided
1/4 cup unsweetened cocoa
1 1/2 teaspoons xanthan gum
12 large egg whites
1 teaspoon cream of tartar
1/4 teaspoon salt
1 1/2 teaspoons almond extract

**Glaze:**
1 cup powdered sugar
2 tablespoons unsweetened cocoa
2 tablespoons fat-free milk
1 teaspoon butter, melted
1/4 teaspoon vanilla extract
1/8 teaspoon salt

1. Preheat oven to 375°.

2. To prepare cake, weigh or lightly spoon white rice flour, cornstarch, sweet white sorghum flour, and almond meal flour into dry measuring cups; level with a knife. Combine white rice flour, cornstarch, sweet white sorghum flour, almond meal flour, 3/4 cup granulated sugar, cocoa, and xanthan gum in a medium bowl; stir with a whisk.

3. Place egg whites in a large bowl; beat with a mixer at high speed until foamy. Add cream of tartar and salt; beat until soft peaks form. Gradually add 3/4 cup granulated sugar, 2 tablespoons at a time, beating until stiff peaks form. Add almond extract; beat well. Sift flour mixture over egg white mixture, 1/4 cup at a time; fold in.

4. Spoon batter into an ungreased 10-inch tube pan. Break air pockets by cutting through batter with a knife. Bake at 375° for 45 minutes or until cake springs back when lightly touched and small cracks form on top of cake. Invert pan (but don't remove from pan); cool completely. Loosen cake from sides of pan using a narrow metal spatula. Invert cake onto a plate.

5. To prepare glaze, combine powdered sugar and remaining ingredients in a small bowl; stir with a whisk until smooth. Spoon over cake. Let stand 10 minutes or until glaze is set. Cut cake into 12 slices. Serves 12 (serving size: 1 slice)

CALORIES 209; FAT 1.9g (sat 0.5g, mono 0.2g, poly 0g); PROTEIN 5.2g; CARB 45g; FIBER 1.8g; CHOL 1mg; IRON 0.6mg; SODIUM 135mg; CALC 14mg

# STRAWBERRY-ALMOND CAKE ROLL

*Don't panic—this fruit and whipped cream–filled cake is surprisingly easy to roll.*

Cooking spray
1.73 ounces white rice flour (about ⅓ cup)
1.2 ounces almond meal flour (about ⅓ cup)
1 teaspoon xanthan gum
1 teaspoon baking powder
Dash of salt
5 large egg yolks
½ cup granulated sugar
½ teaspoon almond extract
5 large egg whites
2 cups frozen fat-free whipped topping, thawed
3 cups sliced strawberries
1 tablespoon powdered sugar

1. Preheat oven to 375°.

2. Coat a 15 x 10–inch jelly-roll pan with cooking spray; line bottom and sides with parchment paper. Coat parchment paper with cooking spray.

3. Weigh or lightly spoon flours into dry measuring cups; level with a knife. Combine flours, xanthan gum, baking powder, and salt; stir with a whisk.

4. Beat egg yolks in a large bowl with a mixer at high speed 2 minutes. Gradually add granulated sugar, beating until thick and pale (about 2 minutes). Beat in almond extract. Gradually add flour mixture, stirring until well blended.

5. Beat egg whites with a mixer at high speed until stiff peaks form. Gently stir one-fourth of egg whites into egg yolk mixture; gently fold in remaining egg whites. Pour batter into prepared pan. Bake at 375° for 12 minutes or until golden brown and cake pulls away from sides of pan. Cool in pan on a wire rack 5 minutes. Loosen cake from sides of pan; turn out onto a clean piece of parchment paper. Carefully peel off parchment paper from bottom of cake; cool cake 1 minute. Starting at narrow end, roll up cake and parchment paper together. Place, seam side down, on a wire rack; cool completely.

6. Unroll cake carefully; remove parchment paper. Spread whipped topping over cake, leaving a ½-inch border around outside edges. Top with strawberries. Reroll cake; place, seam side down, on a platter. Sprinkle with powdered sugar. Cover and chill until ready to serve. Serves 8 (serving size: 1 slice)

CALORIES 199; FAT 5.6g (sat 1.2g, mono 1.4g, poly 0.8g); PROTEIN 5.6g; CARB 31g; FIBER 2.2g; CHOL 116mg; IRON 1mg; SODIUM 113mg; CALC 79mg

# PINEAPPLE UPSIDE-DOWN CAKE

Hands-on time: 8 min. Total time: 1 hr. 48 min.

*This is a fun and brown-sugary pineapple party cake. It is dedicated to Claire Ward—she's 6 years old, super-sweet, with a perpetual twinkle in her eye and a trick up her sleeve….she can actually eat this cake "upside down!"*

6 tablespoons butter, softened and divided
1/4 cup packed brown sugar
Cooking spray
1 (20-ounce) can pineapple slices in juice
3.9 ounces white rice flour (about 3/4 cup)
2.3 ounces brown rice flour (about 1/2 cup)
1.05 ounces sweet white sorghum flour
    (about 1/4 cup)
1 1/2 teaspoons baking powder
1/2 teaspoon xanthan gum
1/3 cup 1% low-fat milk
3/4 cup granulated sugar
1 teaspoon vanilla extract
2 large eggs

1. Preheat oven to 350°.

2. Combine 2 tablespoons butter and brown sugar in a small saucepan over medium heat, stirring until melted and smooth. Spread brown sugar mixture into bottom of a 9-inch square metal baking pan coated with cooking spray and lined with parchment paper.

3. Drain pineapple, reserving 1/4 cup juice. Top brown sugar mixture with pineapple slices.

4. Weigh or lightly spoon flours into dry measuring cups; level with a knife. Combine flours, baking powder, and xanthan gum, stirring with a whisk. Combine milk and reserved 1/4 cup pineapple juice in a small bowl.

5. Place 4 tablespoons butter and granulated sugar in a large bowl; beat with a mixer at medium speed until light and fluffy. Add vanilla and eggs; beat until blended. Add flour mixture and milk mixture alternately to sugar mixture, beginning and ending with flour mixture, stirring until combined.

6. Pour batter evenly over fruit. Bake at 350° for 40 minutes or until a wooden pick inserted in center comes out clean. Immediately invert cake onto a serving platter. Cool 1 hour. Serves 9 (serving size: 1 piece)

---

CALORIES 301; FAT 9.6g (sat 5.4g, mono 2.7g, poly 0.7g); PROTEIN 3.7g; CARB 51g; FIBER 1.8g; CHOL 62mg; IRON 0.8mg; SODIUM 164mg; CALC 92mg

# BANANAS FOSTER UPSIDE-DOWN CAKE

Hands-on time: 35 min. Total time: 1 hr. 30 min.

*On a trip to New Orleans, I made a point of stopping at Brennan's restaurant, where Bananas Foster originated in the 1950s. It was so unbelievable that it inspired me to create this gluten-free riff on that classic dessert.*

Cooking spray
3.45 ounces brown rice flour (about ¾ cup)
2.6 ounces white rice flour (about ½ cup)
1.05 ounces garbanzo bean flour (about ¼ cup)
1.3 ounces potato starch (about ¼ cup)
2 teaspoons baking powder
1 teaspoon xanthan gum
¼ teaspoon ground cinnamon
⅔ cup packed brown sugar
6 tablespoons butter, softened and divided
½ cup chopped pecans
2 medium-sized ripe bananas
½ cup granulated sugar
2 large eggs
¾ cup 1% low-fat milk
½ cup vanilla fat-free Greek yogurt
2 tablespoons dark rum
1 teaspoon vanilla extract

1. Preheat oven to 350°.

2. Line a 9-inch square metal baking pan with foil, allowing foil to extend over edge of pan; coat foil with cooking spray.

3. Weigh or lightly spoon flours and potato starch into dry measuring cups; level with a knife. Combine flours, potato starch, baking powder, xanthan gum, and cinnamon in a medium bowl; stir with a whisk.

4. Place brown sugar and 3 tablespoons butter in a small saucepan. Cook over low heat 2 minutes or until butter melts and mixture is smooth, stirring constantly. Pour into prepared pan, spreading evenly. Sprinkle with pecans.

5. Cut each banana in half crosswise; cut each half lengthwise into ⅛-inch-thick slices. Arrange banana slices over pecans in pan.

6. Place granulated sugar and 3 tablespoons butter in a large bowl; beat with a mixer at medium speed until light and fluffy. Add eggs, 1 at a time, beating well after each addition. Beat in milk, yogurt, rum, and vanilla until well blended. Gradually add flour mixture, beating at low speed until smooth. Pour batter over bananas in pan. Bake at 350° for 45 minutes or until a wooden pick inserted in center comes out clean. Cool 10 minutes in pan. Place a plate upside down on top of cake; invert onto a plate. Serve warm. Serves 12 (serving size: 1 piece)

CALORIES 283; FAT 10.7g (sat 4.4g, mono 3.9g, poly 1.5g); PROTEIN 4.4g; CARB 44g; FIBER 2.1g; CHOL 47mg; IRON 0.8mg; SODIUM 150mg; CALC 109mg

# APPLE OVEN CAKE

*Using a blender to combine the ingredients ensures a smooth batter. Make this pancake for breakfast or serve it with ice cream for dessert.*

2.3 ounces brown rice flour (about ½ cup)
1.05 ounces tapioca flour (about ¼ cup)
1.3 ounces potato starch (about ¼ cup)
1 teaspoon baking soda
½ teaspoon xanthan gum
¼ teaspoon salt
1⅓ cups low-fat buttermilk
½ teaspoon vanilla extract
2 large eggs
¼ cup packed brown sugar
3 tablespoons butter
Cooking spray
3½ cups sliced peeled Fuji apple (about 1 pound)
⅛ teaspoon ground cinnamon
¼ cup finely chopped pecans
1 tablespoon powdered sugar

1. Preheat oven to 400°.

2. Weigh or lightly spoon flours and potato starch into dry measuring cups; level with a knife. Combine flours, potato starch, baking soda, xanthan gum, and salt in a medium bowl, stirring with a whisk.

3. Place buttermilk, vanilla, and eggs in a blender; process until blended. Add flour mixture; process until thoroughly combined.

4. Melt brown sugar and butter in a 12-inch cast-iron or ovenproof skillet coated with cooking spray over medium-high heat. Add apple and cinnamon; cook 1 to 2 minutes or until apple begins to soften.

5. Pour egg batter evenly over apple in pan; sprinkle with pecans. Bake at 400° for 15 minutes or until top of cake is lightly browned. Remove from oven; sprinkle with powdered sugar. Serves 8 (serving size: 1 slice)

CALORIES 212; FAT 8.9g (sat 4g, mono 3.2g, poly 1.3g); PROTEIN 4.2g; CARB 30g; FIBER 1.5g; CHOL 60mg; IRON 0.6mg; SODIUM 335mg; CALC 62mg

## the beauty of cast iron

Serving this cake directly from the cast-iron skillet makes for an attractive presentation. Beyond the aesthetic appeal, cast iron is also an excellent conductor of heat, which means it cooks evenly, producing a prettier and better-tasting cake.

# BLUEBERRY-YOGURT COFFEE CAKE

Hands-on time: 10 min. Total time: 2 hr. 20 min.

*I have always loved the tangy, sweet combination of blueberries and yogurt. Here, it's incorporated into a scrumptious coffee cake, perfect for the break room at work or with Sunday brunch.*

4.6 ounces brown rice flour (about 1 cup)
2.6 ounces white rice flour (about ½ cup)
1.8 ounces almond meal flour (about ½ cup)
1.3 ounces potato starch (about ¼ cup)
1.15 ounces cornstarch (about ¼ cup)
2 teaspoons baking powder
1 teaspoon xanthan gum
½ teaspoon baking soda
½ teaspoon ground cinnamon
³/₈ teaspoon salt
¾ cup granulated sugar
½ cup unsalted butter, softened
3 large eggs
1 cup vanilla fat-free Greek yogurt
1 teaspoon vanilla extract
1 cup low-fat buttermilk
1½ cups fresh blueberries
Cooking spray
½ cup powdered sugar
2½ tablespoons maple syrup

1. Preheat oven to 350°.

2. Weigh or lightly spoon flours and starches into dry measuring cups; level with a knife. Combine flours, starches, baking powder, and next 4 ingredients (through salt) in a medium bowl; stir with a whisk.

3. Place granulated sugar and butter in a large bowl; beat with a mixer at medium speed until light and fluffy. Add eggs, 1 at a time, beating well after each addition. Beat in yogurt and vanilla. Add flour mixture and buttermilk alternately to sugar mixture, beginning and ending with flour mixture. Fold in blueberries.

4. Spoon batter into a 10-inch tube pan coated with cooking spray. Bake at 350° for 55 minutes or until a wooden pick inserted in center comes out clean. Cool 30 minutes in pan. Loosen cake from sides of pan using a narrow metal spatula; turn out onto a wire rack. Cool completely on wire rack.

5. Combine powdered sugar and maple syrup in a small bowl; stir with a whisk. Drizzle over cake. Serves 16 (serving size: 1 slice)

CALORIES 233; FAT 8.8g (sat 4.2g, mono 2.1g, poly 0.5g); PROTEIN 4.5g; CARB 35g; FIBER 1.4g; CHOL 51mg; IRON 0.5mg; SODIUM 187mg; CALC 92mg

# CHOCOLATE VELVET BEET CAKE

Hands-on time: 13 min. Total time: 2 hr. 48 min.

*If you don't mention it, no one will ever suspect that this incredible chocolate dessert, with its smooth texture and rich flavor, is made with beets. My kids won't eat beets, but they devour this dessert.*

**Cake:**
3.6 ounces almond meal flour (about 1 cup)
1/2 cup sugar
1/4 cup unsweetened cocoa
1 1/4 teaspoons baking powder
1/2 teaspoon xanthan gum
1/4 teaspoon salt
6 ounces semisweet chocolate, finely chopped
3 tablespoons unsalted butter
6 ounces canned sliced beets (about 1 cup)
2 tablespoons canola oil
1 teaspoon vanilla extract
3 large eggs
Cooking spray

**Sour Cream Topping:**
1/2 cup reduced-fat sour cream
2 teaspoons sugar
1/4 teaspoon vanilla extract
3 1/2 cups fresh blueberries

1. Preheat oven to 350°.

2. To prepare cake, weigh or lightly spoon almond meal flour into a dry measuring cup; level with a knife. Place almond meal flour in a food processor; pulse 10 times or until very finely ground. Combine almond meal flour, 1/2 cup sugar, and next 4 ingredients (through salt) in a medium bowl; stir with a whisk.

3. Combine chocolate and butter in a small microwave-safe bowl; microwave at HIGH 1 minute or until melted, stirring after 30 seconds. Stir until smooth.

4. Place chocolate mixture, beets, canola oil, 1 teaspoon vanilla, and eggs in a food processor; process until smooth. Add flour mixture; process 30 seconds or until smooth.

5. Pour batter into an 8-inch springform pan coated with cooking spray, spreading evenly. Bake at 350° for 50 minutes or until a wooden pick inserted in center comes out clean. Cool 5 minutes in pan on a wire rack; remove sides of pan. Cool completely on wire rack.

6. To prepare topping, combine sour cream, 2 teaspoons sugar, and 1/4 teaspoon vanilla in a small bowl; stir with a whisk until smooth. Serve blueberries and topping with cake. Serves 14 (serving size: 1 slice cake, 1/4 cup blueberries, and about 2 teaspoons topping)

---

CALORIES 233; FAT 14.5g (sat 5.4g, mono 6.5g, poly 2g); PROTEIN 4.8g; CARB 25.4g; FIBER 3.2g; CHOL 50mg; IRON 1.4mg; SODIUM 131mg; CALC 74mg

# STRAWBERRY-BLUEBERRY CHEESECAKE

Hands-on time: 18 min. Total time: 11 hr. 23 min.

*This luscious cheesecake is a showcase for the season's freshest berries. With all its red, white, and blue, it's perfect to take to the annual Fourth of July party at the Gervais home. Enjoy it at your next summer gathering.*

**Crust:**
2 cups gluten-free graham cracker crumbs
1/4 cup unsalted butter, melted
2 tablespoons sugar
1/2 teaspoon ground cinnamon
Cooking spray

**Cheesecake:**
2 (8-ounce) blocks fat-free cream cheese, softened
1 (8-ounce) block 1/3-less-fat cream cheese, softened
1 cup sugar
1 cup fat-free sour cream
2 teaspoons grated lemon rind
1 teaspoon vanilla extract
3 large eggs

**Topping:**
3/4 cup fresh blueberries
3/4 cup sliced fresh strawberries
2 tablespoons sugar
1 tablespoon grated lemon rind
3 tablespoons fresh lemon juice
3/4 cup strawberry preserves

1. Preheat oven to 325°.

2. To prepare crust, combine crumbs, melted butter, 2 tablespoons sugar, and cinnamon in a medium bowl.

3. Wrap 2 layers of foil around bottom and outside of a 9-inch springform pan; coat inside of pan with cooking spray. Firmly press crust mixture into bottom and 1/2 inch up sides of pan.

4. Bake at 325° for 10 minutes. Cool completely on a wire rack.

5. To prepare cheesecake, place cheeses in a large bowl; beat with a mixer at medium speed until smooth. Add sugar and next 3 ingredients (through vanilla); beat well. Add eggs, 1 at a time, beating well after each addition.

6. Pour cheesecake batter over cooled crust. Place springform pan in a shallow roasting pan; add enough hot water to come halfway up sides of springform pan.

7. Bake at 325° for 1 hour and 20 minutes or until center barely moves when pan is touched. Remove cheesecake from oven; run a knife around outside edge. Cool to room temperature. Cover and chill at least 8 hours.

8. To prepare topping, combine berries, sugar, lemon rind, and lemon juice in a small bowl; let stand 30 minutes. Spread preserves over top of cheesecake; top with fruit mixture. Serves 14 (serving size: 1 slice)

CALORIES 305; FAT 8.5g (sat 4.7g, mono 2.2g, poly 0.6g); PROTEIN 9.1g; CARB 48g; FIBER 1.4g; CHOL 66mg; IRON 0.5mg; SODIUM 375mg; CALC 212mg

# KEY LIME CHEESECAKE

Hands-on time: 10 min. Total time: 11 hr. 50 min.

**Crust:**
1½ cups certified gluten-free quick-cooking oats
2 tablespoons sweet white sorghum flour
2 tablespoons almond meal flour
2 tablespoons sugar
½ teaspoon ground cinnamon
3 tablespoons canola oil
Cooking spray

**Cheesecake:**
2 (8-ounce) blocks ⅓-less-fat cream cheese,
    softened
4 ounces fat-free cream cheese (about ½ cup),
    softened
1 cup sugar
1 cup fat-free sour cream
1 tablespoon cornstarch
1 tablespoon grated Key lime rind
2 teaspoons vanilla extract
⅛ teaspoon salt
3 large eggs
½ cup fresh or bottled Key lime juice
Lime slices, halved

1. Preheat oven to 325°.

2. To prepare crust, place first 5 ingredients in a food
   processor; process until finely ground. Add oil; pulse
   2 to 3 times or until combined.

3. Wrap 2 layers of foil around bottom and outside
   of a 9-inch springform pan; coat inside of pan
   with cooking spray. Firmly press crust mixture into
   bottom and ½ inch up sides of pan. Bake at 325°
   for 5 minutes. Cool completely on a wire rack.

4. To prepare cheesecake, place cheeses in a large bowl;
   beat with a mixer at medium speed until smooth.
   Add sugar and next 5 ingredients (through salt);
   beat well. Add eggs, 1 at a time, beating well after
   each addition. Add lime juice, beating at low speed
   until blended.

5. Pour cheesecake batter over cooled crust. Place
   springform pan in a shallow roasting pan; add
   enough hot water to come halfway up sides of
   springform pan. Bake at 325° for 1 hour and
   5 minutes or until center barely moves when pan
   is touched. Turn oven off; cool cheesecake in closed
   oven 30 minutes. Remove cheesecake from oven;
   run a knife around outside edge. Cool to room
   temperature. Cover and chill at least 8 hours.
   Garnish with lime. Serves 16 (serving size: 1 slice)

CALORIES 228; FAT 11.1g (sat 4.3g, mono 3.9g, poly 1.4g);
PROTEIN 7.1g; CARB 26g; FIBER 1.1g; CHOL 58mg;
IRON 0.7mg; SODIUM 200mg; CALC 88mg

## a flavorful little lime

Key limes are smaller than the limes typically found in the grocery store. They have a
greenish-yellow rind and a much stronger, more
sour-acidic flavor. They do have a short growing
season, usually June through August. If they're
not in season, you can substitute bottled Key
lime juice and Persian lime zest.

# BANANA-TOFFEE CUPCAKES

Hands-on time: 23 min. Total time: 68 min.

*Sticky, sweet, and bursting with bananas, these cupcakes provide the perfect antidote for the after-school "hungries."*

**Cupcakes:**
5.2 ounces white rice flour (about 1 cup)
2.1 ounces sweet white sorghum flour (about 1/2 cup)
2.3 ounces cornstarch (about 1/2 cup)
1 teaspoon baking powder
1/2 teaspoon xanthan gum
1/2 teaspoon baking soda
1/2 teaspoon salt
1/8 teaspoon ground cinnamon
3/4 cup granulated sugar
3/4 cup mashed ripe banana (about 2 small bananas)
1/2 cup canola oil
2 large eggs
1 teaspoon vanilla extract
1/2 cup 2% reduced-fat milk
Cooking spray

**Frosting:**
1/4 cup butter
2 cups powdered sugar
2 tablespoons 2% reduced-fat milk
1 teaspoon vanilla extract

**Remaining Ingredient:**
2 tablespoons almond brickle chips (such as Heath)

1. Preheat oven to 350°.

2. To prepare cupcakes, weigh or lightly spoon flours and cornstarch into dry measuring cups; level with a knife. Combine flours, cornstarch, baking powder, and next 4 ingredients (through cinnamon) in a medium bowl; stir with a whisk.

3. Combine granulated sugar, banana, and canola oil in a large bowl; beat with a mixer at medium speed until smooth. Add eggs, 1 at a time, beating well after each addition. Beat in 1 teaspoon vanilla. Add flour mixture and 1/2 cup milk alternately to sugar mixture, beginning and ending with flour mixture.

4. Place 18 paper muffin cup liners in muffin cups; coat liners with cooking spray. Spoon batter into prepared cups. Bake at 350° for 24 minutes or until a wooden pick inserted in center comes out clean. Cool 5 minutes in pans on a wire rack; remove from pans. Cool completely on wire rack.

5. To prepare frosting, heat butter in a small saucepan over medium heat; cook 2 minutes or until browned, stirring constantly. Remove from heat; cool 5 minutes.

6. Place browned butter, powdered sugar, 2 tablespoons milk, and 1 teaspoon vanilla in a medium bowl; beat with a mixer at low speed until smooth. Spread frosting over cupcakes, and sprinkle with brickle chips. Serves 18 (serving size: 1 cupcake)

CALORIES 250; FAT 10.3g (sat 2.6g, mono 5g, poly 2g); PROTEIN 2.1g; CARB 38g; FIBER 0.9g; CHOL 29mg; IRON 0.3mg; SODIUM 167mg; CALC 34mg

# PEACHES AND CREAM MINI CUPCAKES

Hands-on time: 21 min. Total time: 1 hr. 37 min.

*These lovely little cupcakes are dedicated to Mae Charlotte, Angela's cousin's daughter. Mae's father has been courageously battling a rare form of lymphoma for the past few years. At her very young age, Mae has been incredibly brave, supportive, understanding, and even stoic. These dainty cupcakes are nearly as elegant and intrinsically sweet as our dear Mae. If you don't have a pastry bag, just dollop the whipped topping on each mini cupcake.*

2.6 ounces white rice flour (about 1/2 cup)
2.3 ounces cornstarch (about 1/2 cup)
2.1 ounces sweet white sorghum flour (about 1/2 cup)
1 1/2 teaspoons baking powder
3/4 teaspoon xanthan gum
1/4 teaspoon salt
1/2 cup sugar
6 tablespoons non-dairy buttery spread (such as Earth Balance), softened
2 large eggs
1 large egg white
1/2 teaspoon vanilla extract
1/2 cup vanilla soy milk
Cooking spray
6 tablespoons peach preserves
2 cups frozen reduced-calorie whipped topping, thawed
6 peach slices, cut into thirds

1. Preheat oven to 375°.

2. Weigh or lightly spoon white rice flour, cornstarch, and sweet white sorghum flour into dry measuring cups; level with a knife. Combine white rice flour, cornstarch, sweet white sorghum flour, baking powder, xanthan gum, and salt in a medium bowl; stir with a whisk.

3. Place sugar and buttery spread in a large bowl; beat with a mixer at medium speed until blended. Add eggs and egg white, 1 at a time, beating well after each addition. Beat in vanilla. Add flour mixture and soy milk alternately to sugar mixture, beginning and ending with flour mixture.

4. Place 36 paper muffin cup liners in miniature muffin cups; coat liners with cooking spray. Spoon two-thirds of batter into prepared cups, filling each cup halfway. Spoon 1/2 teaspoon peach preserves over batter in cups; top with remaining batter. Bake at 375° for 15 minutes or until cupcakes spring back when lightly touched in center. Cool 2 minutes in pans on a wire rack; remove from pan. Cool completely on wire rack.

5. Spoon whipped topping into a pastry bag fitted with a small star tip; pipe whipped topping onto cupcakes. Top cupcakes with peaches. Serves 36 (serving size: 1 mini cupcake)

CALORIES 75; FAT 2.8g (sat 1.1g, mono 1g, poly 0.6g); PROTEIN 0.9g; CARB 12g; FIBER 0.4g; CHOL 10mg; IRON 0.2mg; SODIUM 58mg; CALC 20mg

# SOUR CREAM-COCOA CUPCAKES

Hands-on time: 16 min. Total time: 1 hr. 36 min.

2.1 ounces sweet white sorghum flour (about ½ cup)
1.15 ounces brown rice flour (about ¼ cup)
1.05 ounces tapioca flour (about ¼ cup)
½ cup unsweetened cocoa
1 teaspoon xanthan gum
½ teaspoon baking soda
½ teaspoon baking powder
½ teaspoon salt
¾ cup granulated sugar
¼ cup unsalted butter, softened
2 large eggs
1 cup fat-free sour cream
½ teaspoon vanilla extract
Cooking spray
1 cup powdered sugar
2 tablespoons unsalted butter, softened
1 tablespoon 1% low-fat milk
½ teaspoon vanilla extract

1. Preheat oven to 375°.

2. Weigh or lightly spoon flours into dry measuring cups; level with a knife. Combine flours, cocoa, and next 4 ingredients in a bowl; stir with a whisk.

3. Place sugar and ¼ cup butter in a large bowl; beat with a mixer at medium speed until blended. Add eggs, 1 at a time, beating well after each addition. Beat in sour cream and vanilla. Gradually add flour mixture, beating at low speed until smooth (batter will be very thick).

4. Place 12 paper muffin cup liners in muffin cups; coat liners with cooking spray. Spoon batter into prepared cups (cups will be almost full). Bake at 375° for 20 minutes or until a wooden pick inserted in center comes out clean. Cool 10 minutes in pan on a wire rack; remove from pan. Cool completely on wire rack.

5. Combine powdered sugar, 2 tablespoons butter, milk, and ½ teaspoon vanilla in a medium bowl; beat with a mixer at low speed until blended. Increase speed to medium; beat until smooth. Spread frosting over cupcakes. Serves 12 (serving size: 1 cupcake)

CALORIES 218; FAT 7.7g (sat 4.4g, mono 2.1g, poly 0.4g); PROTEIN 3.6g; CARB 36g; FIBER 2g; CHOL 48mg; IRON 1mg; SODIUM 199mg; CALC 57mg

## creating a better cupcake

When you bake, don't skip the softening step. Softened butter mixes with flours and sugars more easily than cold butter fresh out of the refrigerator. The butter should sit out at room temperature for about 30 minutes or until you can press your fingertip into it easily. It should still hold its shape but no part should be melted. If you're short on time, butter will soften more quickly if you cut it into cubes.

# RED VELVET WHOOPIE PIES

Hands-on time: 17 min. Total time: 1 hr. 26 min.

*This hand-held version of the classic cake is a yummy favorite for children of all ages—guaranteed to generate smiles.*

**Cake:**
4.8 ounces oat flour (about 1⅓ cups)
3.06 ounces brown rice flour (about ⅔ cup)
2 tablespoons unsweetened cocoa
1¼ teaspoons baking soda
1 teaspoon xanthan gum
¼ teaspoon baking powder
1 cup granulated sugar
1 cup plain fat-free Greek yogurt
1 teaspoon vanilla extract
3 large eggs
1 (1-ounce) bottle red food coloring
¾ cup water

**Filling:**
1 cup powdered sugar
1 cup marshmallow creme
3 tablespoons butter, softened
2 tablespoons vegetable shortening
1 teaspoon vanilla extract

**Remaining Ingredient:**
¼ cup powdered sugar

1. Preheat oven to 350°.

2. To prepare cake, weigh or lightly spoon flours into dry measuring cups; level with a knife. Combine flours, cocoa, baking soda, xanthan gum, and baking powder in a medium bowl; stir with a whisk.

3. Combine granulated sugar and next 4 ingredients (through food coloring) in a large bowl; beat with a mixer at medium speed until well blended. Add flour mixture and ¾ cup water alternately to sugar mixture, beginning and ending with flour mixture.

4. Spoon 2 tablespoonfuls batter into 24 mounds 2 inches apart onto baking sheets lined with parchment paper. Bake at 350° for 12 minutes or until cakes spring back when lightly touched. Cool completely on pans on wire racks.

5. To prepare filling, combine 1 cup powdered sugar and next 4 ingredients (through vanilla) in a medium bowl. Beat with a mixer at medium speed until light and fluffy. Spread about 1½ tablespoons filling onto bottoms of 12 cakes; top with remaining cakes, bottom sides down. Dust both sides of whoopie pies with ¼ cup powdered sugar just before serving. Serves 12 (serving size: 1 whoopie pie)

CALORIES 289; FAT 7.4g (sat 3g, mono 2.3g, poly 1.3g); PROTEIN 5.6g; CARB 51g; FIBER 1.6g; CHOL 54mg; IRON 1mg; SODIUM 201mg; CALC 36mg

chapter 7

PIES
AND
TARTS

**P**ies and tarts are usually associated with festive times: holidays, picnics, parties, fairs. Everyone, including those who are gluten free, knows how awesome these fruit, nut, meat, or cream-filled desserts can taste.

The gluten-free challenge comes down to the crusts—they don't behave the same way as traditional crusts and require that you handle them with care. You can't simply roll them out on your kitchen counter with a rolling pin because these delicate doughs will fall apart. But a few simple steps go a long way toward making perfect gluten-free

pies and tarts. Things like refrigerating the dough, which helps the butter or shortening firm back up, makes the dough easier to roll. Placing the dough between wax or parchment paper to roll it out provides another layer of protection.

But, handled properly, these crusts will stand the test of time and hold any favorite filling that you happen to crave. Be prepared to sink your teeth into some of the best pies and tarts you have ever tried.

# MAPLE-PECAN PIE

Hands-on time: 13 min. Total time: 4 hr. 8 min.

*No Thanksgiving dinner is complete without a pecan pie. Every November we dedicate this brown sugar and maple pecan pie to the Loucraft family, whose newest endeavor is to harvest sweet and dark maple syrup right from their own Connecticut maple trees.*

**Crust:**
1.7 ounces potato starch (about ⅓ cup)
1.4 ounces tapioca flour (about ⅓ cup)
1 tablespoon granulated sugar
½ teaspoon salt
3 tablespoons chilled butter, cut into small pieces
3½ tablespoons 1% low-fat milk
Cooking spray

**Filling:**
½ cup maple syrup
½ cup light-colored corn syrup
½ cup packed brown sugar
2 tablespoons butter, melted
1 teaspoon vanilla extract
3 large eggs
1½ cups chopped pecans

1. To prepare crust, weigh or lightly spoon potato starch and flour into dry measuring cups; level with a knife. Combine potato starch, flour, granulated sugar, and salt in a medium bowl; stir with a whisk. Cut in butter with a pastry blender or 2 knives until mixture resembles coarse meal. Add milk; toss with a fork until moist. Gently press mixture into a 4-inch circle on 2 sheets of heavy-duty plastic wrap that overlap; cover with additional overlapping plastic wrap. Chill 1 hour.

2. Preheat oven to 350°.

3. Roll dough, still covered, into a 12-inch circle. Fit dough, plastic wrap side up, into a 9-inch pie plate coated with cooking spray. Remove remaining plastic wrap. Press dough against bottom and sides of pan. Fold edges under or flute decoratively. Chill until ready to fill.

4. To prepare filling, combine maple syrup and next 5 ingredients (through eggs) in a large bowl, stirring with a whisk. Stir in pecans; pour into prepared piecrust. Bake at 350° for 30 minutes. Shield edges of piecrust with foil; bake an additional 25 minutes or until filling is puffed and golden brown. Cool completely on a wire rack. Serves 14 (serving size: 1 slice)

CALORIES 256; FAT 13.7g (sat 3.7g, mono 6.3g, poly 2.9g); PROTEIN 2.6g; CARB 33g; FIBER 1.1g; CHOL 51mg; IRON 0.6mg; SODIUM 149mg; CALC 40mg

## pies vs. tarts

Pie and tart crusts are very similar. Piecrusts tend to be flaky and light, and are usually fluted around the edges. They're baked in pie plates with shallow sloped sides in varying sizes. You'll see pies made with crusts on the bottom, on the top, or both. Tarts, on the other hand, rarely have crusts on top, and the crusts themselves tend to be thicker and slightly more dense than piecrusts. Tart crusts are usually made in a round or square pan with very shallow sides.

# SWEET POTATO PIE

Hands-on time: 23 min. Total time: 2 hr. 51 min.

*An alternative to the old-fashioned pumpkin pie, this sweet potato dessert is seasoned to perfection with cinnamon, ginger, nutmeg, and cloves. Serve with a large dollop of light whipped topping dusted with nutmeg, and savor each heavenly bite.*

Crust:

6.5 ounces white rice flour (about 1¼ cups)
4.2 ounces tapioca flour (about 1 cup)
1½ teaspoons sugar
½ teaspoon baking soda
½ teaspoon xanthan gum
¼ cup chilled butter, cut into small pieces
2 tablespoons vegetable shortening
9 tablespoons 1% low-fat milk
Cooking spray

Filling:

1 pound sweet potatoes
¾ cup sugar
½ teaspoon ground cinnamon
½ teaspoon ground ginger
½ teaspoon salt
¼ teaspoon ground nutmeg
⅛ teaspoon ground cloves
2 large eggs
1 (12-ounce) can evaporated low-fat milk
¾ cup frozen reduced-calorie whipped topping, thawed
Grated fresh nutmeg (optional)

1. To prepare crust, weigh or lightly spoon flours into dry measuring cups; level with a knife. Combine flours, 1½ teaspoons sugar, baking soda, and xanthan gum in a medium bowl; stir with a whisk. Cut in butter and shortening with a pastry blender or 2 knives until mixture resembles coarse meal. Add 9 tablespoons 1% low-fat milk; toss with a fork until moist. Gently press mixture into a 4-inch circle on 2 sheets of heavy-duty plastic wrap that overlap; cover with additional overlapping plastic wrap. Chill 30 minutes.

2. Roll dough, still covered, into a 12-inch circle. Fit dough, plastic wrap side up, into a 9-inch pie plate coated with cooking spray. Remove remaining plastic wrap. Press dough against bottom and sides of pan. Fold edges under or flute decoratively. Chill until ready to fill.

3. Preheat oven to 400°.

4. While crust chills, pierce potatoes with a fork; bake at 400° for 1 hour or until tender. Cool. Peel potatoes; mash.

5. Combine mashed potato, ¾ cup sugar, and next 6 ingredients (through eggs) in a large mixing bowl; beat with a mixer at medium speed until well blended. Slowly stir in evaporated milk. Pour filling into prepared crust. Bake at 400° for 15 minutes. Reduce oven temperature to 350° (do not remove pie from oven); bake an additional 45 minutes or until center is set. Cool completely. Serve with whipped topping, and sprinkle with nutmeg, if desired. Serves 12 (serving size: 1 slice and 1 tablespoon whipped topping)

CALORIES 257; FAT 7.5g (sat 3.4g, mono 2.1g, poly 0.9g); PROTEIN 4.8g; CARB 43g; FIBER 1.3g; CHOL 47mg; IRON 0.6mg; SODIUM 245mg; CALC 111mg

# CHEDDAR-APPLE PIE

Hands-on time: 1 hr. 10 min. Total time: 3 hr. 30 min.

*Tart and tangy, sweet and spiced, this intensely flavored homemade apple pie is thickly layered into a sharp cheddar cheese–enhanced crust.*

## Crust:

1.7 ounces potato starch (about 1/3 cup)
1.4 ounces tapioca flour (about 1/3 cup)
1 tablespoon sugar
1/2 teaspoon salt
3 tablespoons chilled unsalted butter, cut into small pieces
3 tablespoons 1% low-fat milk

## Filling:

2 pounds Granny Smith apples, peeled, cored, and thinly sliced
1/3 cup granulated sugar
1/3 cup packed dark brown sugar
2 tablespoons fresh lemon juice
1 tablespoon cornstarch
1 teaspoon ground cinnamon
1/4 teaspoon salt
1/8 teaspoon ground nutmeg
Cooking spray
2 ounces sharp cheddar cheese, shredded (about 1/2 cup) and divided
1 tablespoon chilled unsalted butter, cut into small pieces

## Topping:

1/4 cup granulated sugar
1/4 cup packed brown sugar
1/4 teaspoon salt
3/4 cup certified gluten-free quick-cooking oats
4 ounces gluten-free arrowroot cookies
4 tablespoons chilled unsalted butter, cut into small pieces

1. To prepare crust, weigh or lightly spoon potato starch and flour into dry measuring cups; level with a knife. Combine potato starch, flour, 1 tablespoon sugar, and salt in a bowl; stir with a whisk. Cut in butter with a pastry blender or 2 knives until mixture resembles coarse meal. Add milk; toss with a fork until moist. Gently press mixture into a 4-inch circle on 2 sheets of heavy-duty plastic wrap that overlap; cover with additional overlapping plastic wrap. Chill 1 hour.

2. To prepare filling, place apples and next 7 ingredients (through nutmeg) in a large bowl; toss to combine.

3. Preheat oven to 350°.

4. Roll dough, still covered, into a 12-inch circle. Fit dough, plastic wrap side up, into a 9-inch pie plate coated with cooking spray. Remove remaining plastic wrap. Press dough against bottom and sides of pan. Fold edges under or flute decoratively.

5. Sprinkle 1/4 cup cheese over piecrust. Spoon apple mixture over cheese; top with 1 tablespoon butter pieces. Bake at 350° for 20 minutes.

6. To prepare topping, place 1/4 cup granulated sugar, 1/4 cup brown sugar, and 1/4 teaspoon salt in a food processor; process until combined. Add oats, cookies, and 4 tablespoons butter; pulse 2 times or until crumbly. Remove pie from oven; sprinkle with 1/4 cup cheese and topping, pressing gently to adhere. Bake an additional 30 minutes or until golden brown. Cool on a wire rack. Serves 14 (serving size: 1 slice)

CALORIES 250; FAT 9.5g (sat 5.4g, mono 2.3g, poly 0.5g); PROTEIN 2.7g; CARB 42.5g; FIBER 1.8g; CHOL 25mg; IRON 0.6mg; SODIUM 250mg; CALC 53mg

# LEMON MERINGUE PIE

Hands-on time: 45 min. Total time: 11 hr. 52 min.

**Crust:**
1.7 ounces potato starch (about ⅓ cup)
1.53 ounces brown rice flour (about ⅓ cup)
1.4 ounces tapioca flour (about ⅓ cup)
1.2 ounces almond meal flour (about ⅓ cup)
1 tablespoon sugar
½ teaspoon salt
3 tablespoons chilled butter, cut into small pieces
3 tablespoons 1% low-fat milk
Cooking spray

**Filling:**
½ cup fresh lemon juice
1.15 ounces cornstarch (about ¼ cup)
4 large egg yolks
2 cups 1% low-fat milk
⅔ cup sugar
2 tablespoons grated lemon rind
2 tablespoons butter

**Meringue:**
4 large egg whites
¼ teaspoon cream of tartar
¼ cup sugar

1. To prepare crust, weigh or lightly spoon potato starch and flours into dry measuring cups; level with a knife. Combine potato starch, flours, 1 tablespoon sugar, and salt in a medium bowl; stir with a whisk. Cut in butter with a pastry blender or 2 knives until mixture resembles coarse meal. Add 3 tablespoons milk; toss with a fork until moist. Gently press mixture into a 4-inch circle on 2 sheets of heavy-duty plastic wrap that overlap; cover with additional overlapping plastic wrap. Chill 1 hour.

2. Preheat oven to 375°.

3. Roll dough, still covered, into a 12-inch circle. Fit dough, plastic wrap side up, into a 9-inch pie plate coated with cooking spray. Remove remaining plastic wrap. Press dough against bottom and sides of pan. Fold edges under or flute decoratively. Line bottom of dough with parchment paper; arrange pie weights or dried beans on paper. Bake at 375° for 22 minutes or until edges are lightly browned. Cool completely.

4. To prepare filling, combine lemon juice and cornstarch, stirring with a whisk. Add egg yolks, stirring with a whisk to combine.

5. Place 2 cups milk, ⅔ cup sugar, and rind in a large saucepan over medium-low heat, stirring occasionally with a whisk until mixture comes to a boil. Slowly pour one-third of milk mixture into lemon juice mixture, stirring with a whisk. Slowly pour lemon juice mixture into milk mixture, and boil 1 minute or until mixture thickens, stirring constantly with a whisk. Pour into a bowl; add 2 tablespoons butter, stirring until melted. Pour hot filling into cooled crust.

6. To prepare meringue, place egg whites and cream of tartar in a bowl; beat with a mixer at high speed until soft peaks form. Add ¼ cup sugar, beating until stiff peaks form. Spread evenly over filling, sealing to edge of crust. Bake at 375° for 10 minutes or until lightly browned on top. Cool 1 hour on a wire rack. Chill overnight. Serves 10 (serving size: 1 slice)

CALORIES 226; FAT 8.3g (sat 4.7g, mono 2.6g, poly 0.6g); PROTEIN 4.5g; CARB 34g; FIBER 0.2g; CHOL 92mg; IRON 0.3mg; SODIUM 218mg; CALC 81mg

# CHOCOLATE CREAM PIE

Hands-on time: 28 min. Total time: 6 hr. 21 min.

*My wife's brother, Eddie, has a reputation for being a major chocoholic and pie connoisseur. Since he has tasted so many varieties, he knows what he's talking about when he says, with a mouth full of chocolate, "Dude, this is awwwwwwesome."*

3.45 ounces brown rice flour (about ¾ cup)
1.8 ounces almond meal flour (about ½ cup)
2 tablespoons potato starch
2 tablespoons cornstarch
1 teaspoon sugar
½ teaspoon xanthan gum
½ teaspoon baking soda
½ teaspoon salt
5 tablespoons chilled unsalted butter, cut into small pieces
¼ cup 1% low-fat milk
Cooking spray
⅔ cup sugar
1.15 ounces cornstarch (about ¼ cup)
¼ teaspoon salt
3 large egg yolks
1¾ cups 1% low-fat milk
3 ounces bittersweet chocolate, melted
¼ cup unsweetened cocoa
1 teaspoon unsalted butter, melted
1 teaspoon vanilla extract
1 cup frozen fat-free whipped topping, thawed

1. Weigh or lightly spoon flours into dry measuring cups; level with a knife. Combine flours, potato starch, and next 5 ingredients (through salt) in a medium bowl; stir with a whisk. Cut in butter with a pastry blender or 2 knives until mixture resembles coarse meal. Add ¼ cup milk; toss with a fork until moist. Press mixture into a 4-inch circle on 2 sheets of heavy-duty plastic wrap that overlap; cover with additional overlapping plastic wrap. Freeze 30 minutes.

2. Preheat oven to 350°.

3. Roll dough, still covered, into a 12-inch circle. Fit dough, plastic wrap side up, into a 9-inch pie plate coated with cooking spray. Remove remaining plastic wrap. Press dough against bottom and sides of pan. Flute decoratively. Pierce dough with a fork; bake at 350° for 18 minutes or until crust is golden brown. Cool completely on a wire rack.

4. Combine ⅔ cup sugar, ¼ cup cornstarch, ¼ teaspoon salt, and egg yolks in a medium saucepan; stir with a whisk until blended. Add 1¾ cups milk, stirring with a whisk. Bring to boil over medium-high heat, stirring occasionally with a whisk. Reduce heat to low, and cook 1 minute or until filling thickens.

5. Press filling through a fine sieve over a bowl; discard solids. Add chocolate, cocoa, 1 teaspoon butter, and vanilla to filling, stirring with a whisk. Cool 5 minutes.

6. Spoon filling into prepared crust. Cover surface of filling with plastic wrap coated with cooking spray. Chill 4 hours. Remove plastic wrap; spread whipped topping over filling. Serves 14 (serving size: 1 slice)

CALORIES 219; FAT 10.6g (sat 5.2g, mono 2.5g, poly 0.5g); PROTEIN 3.8g; CARB 28g; FIBER 1.4g; CHOL 53mg; IRON 0.8mg; SODIUM 195mg; CALC 63mg

*Pressing the chocolate filling through a fine mesh sieve removes any lumps of cornstarch and egg and creates a smooth, creamy filling.*

# DOUBLE-BANANA CREAM PIE

Hands-on time: 21 min. Total time: 3 hr. 21 min.

*When Grandpa FitzGerald heard this book was in the works, he insisted that we include this dreamy pie. Thick, vanilla custard layered with ripe bananas in a sweet arrowroot cookie crust. You'll hear, "Mmmmmm" with each bite.*

**Crust:**

5 ounces gluten-free arrowroot cookies (about 50 cookies)
2 tablespoons sugar
¼ cup unsalted butter, melted
Cooking spray

**Filling:**

½ cup sugar
3½ tablespoons cornstarch
⅛ teaspoon salt

2½ cups 1% low-fat milk
3 large egg yolks
1 teaspoon vanilla extract
½ teaspoon banana extract
2 tablespoons unsalted butter
3 ripe bananas, peeled and cut into ¼-inch slices
1½ cups frozen fat-free whipped topping, thawed
1 tablespoon almond brickle chips (such as Heath)

1. Preheat oven to 350°.

2. To prepare crust, place cookies and 2 tablespoons sugar in a food processor; process until finely ground. Add ¼ cup melted butter; process until blended and moist. Press into bottom and up sides of a 9-inch pie plate coated with cooking spray. Bake at 350° for 8 to 10 minutes or until lightly browned. Cool completely on a wire rack.

3. To prepare filling, combine ½ cup sugar, cornstarch, and salt in a heavy saucepan over medium heat, stirring to combine. Add milk and egg yolks, stirring with a whisk. Cook 6 minutes or until mixture starts to boil and begins to thicken, stirring occasionally. Remove from heat. Stir in extracts and 2 tablespoons butter. Place pan in a bowl of ice to cool.

4. Arrange half of bananas slices in a single layer over crust; top with half of filling mixture. Repeat layers. Cover surface of filling with plastic wrap coated with cooking spray. Chill at least 3 hours. Uncover, and spread whipped topping over filling. Sprinkle with brickle bits. Serves 12 (serving size: 1 slice)

CALORIES 237; FAT 9.6g (sat 5g, mono 2.3g, poly 0.5g); PROTEIN 3.7g; CARB 37g; FIBER 1.6g; CHOL 68mg; IRON 0.5mg; SODIUM 94mg; CALC 80mg

# BLACK BOTTOM PIE

Hands-on time: 25 min. Total time: 5 hr. 28 min.

*Grandma Laurel sent this family favorite recipe from Texas. With a few changes, all those on a gluten-free diet who crave old-fashioned vanilla pudding layered over a bittersweet chocolate crust can now indulge.*

Crust:

1.7 ounces potato starch (about 1/3 cup)
1.4 ounces tapioca flour (about 1/3 cup)
1 tablespoon sugar
1/2 teaspoon salt
3 tablespoons chilled butter, cut into small pieces
1/4 cup 1% low-fat milk
Cooking spray
2/3 cup semisweet chocolate chips

Filling:

4 large egg yolks, lightly beaten
2 cups 1% low-fat milk
3/4 cup sugar
2 tablespoons cornstarch
1 teaspoon vanilla extract
1/2 ounce semisweet chocolate, grated

1. To prepare crust, weigh or lightly spoon potato starch and flour into dry measuring cups; level with a knife. Combine potato starch, flour, 1 tablespoon sugar, and salt in a medium bowl; stir with a whisk. Cut in butter with a pastry blender or 2 knives until mixture resembles coarse meal. Add 1/4 cup milk; toss with a fork until moist. Gently press mixture into a 4-inch circle on 2 sheets of heavy-duty plastic wrap that overlap; cover with additional overlapping plastic wrap. Chill 1 hour.

2. Preheat oven to 375°.

3. Roll dough, still covered, into a 12-inch circle. Fit dough, plastic wrap side up, into a 9-inch pie plate coated with cooking spray. Remove remaining plastic wrap. Press dough against bottom and sides of pan. Fold edges under or flute decoratively. Line bottom of dough with parchment paper; arrange pie weights or dried beans on paper. Bake at 375° for 22 minutes or until edges are lightly browned. Sprinkle chocolate chips over hot crust; spread with a spatula when melted. Cool completely.

4. To prepare filling, place egg yolks in a medium bowl. Combine 2 cups milk, 3/4 cup sugar, and cornstarch in a 4-quart saucepan. Bring to a boil; cook 1 minute, stirring constantly. Pour one-fourth of milk mixture into egg yolks, stirring with a whisk. Pour egg yolk mixture into milk mixture. Boil 2 to 3 minutes or until mixture thickens, stirring constantly. Remove from heat; stir in vanilla.

5. Pour filling mixture into cooled crust. Cover surface of filling with plastic wrap. Chill at least 3 hours. Sprinkle with grated chocolate. Serves 10 (serving size: 1 slice)

CALORIES 239; FAT 9.8g (sat 5.5g, mono 3.1g, poly 0.6g); PROTEIN 3.5g; CARB 37g; FIBER 0.8g; CHOL 86mg; IRON 0.6mg; SODIUM 178mg; CALC 82mg

# WHITE CHOCOLATE-RASPBERRY PIE

Hands-on time: 13 min. Total time: 12 hr. 56 min.

### Crust:

**5 ounces gluten-free arrowroot cookies (about 50 cookies)**
**2 tablespoons sugar**
**3 tablespoons unsalted butter, melted**
**Cooking spray**

### Filling:

**⅔ cup white chocolate chips**
**⅓ cup sugar**
**⅓ cup vanilla fat-free Greek yogurt**
**1 (8-ounce) block ⅓-less-fat cream cheese, softened**
**1 teaspoon vanilla extract**
**8 ounces fresh raspberries**

1. Preheat oven to 350°.

2. To prepare crust, place cookies and 2 tablespoons sugar in a food processor; process until finely ground. Add butter; process until blended and moist. Press into bottom and up sides of a 9-inch pie plate coated with cooking spray. Bake at 350° for 8 to 10 minutes or until lightly browned. Cool completely on a wire rack.

3. To prepare filling, place white chocolate chips in the top of a double boiler; place over simmering water. Heat chips until melted and smooth, stirring often. Remove from heat. Place ⅓ cup sugar, yogurt, and cream cheese in a medium bowl; beat with a mixer at medium speed until light and frothy. Add vanilla and melted chocolate; beat until blended.

4. Spoon filling into cooled crust. Cover loosely with foil, and chill overnight. Top filling with a single layer of raspberries. Refrigerate until ready to serve. Serves 14 (serving size: 1 slice)

CALORIES 191; FAT 10.3g (sat 5.5g, mono 2.4g, poly 0.4g); PROTEIN 3.3g; CARB 25g; FIBER 1.7g; CHOL 24mg; IRON 0.4mg; SODIUM 92mg; CALC 51mg

# ALL-PURPOSE LIGHT PIECRUST

Hands-on time: 14 min. Total time: 2 hr. 34 min.

*This piecrust has just the right amount of butter for flavor and shortening for flakiness. It is versatile enough to complement any fruit, cream, nut, or pudding fillings that you'd like.*

6.5 ounces white rice flour (about 1¼ cups)
4.2 ounces tapioca flour (about 1 cup)
1 tablespoon sugar
½ teaspoon baking soda
½ teaspoon xanthan gum
½ teaspoon salt
¼ cup chilled butter, cut into small pieces
3 tablespoons vegetable shortening
9 tablespoons 1% low-fat milk
Cooking spray

1. Weigh or lightly spoon flours into dry measuring cups; level with a knife. Combine flours, sugar, and next 3 ingredients (through salt) in a large bowl; stir with a whisk. Cut in butter and shortening with a pastry blender or 2 knives until mixture resembles coarse meal. Add milk; toss with a fork until moist. Gently press mixture into a 4-inch circle on 2 sheets of heavy-duty plastic wrap that overlap; cover with additional overlapping plastic wrap. Chill at least 2 hours.

2. Preheat oven to 375°.

3. Roll dough, still covered, into a 12-inch circle. Fit dough, plastic wrap side up, into a 9-inch pie plate coated with cooking spray. Remove remaining plastic wrap. Press dough against bottom and sides of pan. Fold edges under or flute decoratively.

4. Line bottom of dough with parchment paper; arrange pie weights or dried beans on paper. Bake at 375° for 12 minutes. Remove pie weights and paper; bake an additional 8 minutes or until edge is lightly browned. Cool on a wire rack. Serves 10 (serving size: ⅒ of piecrust)

CALORIES 192; FAT 8.6g (sat 4g, mono 2.5g, poly 1.2g); PROTEIN 1.6g; CARB 27g; FIBER 0.6g; CHOL 13mg; IRON 0.2mg; SODIUM 228mg; CALC 20mg

## stay a step ahead

If making a pie is in your near future, you can prepare this crust through step 1 and freeze it. In addition to covering the dough with plastic wrap, place it in a heavy-duty zip-top plastic bag to keep it freezer-safe. It'll keep up to three months. Let the dough thaw in the refrigerator for two days before continuing with step 2.

# CHERRY TART
## WITH ALMOND STREUSEL TOPPING

Hands-on time: 46 min. Total time: 2 hr. 11 min.

*Our friends, the Siwkos, have two little girls, Isabella and Mariella, who love tea parties. They sit at a pretty table, and their mom helps them serve this tart. Then, after a refined tea service, they aren't afraid to wrestle their three hungry brothers who try to run off with any leftover fare.*

6.5 ounces white rice flour (about 1¼ cups)
4.2 ounces tapioca flour (about 1 cup)
1½ teaspoons granulated sugar
½ teaspoon baking soda
½ teaspoon xanthan gum
¼ cup chilled butter, cut into small pieces
2 tablespoons vegetable shortening
9 tablespoons 1% low-fat milk
Cooking spray
¾ cup granulated sugar
3 tablespoons cornstarch
1½ pounds pitted fresh sweet cherries or frozen
   sweet cherries, thawed (about 4 cups)
1.7 ounces white rice flour (about ⅓ cup)
¼ cup packed brown sugar
2 tablespoons sliced almonds
2 tablespoons butter, diced
¼ teaspoon ground cinnamon

1. Weigh or lightly spoon 6.5 ounces white rice flour (about 1¼ cups) and tapioca flour into dry measuring cups; level with a knife. Combine flours, 1½ teaspoons granulated sugar, baking soda, and xanthan gum in a medium bowl; stir with a whisk. Cut in butter and shortening with a pastry blender or 2 knives until mixture resembles coarse meal. Add milk; toss with a fork until moist. Gently press mixture into a 4-inch circle on 2 sheets of heavy-duty plastic wrap that overlap; cover with additional plastic wrap. Chill 30 minutes.

2. Preheat oven to 400°.

3. Roll dough, still covered, into a 13-inch circle. Fit dough, plastic wrap side up, into a 10-inch removable-bottom tart pan coated with cooking spray. Remove remaining plastic wrap. Press dough against bottom and sides of pan. Line bottom of dough with parchment paper; fill with pie weights or dried beans. Bake at 400° for 8 to 10 minutes; remove parchment paper, and cool on a wire rack.

4. Reduce oven temperature to 350°.

5. Combine ¾ cup granulated sugar and cornstarch in a small bowl. Place cherries in a medium saucepan over medium-low heat; cook 5 minutes. Stir in sugar mixture. Reduce heat to low; cook 10 to 15 minutes or until mixture thickens, stirring frequently. Remove from heat; cool completely.

6. Weigh or lightly spoon 1.7 ounces white rice flour (about ⅓ cup) into a dry measuring cup; level with a knife. Place flour, brown sugar, and remaining ingredients in a food processor; process until coarsely ground.

7. Spoon cooled cherry mixture into crust. Sprinkle brown sugar mixture over filling. Bake at 350° for 40 minutes or until crust and topping are browned and filling is bubbly. Serves 12 (serving size: 1 slice)

CALORIES 297; FAT 8.9g (sat 4.4g, mono 2.7g, poly 1g); PROTEIN 2.4g; CARB 54g; FIBER 1.9g; CHOL 16mg; IRON 0.5mg; SODIUM 110mg; CALC 32mg

# CRANBERRY-WALNUT TART

Hands-on time: 30 min. Total time: 1 hr. 53 min.

*This tart has a great basic crust. The white rice flour and tapioca flour have a neutral taste that allows the flavor of the butter to stand out. The shortening ensures flakiness.*

**Crust:**
6.5 ounces white rice flour (about 1¼ cups)
4.2 ounces tapioca flour (about 1 cup)
1½ teaspoons granulated sugar
½ teaspoon baking soda
½ teaspoon xanthan gum
¼ cup chilled butter, cut into small pieces
2 tablespoons vegetable shortening
9 tablespoons 1% low-fat milk
Cooking spray

**Filling:**
⅔ cup light-colored corn syrup
⅓ cup granulated sugar
⅓ cup packed brown sugar
1 teaspoon vanilla extract
¼ teaspoon salt
3 large eggs
1¼ cups fresh cranberries
⅔ cup chopped walnuts

1. To prepare crust, weigh or lightly spoon flours into dry measuring cups; level with a knife. Combine flours, 1½ teaspoons granulated sugar, baking soda, and xanthan gum in a medium bowl; stir with a whisk. Cut in butter and shortening with a pastry blender or 2 knives until mixture resembles coarse meal. Add milk; toss with a fork until moist. Gently press mixture into a 4-inch circle on 2 sheets of heavy-duty plastic wrap that overlap; cover with additional overlapping plastic wrap. Chill 30 minutes.

2. Preheat oven to 400°.

3. Roll dough, still covered, into a 13-inch circle. Fit dough, plastic wrap side up, into a 10-inch removable-bottom tart pan coated with cooking spray. Remove remaining plastic wrap. Press dough against bottom and sides of pan. Line bottom of dough with parchment paper; arrange pie weights or dried beans on paper. Bake at 400° for 8 to 10 minutes; carefully remove parchment paper, and cool crust 5 minutes on a wire rack.

4. Reduce oven temperature to 350°.

5. To prepare filling, combine corn syrup and next 5 ingredients (through eggs), stirring with a whisk. Fold in cranberries and walnuts. Pour filling into crust. Bake at 350° for 45 minutes or until center is set and crust is slightly golden. Cool completely in pan. Serves 14 (serving size: 1 slice)

CALORIES 271; FAT 10.1g (sat 3.3g, mono 2.5g, poly 3.5g); PROTEIN 3.4g; CARB 44g; FIBER 1.2g; CHOL 49mg; IRON 0.6mg; SODIUM 148mg; CALC 33mg

# PEAR AND APRICOT TART

Hands-on time: 30 min. Total time: 1 hr. 53 min.

*In the late 19th century, the families of Sicily came to America bringing their most cherished Italian customs and cooking. Prominent among them were flavorful, fresh fruit desserts, such as this lovely pear and apricot tart. Serve with a scoop of vanilla ice cream or, even better, gelato.*

**Crust:**

6.5 ounces white rice flour (about 1¼ cups)
4.2 ounces tapioca flour (about 1 cup)
1½ teaspoons granulated sugar
½ teaspoon baking soda
½ teaspoon xanthan gum
¼ cup chilled butter, cut into small pieces
2 tablespoons vegetable shortening
9 tablespoons 1% low-fat milk
Cooking spray

**Filling:**

½ cup lightly packed brown sugar
2 tablespoons cornstarch
1 tablespoon fresh lemon juice
⅛ teaspoon ground cinnamon
4 pears, peeled, cored and cut lengthwise into ¼-inch-thick slices

**Glaze:**

½ cup apricot preserves
1 tablespoon fresh orange juice

1. To prepare crust, weigh or lightly spoon flours into dry measuring cups; level with a knife. Combine flours, granulated sugar, baking soda, and xanthan gum in a medium bowl; stir with a whisk. Cut in butter and shortening with a pastry blender or 2 knives until mixture resembles coarse meal. Add milk; toss with a fork until moist. Gently press mixture into a 4-inch circle on 2 sheets of heavy-duty plastic wrap that overlap; cover with additional overlapping plastic wrap. Chill 30 minutes.

2. Preheat oven to 400°.

3. Roll dough, still covered, into a 12-inch square. Fit dough, plastic wrap side up, into a 10-inch square removable-bottom tart pan coated with cooking spray. Remove remaining plastic wrap. Press dough against bottom and sides of pan. Line bottom of dough with a piece of foil; arrange pie weights or dried beans on foil. Bake at 400° for 8 minutes. Remove pie weights and foil; bake an additional 3 minutes. Cool 5 minutes on a wire rack.

4. Reduce oven temperature to 350°.

5. To prepare filling, combine brown sugar, cornstarch, lemon juice, and cinnamon in a large bowl. Add pears, tossing to coat. Spoon pear mixture in prepared crust. Bake at 350° for 45 minutes. Cool in pan on wire rack.

6. To prepare glaze, place preserves and orange juice in a small bowl, stirring to combine. Brush glaze over tart. Cool completely before serving. Serves 12 (serving size: 1 slice)

CALORIES 258; FAT 6.4g (sat 3.1g, mono 1.9g, poly 0.7g); PROTEIN 1.7g; CARB 50g; FIBER 2.4g; CHOL 11mg; IRON 0.4mg; SODIUM 100mg; CALC 33mg

# STRAWBERRY-ORANGE TART

Hands-on time: 20 min. Total time: 4 hr. 5 min.

*This berry and citrus combination makes for an intense burst of flavor that dances on the taste buds. It's as wonderful to look at as it is to serve and eat.*

**Crust:**
5 ounces gluten-free arrowroot cookies (about 50 cookies)
2 tablespoons sugar
¼ cup unsalted butter, melted
Cooking spray

**Filling:**
2 cups 1% low-fat milk
4 large egg yolks
½ cup sugar
¼ cup cornstarch
2 tablespoons butter
1 teaspoon grated orange rind
1 teaspoon vanilla extract
3 cups sliced strawberries

1. Preheat oven to 350°.

2. To prepare crust, place cookies and 2 tablespoons sugar in a food processor; process until finely ground. Add butter; process until blended and moist. Press into bottom and up sides of a 9-inch pie plate coated with cooking spray. Bake at 350° for 8 to10 minutes or until lightly browned. Cool 30 minutes on a wire rack.

3. To prepare filling, combine milk and egg yolks in a medium bowl, stirring with a whisk. Combine ½ cup sugar and cornstarch in a medium saucepan over medium heat. Slowly pour milk mixture into sugar mixture, stirring with a whisk until mixture comes to a boil. Boil 1 to 2 minutes or until mixture thickens, stirring constantly. Remove from heat; stir in butter, orange rind, and vanilla. Pour filling into cooled crust. Cover surface of filling with plastic wrap. Chill at least 3 hours.

4. Uncover; top filling with strawberry slices. Chill until ready to serve. Serves 12 (serving size: 1 slice)

CALORIES 204; FAT 9.5g (sat 4.9g, mono 2.4g, poly 0.6g); PROTEIN 3.4g; CARB 30g; FIBER 1.7g; CHOL 83mg; IRON 0.6mg; SODIUM 72mg; CALC 75mg

## keeping a silky texture

When custard is exposed to air, a thick skin will form on the surface, which isn't an ideal pairing for the silky smooth texture of this dessert. To prevent this from happening, press a sheet of plastic wrap directly on the surface of the custard before chilling it.

# DOUBLE NUT-CHOCOLATE TART

Hands-on time: 10 min. Total time: 60 min.

*This dark, almondy, and rich-tasting tart requires much less sugar and butter than the standard fare. It's almost a flourless chocolate cake, but I added a little bit of brown rice flour to give it some structure so it would develop a nice crust.*

5 ounces bittersweet chocolate, chopped
5 tablespoons unsalted butter
½ cup packed brown sugar
2 tablespoons granulated sugar
1 teaspoon vanilla extract
¼ teaspoon salt
2 large eggs, lightly beaten
2.3 ounces brown rice flour (about ½ cup)
½ cup sliced almonds, toasted
½ cup chopped walnuts, toasted
1 teaspoon xanthan gum

Cooking spray
1 cup frozen reduced-calorie whipped topping, thawed

1. Preheat oven to 350°.

2. Place chocolate and butter in a medium microwave-safe bowl; microwave at HIGH 1 minute, stirring until smooth. Cool 2 minutes.

3. Combine brown sugar and next 4 ingredients (through eggs) in a large bowl, stirring with a whisk. Add chocolate mixture, stirring to combine.

4. Weigh or lightly spoon flour into a dry measuring cup; level with a knife. Add flour, nuts, and xanthan gum to sugar mixture, stirring with a whisk. Pour batter evenly into a 9-inch round removable-bottom tart pan coated with cooking spray. Bake at 350° for 20 minutes or until a wooden pick inserted in center comes out clean. Cool 30 minutes in pan on a wire rack. Cut into 16 slices. Top with whipped topping. Serves 16 (serving size: 1 slice and 1 tablespoon whipped topping)

CALORIES 194; FAT 12.4g (sat 5.6g, mono 3.4g, poly 2.5g); PROTEIN 2.9g; CARB 19g; FIBER 1g; CHOL 33mg; IRON 0.7mg; SODIUM 49mg; CALC 25mg

# TOASTED ALMOND-APRICOT TORTE

Hands-on time: 19 min. Total time: 1 hr. 14 min.

1.5 ounces brown rice flour (about ⅓ cup)
1.4 ounces tapioca flour (about ⅓ cup)
½ cup whole blanched almonds, toasted
½ cup dried apricots (about 14)
½ teaspoon ground cinnamon
½ teaspoon baking powder
¼ teaspoon ground nutmeg
¼ teaspoon salt
⅔ cup granulated sugar, divided
6 large egg yolks
6 large egg whites
1 teaspoon vanilla extract
Cooking spray
Tapioca flour, for dusting
4 ounces ⅓-less-fat cream cheese, softened
    (about ½ cup)
1 tablespoon butter, softened
3 cups powdered sugar
1 teaspoon vanilla extract
1 cup apricot preserves
2 tablespoons sliced almonds, toasted
4 dried apricots, chopped

1. Preheat oven to 350°.

2. Weigh or lightly spoon flours into dry measuring cups; level with a knife. Place flours, almonds, and next 5 ingredients (through salt) in a food processor; process 1 minute or until finely chopped.

3. Combine ⅓ cup granulated sugar and egg yolks in a large bowl; beat with a mixer at high speed 2 minutes or until mixture is very thick and pale in color.

4. Place egg whites in a large bowl; beat at high speed until stiff peaks form using clean, dry beaters. Slowly add ⅓ cup granulated sugar and 1 teaspoon vanilla; beat 4 minutes or until stiff peaks form.

5. Add flour mixture and one-third of egg white mixture to egg yolk mixture, stirring gently to combine. Fold in remaining egg white mixture, being careful not to deflate batter. Pour batter into a 9-inch springform pan coated with cooking spray and lightly dusted with tapioca flour.

6. Bake at 350° for 35 to 38 minutes or until top springs back when pressed in center. Cool 15 minutes in pan; remove torte from pan, and cool completely.

7. Place cream cheese and butter in a large bowl; beat with a mixer at high speed until light and fluffy. Slowly add powdered sugar, beating at medium speed until smooth. Beat in 1 teaspoon vanilla.

8. Cut cake in half horizontally, using a serrated knife; place bottom layer cut side up on a plate. Spread preserves over cut side of bottom layer. Top with remaining cake layer. Spread cream cheese mixture over top of cake; sprinkle with sliced almonds and chopped apricots. Cover loosely with plastic wrap; store in refrigerator. Serves 16 (serving size: 1⁄16 of torte)

CALORIES 297; FAT 7g (sat 2.3g, mono 3.5g, poly 1.2g); PROTEIN 4.8g; CARB 55g; FIBER 1.2g; CHOL 76mg; IRON 1mg; SODIUM 115mg; CALC 52mg

chapter 8

# COBBLERS

AND

# CRISPS

utumn is my favorite time of the year in New England. The air becomes cool and crisp; the leaves turn brilliantly yellow, red, and orange; and the apple varieties reach their peak of tartness or sweetness.

Cobblers, crisps, grunts, and buckles—also known as "good ole-fashioned New England desserts"—are my fall go-to recipes because they're warming and hearty. You'll notice the batter of these desserts is wetter than traditional versions. Gluten holds onto moisture, so in its absence, you need a batter with more moisture so the topping doesn't dry out and harden as it bakes. In this chapter you'll find a number of different topping options that you can pair with fresh produce from any season.

# APPLE-CHERRY COBBLER
## WITH SWEET SPIRAL BISCUITS

Hands-on time: 45 min. Total time: 1 hr. 25 min.

*We brought this to a party at Bryce and Dinah Dietz's home, a busy household with eight children. Bryce gave his ultimate approval, "Dude, this is to die for," as we began to spoon seconds onto the empty plates of the line of kids formed behind him.*

**Filling:**

4 large Fuji apples, peeled and cut into 1/4-inch slices (about 6 cups)
1 (12-ounce) package frozen pitted dark sweet cherries, thawed and drained
1 cup granulated sugar
1 1/2 tablespoons cornstarch
2 tablespoons fresh lemon juice
1/2 teaspoon ground cinnamon
Cooking spray

**Biscuits:**

2.3 ounces brown rice flour (about 1/2 cup)
1.8 ounces oat flour (about 1/2 cup)
1.15 ounces cornstarch (about 1/4 cup)
2 tablespoons granulated sugar
1 1/2 teaspoons xanthan gum
1 1/2 teaspoons baking powder
1/4 teaspoon salt
1/3 cup non-dairy buttery spread (such as Earth Balance)
2 tablespoons vanilla rice milk
1 large egg, lightly beaten
Brown rice flour, for dusting
1 tablespoon non-dairy buttery spread, melted
1/3 cup packed brown sugar

1. Preheat oven to 400°.

2. To prepare filling, combine first 6 ingredients in a large bowl; toss gently to combine. Spoon mixture into a 9-inch square glass or ceramic baking dish coated with cooking spray.

3. To prepare biscuits, weigh or lightly spoon flours and cornstarch into dry measuring cups; level with a knife. Combine flours, cornstarch, 2 tablespoons granulated sugar, and next 3 ingredients (through salt) in a medium bowl, stirring with a whisk; cut in 1/3 cup buttery spread with a pastry blender or 2 knives until mixture resembles coarse meal. Make a well in center of flour mixture; add rice milk and egg, stirring just until moist.

4. Turn dough out onto a heavily floured surface; knead lightly 5 to 6 times. Roll dough into a 12 x 12–inch square. Brush 1 tablespoon melted buttery spread over dough; sprinkle evenly with brown sugar. Roll up dough tightly, jelly-roll fashion. Pinch seams and ends to seal. Cut into 12 (1-inch) slices; place in a single layer on top of filling. Bake at 400° for 40 minutes or until biscuits are golden brown. Serves 12 (serving size: 1 biscuit and 1/2 cup apple mixture)

CALORIES 260; FAT 7g (sat 1.8g, mono 3.1g, poly 1.9g); PROTEIN 2g; CARB 49g; FIBER 2.4g; CHOL 16mg; IRON 0.6mg; SODIUM 167mg; CALC 59mg

*This biscuit dough is drier, so you will be able to knead and roll it up.*

The cornstarch mixed into the fresh fruit acts as a thickener, preventing the filling from becoming too runny.

# BLACKBERRY-ALMOND COBBLER

Hands-on time: 8 min. Total time: 48 min.

*This cobbler made me realize that I was spending too much time reading cookbooks and not enough time reading nursery rhymes to my three young sons. As Andrew began eating this cobbler, he sang out, "Sing a song of sixpence, a pocket full of rye…four and twenty BLACKBERRIES baked in a pie!"*

**Filling:**
4 cups fresh blackberries
3 tablespoons sugar
1 tablespoon cornstarch
1 tablespoon fresh lemon juice
Cooking spray

**Topping:**
2.3 ounces brown rice flour (about ½ cup)
1.8 ounces almond meal flour (about ½ cup)
¼ cup sugar
1 teaspoon baking powder
⅛ teaspoon salt
1 large egg, lightly beaten
4 tablespoons butter, melted and cooled
2 cups vanilla light ice cream

1. Preheat oven to 375°.

2. To prepare filling, combine first 4 ingredients in a large bowl, tossing to coat. Pour mixture into an 8-inch square glass or ceramic baking dish coated with cooking spray.

3. To prepare topping, weigh or lightly spoon flours into dry measuring cups; level with a knife. Combine flours, ¼ cup sugar, baking powder, and salt in a large bowl, stirring with a whisk. Add egg, stirring to combine. Add butter, stirring just until moist.

4. Drop batter by teaspoonfuls onto blackberry mixture. Bake at 375° for 30 minutes or until topping is lightly browned. Cool 10 minutes. Serve with ice cream. Serves 8 (serving size: ⅛ of cobbler and ¼ cup ice cream)

CALORIES 276; FAT 12.2g (sat 5.3g, mono 2.5g, poly 0.7g); PROTEIN 5.6g; CARB 38g; FIBER 4.8g; CHOL 49mg; IRON 1.1mg; SODIUM 183mg; CALC 143mg

## homemade almond meal flour

Making your own almond meal flour doesn't take long. Simply place blanched, unsalted almonds in a food processor, and process until they're a flour-like consistency. Pulse in one-second bursts, and check the flour consistency often. Blending too long can cause the almonds to release their natural oils and make the flour moist and clumpy.

# BLUEBERRY-PEACH COBBLER WITH PECANS

Hands-on time: 25 min. Total time: 60 min.

*My friend, Patty Charpentier, makes this cobbler with fresh or frozen berries along with the sweet peaches she lovingly preserves by hand. You can re-create this at home using frozen berries and peaches.*

⅓ cup granulated sugar
1 teaspoon cornstarch
½ teaspoon ground cinnamon
1½ pounds fresh peaches, peeled, pitted, and thinly sliced (about 4)
2 cups fresh or frozen blueberries
Cooking spray
2.6 ounces white rice flour (about ½ cup)
2.3 ounces brown rice flour (about ½ cup)
0.9 ounce oat flour (about ¼ cup)
2 tablespoons granulated sugar
1 teaspoon baking powder
½ teaspoon baking soda
½ teaspoon xanthan gum
⅛ teaspoon salt
¼ cup chilled unsalted butter, cut into small pieces
¾ cup low-fat buttermilk
¼ cup chopped pecans
½ teaspoon vanilla extract
1 teaspoon turbinado sugar
Vanilla light ice cream (optional)

1. Preheat oven to 375°.

2. Combine first 3 ingredients in a large bowl; add peaches and blueberries, tossing to coat. Pour mixture into a 1½-quart glass or ceramic baking dish coated with cooking spray.

3. Weigh or lightly spoon flours into dry measuring cups; level with a knife. Combine flours, 2 tablespoons granulated sugar, and next 4 ingredients (through salt) in a bowl, stirring with a whisk. Cut in butter with a pastry blender or 2 knives until mixture resembles coarse meal. Add buttermilk, pecans, and vanilla, stirring just until moist.

4. Drop 9 spoonfuls of batter over fruit mixture; sprinkle with turbinado sugar. Bake at 375° for 35 minutes or until topping is browned. Serve with ice cream, if desired. Serves 9 (serving size: ⅑ of cobbler)

CALORIES 237; FAT 8.7g (sat 3.7g, mono 3g, poly 1.2g); PROTEIN 3.5g; CARB 39g; FIBER 3g; CHOL 15mg; IRON 0.7mg; SODIUM 177mg; CALC 72mg

# APPLE, PEAR, AND CRANBERRY CRISP

Hands-on time: 16 min. Total time: 1 hr. 11 min.

*The tart and tangy cranberries complement the sweet apples and pears in this streusel-topped delight. This warm crisp served à la mode quickly became a Thanksgiving favorite for our family the first time it was served.*

1/3 cup granulated sugar
2 tablespoons cornstarch
1 tablespoon fresh lemon juice
1 tablespoon fresh orange juice
1/2 teaspoon ground cinnamon
1/4 teaspoon ground nutmeg
1 pound Fuji apples, peeled and thinly sliced
1 pound Bosc pears, peeled and thinly sliced
1/2 cup dried cranberries
Cooking spray
3.45 ounces brown rice flour (about 3/4 cup)
1 cup certified gluten-free old-fashioned rolled oats
1/2 cup packed brown sugar
6 tablespoons unsalted butter, melted
1 teaspoon vanilla extract
1/2 teaspoon salt

1. Preheat oven to 375°.

2. Combine first 6 ingredients in a medium bowl, stirring with a whisk. Add apples, pears, and cranberries, stirring to coat fruit. Pour mixture into an 11 x 7–inch glass or ceramic baking dish coated with cooking spray.

3. Weigh or lightly spoon flour into dry measuring cups; level with a knife. Combine flour and remaining ingredients in a bowl, stirring to combine.Spoon flour mixture over fruit mixture. Bake at 375° for 45 minutes or until topping is golden brown. Cool 10 minutes. Serves 9 (serving size: 1/9 of crisp)

---

CALORIES 303; FAT 9g (sat 5.1g, mono 2.5g, poly 0.7g); PROTEIN 2.8g; CARB 55g; FIBER 4g; CHOL 20mg; IRON 0.9mg; SODIUM 138mg; CALC 23mg

# GRAHAM CRACKER-APPLE CRISP

Hands-on time: 10 min. Total time: 40 min.

*This crisp has become a huge hit when served for breakfast. Ava, a 9-year-old family friend who lives in Texas, made us laugh when she drawled in her precious Southern twang, "This is highly unusual for all of us Bolligs. We eat oatmeal every morning for breakfast during the week, but I'd take this apple crisp instead, any day!"*

2 pounds Fuji apples, peeled and cut into ½-inch slices (about 5 cups)
1 tablespoon granulated sugar
1 tablespoon fresh lemon juice
½ teaspoon ground cinnamon
¼ teaspoon ground nutmeg

Cooking spray
½ cup packed brown sugar
¼ cup certified gluten-free quick-cooking oats
2 tablespoons brown rice flour
2 tablespoons potato starch
5 gluten-free graham cracker sheets, broken into fourths
6 tablespoons non-dairy buttery spread (such as Earth Balance), melted
½ cup frozen reduced-calorie whipped topping, thawed
Ground cinnamon (optional)

1. Preheat oven to 400°.

2. Combine first 5 ingredients in a large bowl, tossing to coat. Spoon mixture into an 11 x 7–inch glass or ceramic baking dish coated with cooking spray.

3. Place brown sugar and next 4 ingredients (through graham crackers) in a food processor; pulse until crackers are coarsely chopped. Add melted buttery spread; pulse 6 to 7 times or until combined.

4. Spoon brown sugar mixture over apples. Bake at 400° for 25 to 30 minutes or until topping is browned and crisp and apples are tender. Top each serving with whipped topping; sprinkle with cinnamon, if desired. Serves 8 (serving size: ⅛ of crisp and 1 tablespoon whipped topping)

CALORIES 259; FAT 9.7g (sat 3g, mono 4.1g, poly 2.5g); PROTEIN 1.2g; CARB 43g; FIBER 2.4g; CHOL 0mg; IRON 0.5mg; SODIUM 196mg; CALC 52mg

# STRAWBERRY, RHUBARB, AND GINGER CRISP

Hands-on time: 15 min. Total time: 1 hour 15 min.

**Filling:**
1 (1-pound) package frozen rhubarb, cut into 1-inch pieces
1 pound strawberries, hulled and halved
³/₄ cup granulated sugar
3 tablespoons cornstarch
1 teaspoon grated orange rind
Cooking spray

**Topping:**
0.9 ounce oat flour (about ¹/₄ cup)
¹/₄ cup granulated sugar
¹/₄ cup packed brown sugar
¹/₄ teaspoon salt
³/₄ cup certified gluten-free quick-cooking oats
4 ounces gluten-free gingersnaps
6 tablespoons unsalted butter, cut into small pieces

1. Preheat oven to 350°.

2. To prepare filling, combine first 5 ingredients in a large bowl, tossing to coat. Pour mixture into an 11 x 7–inch glass or ceramic baking dish coated with cooking spray.

3. To prepare topping, weigh or lightly spoon flour into a dry measuring cup; level with a knife. Place flour, ¼ cup granulated sugar, brown sugar, and salt in a food processor; process until combined. Add oats, gingersnaps, and butter; pulse 2 times or until crumbly.

4. Sprinkle topping over fruit mixture. Bake at 350° for 50 minutes or until filling is bubbly and topping is golden brown. Cool 10 minutes. Serve warm. Serves 9 (serving size: ⅑ of crisp)

CALORIES 313; FAT 11.3g (sat 5g, mono 2.4g, poly 0.7g); PROTEIN 3.1g; CARB 52.4g; FIBER 3.2g; CHOL 20mg; IRON 1.1mg; SODIUM 107mg; CALC 123mg

## choice ingredient: rhubarb

Rhubarb is a harbinger of spring. The celery-like red and green stalks are the edible portion of the plant; the leaves, which contain oxalic acid, are mildly toxic and should be avoided. Without a sweetener, rhubarb is bracingly sour, which is why it's often paired with fruits like strawberries and citrus. Fresh rhubarb is usually available from April through June, but you'll find frozen year-round.

# WILDBERRY BUCKLE

Hands-on time: 25 min. Total time: 1 hr. 15 min.

*As this bakes, the cake batter rises and buckles around the fruit, giving it a wrinkled appearance.*

**Filling:**
2.3 ounces millet flour (about ½ cup)
2.3 ounces brown rice flour (about ½ cup)
1.3 ounces white rice flour (about ¼ cup)
1.05 ounces tapioca flour (about ¼ cup)
2 teaspoons xanthan gum
1 teaspoon baking powder
¼ teaspoon baking soda
¼ teaspoon salt
½ cup granulated sugar
¼ cup butter, softened
2 tablespoons canola oil
1 teaspoon vanilla extract
2 large eggs
1 cup low-fat buttermilk

2 cups mixed berries (such as blueberries, blackberries, and raspberries)
Cooking spray

**Topping:**
½ cup chopped pecans
¼ cup packed brown sugar
1 tablespoon butter, melted
¼ teaspoon ground cinnamon
¼ teaspoon ground allspice

1. Preheat oven to 350°.

2. To prepare filling, weigh or lightly spoon flours into dry measuring cups; level with a knife. Combine flours in a bowl, stirring with a whisk. Set aside ¼ cup flour mixture. Add xanthan gum, baking powder, baking soda, and salt, stirring to combine.

3. Place granulated sugar and softened butter in a large bowl; beat with a mixer at medium speed until light and fluffy. Add oil, vanilla, and eggs; beat until blended. Add flour mixture and buttermilk alternately to sugar mixture, beating after each addition until smooth. Fold berries into batter using a rubber spatula. Pour batter into a 9-inch square glass or ceramic baking dish coated with cooking spray.

4. To prepare topping, combine reserved ¼ cup flour mixture, pecans, and remaining ingredients; sprinkle over batter. Bake at 350° for 40 to 45 minutes or until a wooden pick inserted in center comes out clean. Cool 10 minutes. Serves 16 (serving size: 1⁄16 of buckle)

CALORIES 181; FAT 9.1g (sat 3g, mono 3.8g, poly 1.6g); PROTEIN 2.7g; CARB 23g; FIBER 2.3g; CHOL 34mg; IRON 0.6mg; SODIUM 144mg; CALC 51mg

# PLUM AND GINGER GRUNT

Hands-on time: 30 min. Total time: 45 min.

*One favorite of Northeasterners is the grunt. "Grunt" is a dessert made by stewing fresh fruit on the stovetop, dropping dollops of biscuit batter on top, covering it with a lid, and allowing the biscuits to steam until done. Serve with vanilla ice cream.*

2.3 ounces brown rice flour (about ½ cup)
1.53 ounces millet flour (about ⅓ cup)
1.05 ounces tapioca flour (about ¼ cup)
1.3 ounces potato starch (about ¼ cup)
2 teaspoons baking powder
1 teaspoon xanthan gum
¾ teaspoon salt, divided
¼ teaspoon baking soda
4 tablespoons unsalted butter, cut into small pieces
1 cup low-fat buttermilk
2 pounds pitted plums, cut into 1-inch chunks
¾ cup sugar
½ cup water
1 tablespoon fresh lemon juice
2 teaspoons cornstarch
½ teaspoon ground ginger

1. Weigh or lightly spoon flours and potato starch into dry measuring cups; level with a knife. Combine flours, potato starch, baking powder, xanthan gum, ½ teaspoon salt, and baking soda in a large bowl, stirring with a whisk. Cut in butter with a pastry blender or 2 knives until mixture resembles coarse meal. Make a well in center of flour mixture, and slowly add buttermilk, stirring with a wooden spoon until combined. Chill until ready to use.

2. Combine plums, ¼ teaspoon salt, sugar, and remaining ingredients in a large bowl. Pour into a 10- to 12-inch skillet and place over medium-high heat. Bring to a boil, cover with lid, and decrease heat to medium-low. Cook until liquid begins to thicken, about 15 minutes, stirring occasionally.

3. Drop dough by spoonfuls, 2 tablespoons each, onto plum mixture. Cover pan, and cook 15 minutes. Serves 10 (serving size: ⅒ of grunt)

CALORIES 214; FAT 5.2g (sat 3g, mono 1.4g, poly 0g); PROTEIN 2.5g; CARB 41g; FIBER 2.4g; CHOL 13mg; IRON 0mg; SODIUM 320mg; CALC 103mg

chapter 9

# YEAST BREADS
## AND
# PIZZAS

When Angela had to go gluten free, we grieved the loss of Italian bread, focaccia, pumpernickel, and rye since we were in the habit of consuming quite a lot of pizza, and breakfast always included bagels, muffins, or toasted bread of some kind. The dry, flavorless pseudo-breads available at that time were just not going to cut it. I knew that this couldn't be the end of bread, that there had to be a better way to eat and live.

Over the years, I've worked with some very talented bakers and bread makers, gleaning from them the secrets to making really good bread. I used that knowledge to create tasty gluten-free versions. The results

are fantastic, but be warned: The recipe for getting there doesn't look much like wheat-based baking. Yeast bread doughs look more like batters—they're much thinner—and you'll be pouring the batter into a pan rather than shaping a dough. You may say to yourself, "There's no way this is going to bake up into a loaf of bread." Don't be tempted to tinker with the recipe. Trust me on this, and you'll be rewarded with some

stellar yeast breads and pizzas that will have you rejoicing instead of mourning.

# GLAZED GOLDEN RAISIN-CINNAMON ROLLS

Hands-on time: 28 min. Total time: 2 hr. 18 min.

¾ cup low-fat buttermilk

2 tablespoons granulated sugar, divided

1 package dry yeast (about 2¼ teaspoons)

4.6 ounces brown rice flour (about 1 cup)

4.2 ounces tapioca flour (about 1 cup)

2.6 ounces potato starch (about ½ cup)

0.9 ounce flaxseed meal (about ¼ cup)

2 teaspoons xanthan gum

2 teaspoons baking powder

½ teaspoon salt

¼ teaspoon baking soda

¼ teaspoon ground cinnamon

2 tablespoons canola oil

3 tablespoons butter, melted and divided

1 teaspoon vanilla extract

2 large egg whites

1 large egg

Tapicoa flour, for dusting

⅓ cup packed brown sugar

1 teaspoon ground cinnamon

¼ cup golden raisins

Cooking spray

1 cup powdered sugar

2 ounces ⅓-less-fat cream cheese, softened (about ¼ cup)

1 tablespoon 1% low-fat milk

1 teaspoon vanilla extract

1. Combine buttermilk and 1 tablespoon granulated sugar in a small saucepan, stirring with a whisk. Cook over medium heat until thermometer registers 110°. Remove from heat. Dissolve yeast in buttermilk mixture; let stand 5 minutes.

2. Weigh or lightly spoon flours, potato starch, and flaxseed meal into dry measuring cups; level with a knife. Combine flours, potato starch, flaxseed meal, xanthan gum, and next 4 ingredients in a large bowl; beat with a mixer at medium speed until blended. Add buttermilk mixture, oil, 1 tablespoon butter, 1 teaspoon vanilla, egg whites, and egg; beat at low speed until dough pulls away from sides of bowl.

3. Turn dough out onto well-floured parchment paper. Cover with an additional piece of floured parchment paper. Roll dough, still covered, into a 15 x 10–inch rectangle. Remove top sheet of paper; brush dough with 2 tablespoons melted butter.

4. Combine brown sugar, 1 tablespoon granulated sugar, and 1 teaspoon cinnamon in a small bowl, stirring with a whisk until blended. Sprinkle sugar mixture over butter. Sprinkle raisins over sugar mixture.

5. Beginning at short side, roll up dough tightly, jelly-roll fashion, while peeling away paper; pinch seam and ends to seal. Cut dough into 15 (1-inch) slices. Place slices in muffins tins coated with cooking spray. Cover with plastic wrap and let rise in a warm place (85°), free from drafts, 1½ hours or until dough has risen to top of tins.

6. Preheat oven to 375°.

7. Bake at 375° for 20 minutes or until golden brown.

8. Combine powdered sugar and remaining ingredients; stir with a whisk until smooth. Remove rolls from muffin tins; drizzle with glaze. Serve warm. Serves 15 (serving size: 1 roll)

CALORIES 213; FAT 6.5g (sat 2.3g, mono 2.4g, poly 1.3g); PROTEIN 3.1g; CARB 37g; FIBER 1.6g; CHOL 22mg; IRON 0.5mg; SODIUM 221mg; CALC 74mg

# CHOCOLATE BABKA

Hands-on time: 20 min. Total time: 3 hr. 40 min.

**Filling:**
3 ounces bittersweet chocolate, finely grated
1/4 cup granulated sugar
1 1/2 teaspoons unsweetened cocoa
1/4 teaspoon ground cinnamon

**Streusel:**
2 tablespoons powdered sugar
2 tablespoons white rice flour
1/8 teaspoon salt
1 tablespoon unsalted butter, softened

**Dough:**
1 package dry yeast (about 2 1/4 teaspoons)
5 tablespoons granulated sugar, divided
1 1/2 cups warm 1% low-fat milk (100° to 110°)
2 tablespoons unsalted butter, melted
1 tablespoon canola oil
1/2 teaspoon vanilla extract
1 large egg
1 large egg yolk
4.2 ounces sweet white sorghum flour (about 1 cup)
4.2 ounces tapioca flour (about 1 cup)
2.6 ounces potato starch (about 1/2 cup)
2.3 ounces cornstarch (about 1/2 cup)
1 tablespoon xanthan gum
2 teaspoons baking powder
1/2 teaspoon salt
Cooking spray

1. To prepare filling, combine first 4 ingredients in a bowl, stirring with a whisk.

2. To prepare streusel, combine 1 tablespoon filling, powdered sugar, white rice flour, and 1/8 teaspoon salt in a small bowl; cut in 1 tablespoon butter with a pastry blender or 2 knives until mixture resembles coarse meal. Cover and refrigerate.

3. To prepare dough, dissolve yeast and 1 tablespoon granulated sugar in milk in a bowl; let stand 5 minutes.

4. Combine melted butter, oil, vanilla, egg, and egg yolk in a medium bowl; stir with a whisk. Weigh or lightly spoon flours, potato starch, and cornstarch into dry measuring cups; level with a knife. Combine flours, potato starch, cornstarch, 4 tablespoons sugar, xanthan gum, baking powder, and 1/2 teaspoon salt in a large bowl; beat with a mixer at medium speed. Add yeast mixture and egg mixture; beat at low speed until blended. Add 1/3 cup streusel; beat just until blended.

5. Spoon one-third of dough evenly into bottom of a 9 x 5–inch loaf pan coated with cooking spray. Top with half of filling. Repeat procedure ending with dough. Swirl dough together using the tip of a knife. Cover with plastic wrap coated with cooking spray, and let rise in a warm place (85°), free from drafts, 1 hour or until dough reaches top of pan.

6. Preheat oven to 350°.

7. Sprinkle top of dough with streusel. Bake at 350° for 45 minutes or until browned or loaf sounds hollow when tapped. Cool 15 minutes in pan on a wire rack; remove from pan. Cool completely. Serves 16 (serving size: 1 slice)

---

CALORIES 200; FAT 6.5g (sat 3.2g, mono 1.5g, poly 0.5g); PROTEIN 3g; CARB 34g; FIBER 1.5g; CHOL 30mg; IRON 0.7mg; SODIUM 164mg; CALC 77mg

# ORANGE & CINNAMON-DUSTED DONUT HOLES

Hands-on time: 40 min. Total time: 2 hr. 10 min.

1 package yeast (about 2¼ teaspoons)
½ cup sugar, divided
½ cup warm water (100° to 110°)
3.45 ounces brown rice flour (about ¾ cup)
2.6 ounces white rice flour (about ½ cup)
2.6 ounces potato starch (about ½ cup)
1 teaspoon xanthan gum
⅛ teaspoon salt
¼ cup plain fat-free Greek yogurt
1 teaspoon vanilla extract
1 large egg
White rice flour for dusting
Cooking spray
½ teaspoon grated orange rind
⅛ teaspoon ground cinnamon
Peanut oil

1. Dissolve yeast and ¼ cup sugar in ½ cup warm water in a small bowl; let stand 5 minutes.

2. Weigh or lightly spoon flours and potato starch into dry measuring cups; level with a knife. Combine flours, potato starch, xanthan gum, and salt in a large bowl; add yeast mixture, yogurt, vanilla, and egg. Beat at medium-high speed until blended.

3. Turn dough out onto a lightly floured surface; shape into a ball. Place dough in a large bowl coated with cooking spray; cover loosely with plastic wrap, and let rise in a warm place (85°), free from drafts, 1 hour.

4. Turn dough out onto a well-floured surface; knead lightly 4 to 5 times with floured hands. Roll dough to a ½-inch thickness; cut with a 1-inch biscuit cutter. Place on a baking sheet lined with parchment paper. Repeat procedure with remaining dough. Let rise in a warm place (85°), free from drafts, 30 minutes.

5. Place ¼ cup sugar, orange rind, and cinnamon in a food processor; process until well blended.

6. Add oil to a large Dutch oven to a depth of 2 inches. Heat oil over medium-high heat until thermometer registers 360°. Place 8 to 10 donut holes in hot oil; cook 1 minute or until golden brown, stirring occasionally. Remove using slotted spoon; drain on paper towels. Repeat procedure with remaining donut holes.

7. Combine donut holes and sugar mixture in a bowl; toss gently to coat. Serve warm. Serves 20 (serving size: 3 donut holes)

CALORIES 200; FAT 15g (sat 2.6g, mono 7.1g, poly 5g); PROTEIN 2.4g; CARB 16g; FIBER 1.3g; CHOL 9mg; IRON 0.2mg; SODIUM 22mg; CALC 5mg

# BRIOCHE

*Brioche is a flaky, buttery egg bread. The cornstarch makes it light and airy. Use it to make sandwiches, or French toast, or just toast and butter it for breakfast.*

3.4 ounces cornstarch (about ¾ cup)
1.5 ounces brown rice flour (about ⅓ cup)
1.4 ounces tapioca flour (about ⅓ cup)
2 tablespoons sugar
1 tablespoon xanthan gum
1 package dry yeast (about 2¼ teaspoons)
1 teaspoon salt
¼ cup butter, melted
¼ cup warm 2% reduced-fat milk (100° to 110°)
2 tablespoons honey
3 large eggs, lightly beaten
Cooking spray
1 tablespoon water
1 large egg white

1. Weigh or lightly spoon cornstarch and flours into dry measuring cups; level with a knife. Combine cornstarch, flours, sugar, and next 3 ingredients (through salt) in a large bowl, stirring with a whisk. Add butter and next 3 ingredients (through eggs); beat with a mixer at high speed until dough is smooth.

2. Spoon dough into a 9 x 5–inch loaf pan coated with cooking spray. Let rise in a warm place (85°), free from drafts, 20 minutes. Cover with plastic wrap, and refrigerate overnight.

3. Remove dough from refrigerator. Let dough rise in a warm place (85°), free from drafts, 2 to 4 hours or until batter is slightly below rim of pan.

4. Preheat oven to 350°.

5. Bake at 350° for 25 minutes. Combine 1 tablespoon water and egg white in a small bowl, stirring with a whisk. Brush loaf with egg white mixture, and cover with foil. Bake an additional 30 minutes. Cool 15 minutes in pan on a wire rack; remove from pan. Cool completely on wire rack. Serves 16 (serving size: 1 slice)

CALORIES 101; FAT 4.1g (sat 2.2g, mono 1.3g, poly 0.3g); PROTEIN 2g; CARB 14g; FIBER 0.8g; CHOL 43mg; IRON 0.3mg; SODIUM 193mg; CALC 12mg

# CINNAMON-RAISIN BREAD

Hands-on time: 13 min. Total time: 3 hr. 56 min.

*This versatile bread is topnotch. It makes for a stellar French toast—find that recipe on page 41.*

2 cups warm water (100° to 110°), divided
³/₄ cup raisins
1 package dry yeast (about 2¹/₄ teaspoons)
1¹/₂ cups warm 1% low-fat milk (100° to 110°)
4.2 ounces sweet white sorghum flour (about 1 cup)
2.6 ounces white rice flour (about ¹/₂ cup)
2.3 ounces brown rice flour (about ¹/₂ cup)
2.1 ounces tapioca flour (about ¹/₂ cup)
1.8 ounces flaxseed meal (about ¹/₂ cup)
3 teaspoons ground cinnamon, divided
2 teaspoons xanthan gum
¹/₂ teaspoon salt
2 tablespoons unsalted butter, melted
2 tablespoons cider vinegar
¹/₄ cup honey
2 large eggs
¹/₄ cup packed brown sugar
Cooking spray

1. Combine 1 cup warm water and raisins in a medium bowl. Let stand 10 minutes or until raisins are plump; drain.

2. Dissolve yeast in 1 cup warm water and milk in a small bowl; let stand 5 minutes.

3. Weigh or lightly spoon flours and flaxseed meal into dry measuring cups; level with a knife. Place flours, flaxseed meal, 1 teaspoon cinnamon, xanthan gum, and salt in a large bowl; beat with a mixer at medium speed until combined. Add yeast mixture, butter, vinegar, honey, and eggs; beat until blended. Fold in raisins.

4. Combine 2 teaspoons cinnamon and brown sugar in a small bowl.

5. Spoon one-third of batter into a 9 x 5–inch loaf pan coated with cooking spray. Top with half of cinnamon-sugar mixture. Repeat layers once. Spoon remaining one-third of batter over cinnamon-sugar mixture. Cover loosely with plastic wrap, and let rise in a warm place (85°), free from drafts, 1 hour and 45 minutes or until dough is just above top of pan.

6. Preheat oven to 375°.

7. Bake at 375° for 55 minutes or until top is golden brown and bread sounds hollow when tapped. Cool completely in pan. Serves 16 (serving size: 1 slice)

CALORIES 173; FAT 4.1g (sat 1.3g, mono 1g, poly 1.4g); PROTEIN 4.1g; CARB 31.6g; FIBER 2.6g; CHOL 28mg; IRON 0.8mg; SODIUM 95mg; CALC 45mg

# CINNAMON STICKY BREAD

Hands-on time: 21 min. Total time: 2 hr. 21 min.

*This bread—also known as monkey bread, African coffee cake, or bubbleloaf—is served for breakfast at the university where I work.*

1 cup low-fat buttermilk
5 tablespoons granulated sugar, divided
1 package dry yeast (about 2¼ teaspoons)
4.6 ounces brown rice flour (about 1 cup)
4.2 ounces tapioca flour (about 1 cup)
3.9 ounces white rice flour (about ¾ cup)
2 teaspoons baking powder
1¼ teaspoons xanthan gum
¾ teaspoon ground cinnamon, divided
½ teaspoon baking soda
½ teaspoon salt
2 tablespoons canola oil
1 teaspoon vanilla extract
2 large eggs
¼ cup chopped pecans
Cooking spray
⅔ cup packed brown sugar
8 tablespoons butter, melted

1. Combine buttermilk and 1 tablespoon granulated sugar in a small saucepan, stirring with a whisk. Cook over medium heat until thermometer registers 110°. Remove from heat. Dissolve yeast in buttermilk mixture; let stand 5 minutes.

2. Weigh or lightly spoon flours into dry measuring cups; level with a knife. Combine flours, baking powder, xanthan gum, ¼ teaspoon cinnamon, baking soda, and salt in a large bowl; beat with a mixer at medium speed until blended. Add buttermilk mixture, oil, vanilla, and eggs, beating until a soft, sticky dough forms.

3. Sprinkle pecans in bottom of a 10-inch Bundt pan coated with cooking spray. Combine ¼ cup granulated sugar and ½ teaspoon cinnamon in a small bowl.

4. Scoop dough using a 1½-inch ice-cream scoop coated with cooking spray; roll dough ball in cinnamon-sugar mixture, and place in Bundt pan. Repeat procedure with remaining dough and cinnamon-sugar mixture. Cover pan loosely with plastic wrap, and let rise in a warm place (85°), free from drafts, 1½ hours.

5. Preheat oven to 350°.

6. Combine brown sugar and melted butter, stirring until smooth. Pour evenly over dough balls in pan. Bake at 350° for 35 minutes or until top of bread is golden brown. Place a serving plate on top of pan; invert bread onto plate. Cool 15 minutes before serving. Serves 16 (serving size: ¹⁄₁₆ of bread)

---

CALORIES 223; FAT 10g (sat 4g, mono 3.8g, poly 1.3g); PROTEIN 2.8g; CARB 32g; FIBER 1.1g; CHOL 39mg; IRON 0.5mg; SODIUM 248mg; CALC 73mg

# WHOLE-GRAIN HONEY BREAD

Hands-on time: 25 min. Total time: 3 hr. 20 min.

*Montina grass flour, an Indian rice grass that is very high in protein, fiber, and iron, flecks this hearty bread.*

1 package dry yeast (about 2¼ teaspoons)
1 cup warm water (100° to 110°)
½ cup warm 2% reduced-fat milk (100° to 110°)
15.9 ounces gluten-free Montina all-purpose baking flour blend (about 3 cups)
0.9 ounce flaxseed meal (about ¼ cup)
½ cup certified gluten-free old-fashioned rolled oats
1 tablespoon xanthan gum
1½ teaspoons salt
½ teaspoon baking soda
½ cup honey
¼ cup butter, melted
1 teaspoon cider vinegar
3 large eggs yolks
3 large egg whites
Cooking spray

1. Dissolve yeast in 1 cup warm water and milk in a small bowl; let stand 5 minutes.

2. Weigh or lightly spoon flour blend and flaxseed meal into dry measuring cups; level with a knife. Place flour blend, flaxseed meal, oats, and next 3 ingredients (through baking soda) in a large bowl, stirring with a whisk. Slowly add yeast mixture, honey, butter, vinegar, and egg yolks, beating with a mixer at low speed. Increase speed to high; beat 1 to 2 minutes until well blended.

3. Place egg whites in a bowl; beat with a mixer at high speed until soft peaks form using clean, dry beaters. Gently fold egg white mixture into batter. Spoon batter into a 9 x 5–inch loaf pan coated with cooking spray. Cover with plastic wrap, and let rise in a warm place (85°), free from drafts, 1 hour or until dough is just above top of pan.

4. Preheat oven to 375°.

5. Bake at 375° for 10 minutes. Cover with foil; bake an additional 35 minutes or until very browned. Cool 10 minutes in pan on a wire rack; remove from pan. Cool completely on wire rack. Serves 14 (serving size: 1 slice)

CALORIES 223; FAT 6.1g (sat 2.6g, mono 1.6g, poly 0.9g); PROTEIN 5.1g; CARB 40g; FIBER 3.2g; CHOL 49mg; IRON 0.9mg; SODIUM 348mg; CALC 18mg

# QUINOA BREAD

Hands-on time: 10 min. Total time: 3 hr. 5 min.

*Quinoa flour is the star in this hearty and delicious loaf of bread. Slice, toast, and spread with your favorite jam for breakfast.*

2 tablespoons sugar
1 tablespoon dry yeast
1½ cups warm water (100° to 110°)
4.6 ounces brown rice flour (about 1 cup)
3.15 ounces tapioca flour (about ¾ cup)
3 ounces quinoa flour (about ¾ cup)
3.4 ounces cornstarch (about ¾ cup)
1 tablespoon xanthan gum
1 teaspoon baking powder
1 teaspoon salt
¼ cup canola oil
1 teaspoon vinegar
2 large eggs, lightly beaten
Cooking spray

1. Dissolve sugar and yeast in 1½ cups warm water in a small bowl; let stand 5 minutes.

2. Weigh or lightly spoon flours and cornstarch into dry measuring cups; level with a knife. Combine flours, cornstarch, xanthan gum, baking powder, and salt in a large bowl, stirring with a whisk. Add yeast mixture, oil, vinegar, and eggs; beat with a mixer at medium speed 3 minutes or until well blended.

3. Spoon batter into a 9 x 5–inch loaf pan coated with cooking spray; smooth top of dough with a spatula. Cover with plastic wrap coated with cooking spray, and let dough rise in a warm place (85°), free from drafts, 1 hour or until dough reaches top of pan.

4. Preheat oven to 375°.

5. Bake at 375° for 45 minutes or until top is golden brown and loaf sounds hollow when tapped. Cool 10 minutes in pan on a wire rack; remove from pan. Cool completely on wire rack. Serves 16 (serving size: 1 slice)

CALORIES 145; FAT 4.9g (sat 0.5g, mono 2.6g, poly 1.2g); PROTEIN 2.5g; CARB 23g; FIBER 1.9g; CHOL 23mg; IRON 0.7mg; SODIUM 188mg; CALC 27mg

## a great grain

Quinoa flour is made from ground quinoa grains and is considered a complete protein, which is unique in the grain family. It's packed with B vitamins, vitamin E, magnesium, iron, and a dose of calcium.

# CRANBERRY-FLAX BREAD

Hands-on time: 15 min. Total time: 2 hr. 55 min.

*The Bear family lives a busy life, raising six children, homeschooling, and tending to their 50 beautiful acres with gardens and fruit trees in central Connecticut. After waging a successful battle against breast cancer in 2011, Susan and her family decided to fully embrace a more natural and healthy way of eating and living. This wonderful bread fits right into their daily routine. Filled with cranberries, walnuts, and flaxseed meal, this bread offers a strong combination of antioxidants, lignans, fiber, and omega-3 fatty acids, all in one delicious package. Toast it up for breakfast or stack your slices with your favorite meats and cheeses.*

1 package dry yeast (about 2¼ teaspoons)
½ cup warm water (100° to 110°)
4.6 ounces brown rice flour (about 1 cup)
3.4 ounces millet flour (about ¾ cup)
2.6 ounces potato starch (about ½ cup)
2.3 ounces cornstarch (about ½ cup)
0.9 ounce flaxseed meal (about ¼ cup)
2 teaspoons xanthan gum
¾ teaspoon salt
¾ cup 1% low-fat milk
¼ cup non-dairy buttery spread (such as Earth Balance), melted and cooled
2 large eggs, lightly beaten
¾ cup sweetened dried cranberries
¾ cup chopped walnuts
Cooking spray

1. Dissolve yeast in ½ cup warm water in a small bowl; let stand 5 minutes.

2. Weigh or lightly spoon flours, potato starch, cornstarch, and flaxseed meal into dry measuring cups; level with a knife. Combine flours, potato starch, cornstarch, flaxseed meal, xanthan gum, and salt in a large bowl, stirring with a whisk. Add yeast mixture, milk, buttery spread, and eggs; beat with a mixer at low speed until blended. Fold in cranberries and walnuts.

3. Spoon batter into a 9 x 5–inch loaf pan coated with cooking spray. Cover with plastic wrap, and let rise in a warm place (85°), free from drafts, 2 hours or until dough has risen almost to top of pan.

4. Preheat oven to 400°.

5. Bake at 400° for 30 minutes or until bread sounds hollow when tapped. Remove from pan; cool on a wire rack. Serves 16 (serving size: 1 slice)

CALORIES 189; FAT 8.3g (sat 1.4g, mono 2.3g, poly 4g); PROTEIN 3.8g; CARB 25.8g; FIBER 2.8g; CHOL 24mg; IRON 0.7mg; SODIUM 152mg; CALC 24mg

# FIVE-SEED BREAD

Hands-on time: 11 min. Total time: 3 hr. 11 min.

*This recipe offers a number of healthful benefits by incorporating sunflower, chia, caraway, sesame, and poppy seeds in one excellent loaf. The chia seeds also absorb liquid, which helps maintain moisture.*

¼ cup unsalted, roasted sunflower seed kernels
1 tablespoon chia seeds
1 tablespoon caraway seeds
1 tablespoon sesame seeds
1 teaspoon poppy seeds
2 tablespoons honey
1 package dry yeast (about 2¼ teaspoons)
1½ cups warm water (100° to 110°)
4.2 ounces sweet white sorghum flour (about 1 cup)
3.9 ounces potato starch (about ¾ cup)
2.3 ounces cornstarch (about ½ cup)
1 tablespoon xanthan gum
1 teaspoon baking powder
1 teaspoon sea salt
¼ cup canola oil
1 teaspoon white vinegar
2 large eggs, lightly beaten
Cooking spray

1. Combine first 5 ingredients in a small bowl, stirring to combine. Set aside.

2. Dissolve honey and yeast in 1½ cups warm water in a medium bowl; let stand 5 minutes.

3. Weigh or lightly spoon flour, potato starch, and cornstarch into dry measuring cups; level with a knife. Place flour, potato starch, cornstarch, xanthan gum, baking powder, and salt in a large bowl; beat with a mixer at medium speed until blended. Add seed mixture, yeast mixture, oil, vinegar, and eggs; beat at low speed until blended.

4. Spoon batter into a 9 x 5–inch loaf pan coated with cooking spray. Cover with plastic wrap coated with cooking spray, and let rise in a warm place (85°), free from drafts, 45 minutes or until dough reaches top of pan.

5. Preheat oven to 375°.

6. Bake at 375° for 45 minutes or until loaf sounds hollow when tapped. Cool 10 minutes in pan on a wire rack; remove from pan. Cool completely on wire rack. Serves 16 (serving size: 1 slice)

CALORIES 137; FAT 6.1g (sat 0.6g, mono 2.8g, poly 2g); PROTEIN 2.6g; CARB 19g; FIBER 2.1g; CHOL 23mg; IRON 0.7mg; SODIUM 179mg; CALC 37mg

# RUSSIAN BLACK BREAD

Hands-on time: 20 min. Total time: 2 hr. 50 min.

*This bread is a dream come true for the gluten-free lover of pumpernickel bread. The unique combination of cocoa, coffee, and caraway closely mimics the flavor of that old-fashioned loaf.*

1 package dry yeast (about 2¼ teaspoons)
1½ cups warm water (100° to 110°)
4.6 ounces brown rice flour (about 1 cup)
4.2 ounces sweet white sorghum flour (about 1 cup)
4.2 ounces tapioca flour (about 1 cup)
1.8 ounces flaxseed meal (about ½ cup)
2 tablespoons unsweetened cocoa
1 tablespoon brown sugar
1 tablespoon caraway seeds
1 teaspoon instant coffee granules
1 teaspoon xanthan gum
1 teaspoon salt
2 tablespoons unsalted butter, melted
2 tablespoons molasses
2 tablespoons cider vinegar
2 large eggs
Cooking spray

1. Dissolve yeast in 1½ cups warm water in a small bowl; let stand 5 minutes.

2. Weigh or lightly spoon flours and flaxseed meal into dry measuring cups; level with a knife. Combine flours, flaxseed meal, cocoa, and next 5 ingredients (through salt) in the bowl of a stand mixer fitted with a paddle attachment; beat at medium speed until blended. Add yeast mixture, butter, molasses, vinegar, and eggs; beat until blended. Spoon batter in a 9 x 5–inch loaf pan coated with cooking spray. Cover loosely with plastic wrap, and let rise in a warm place (85°), free from drafts, 1 hour or until dough is just above top of pan.

3. Preheat oven to 400°.

4. Bake at 400° for 20 minutes. Cover top of bread with foil; bake an additional 25 minutes. Remove foil from bread; bake 5 minutes. Cool 10 minutes in pan on a wire rack; remove from pans. Cool completely on wire rack. Serves 14 (serving size: 1 slice)

CALORIES 154; FAT 4.7g (sat 1.4g, mono 1.2g, poly 1.4g); PROTEIN 3.8g; CARB 26g; FIBER 2.8g; CHOL 31mg; IRON 1mg; SODIUM 183mg; CALC 16mg

## an extra boost

t
i
p

The addition of an acid such as cider vinegar to the dough acts as a dough conditioner. The vinegar causes the starches and sugars in the dough to break down quicker, giving the yeast more to eat, which allows it to have a better rise with more volume. If you have hard water, the acid mixed with the water also changes the pH level and assists in softening the dough. Many commercial bakeries today still add vinegar to their breads to help extend shelf life.

# BAVARIAN SAUERKRAUT BREAD

*This bread brings back great memories of when my wife and I would head to Vermont for cross-country skiing weekends with our friends the Mylniecs. We often stayed at the Grunberg House, where this bread would have fit right into the German menu.*

1 package dry yeast (about 2¼ teaspoons)
¼ cup warm water (100° to 110°)
4.6 ounces millet flour (about 1 cup)
4.2 ounces sweet white sorghum flour (about 1 cup)
2.6 ounces potato starch (about ½ cup)
2.3 ounces cornstarch (about ½ cup)
2 tablespoons brown sugar

1 tablespoon caraway seeds
2 teaspoons xanthan gum
¼ teaspoon salt
1 cup drained Bavarian-style sauerkraut
½ cup drained sauerkraut liquid
2 tablespoons non-dairy buttery spread (such as Earth Balance), melted
2 large eggs, slightly beaten
Cooking spray

1. Dissolve yeast in ¼ cup warm water in a small bowl; let stand 5 minutes.

2. Weigh or lightly spoon flours, potato starch, and cornstarch into dry measuring cups; level with a knife. Place flours, potato starch, cornstarch, brown sugar, and next 3 ingredients (through salt) in a large bowl; beat with a mixer at medium speed until blended. Add yeast mixture, sauerkraut, sauerkraut liquid, buttery spread, and eggs; beat at low speed until blended.

3. Spoon batter into a 9 x 5–inch loaf pan coated with cooking spray. Cover with plastic wrap, and let rise in a warm place (85°), free from drafts, 1 hour or until dough reaches top of pan.

4. Preheat oven to 400°.

5. Bake at 400° for 38 minutes or until loaf sounds hollow when tapped. Remove from pan; cool on a wire rack. Serves 14 (serving size: 1 slice)

CALORIES 141; FAT 3.1g (sat 0.7g, mono 1.1g, poly 0.6g); PROTEIN 3.2g; CARB 25g; FIBER 3.3g; CHOL 27mg; IRON 0.9mg; SODIUM 249mg; CALC 9mg

# PEPPERONI AND CHEESE BAGUETTES

Hands-on time: 24 min. Total time: 2 hr. 29 min.

2 tablespoons sugar

1 package dry yeast (about 2¼ teaspoons)

1 cup warm water (100° to 110°)

¼ cup olive oil

1 tablespoon cider vinegar

2 large egg yolks

3 ounces part-skim mozzarella cheese, shredded
(about ¾ cup)

3 ounces reduced-fat sharp cheddar cheese,
shredded (about ¾ cup)

7.8 ounces white rice flour (about 1½ cups)

3.45 ounces brown rice flour (about ¾ cup)

2.1 ounces tapioca flour (about ½ cup)

2 ounces quinoa flour (about ½ cup)

1.3 ounces potato starch (about ¼ cup)

0.9 ounce flaxseed meal (about ¼ cup)

1 tablespoon xanthan gum

½ teaspoon salt

White rice flour, for dusting

2 ounces turkey pepperoni

1 tablespoon shredded fresh Parmesan cheese

1 teaspoon dried oregano

2 large egg whites

1. Dissolve sugar and yeast in 1 cup warm water in a small bowl; let stand 5 minutes.

2. Combine oil, vinegar, and egg yolks in a small bowl, stirring with a whisk. Place mozzarella cheese and cheddar cheese in a bowl, stirring to combine. Chill.

3. Weigh or lightly spoon flours, potato starch, and flaxseed meal into dry measuring cups; level with a knife. Combine flours, potato starch, flaxseed meal, xanthan gum, and salt in the bowl of a stand mixer fitted with a paddle attachment; beat at medium speed until blended. Slowly add yeast mixture and oil mixture, beating until blended and dough pulls away from sides of bowl.

4. Turn dough onto a lightly floured surface; divide dough into 4 equal portions. Shape each portion into a ball. Working with 1 portion at a time (cover remaining portions to prevent drying), roll each portion into a 12 x 6–inch rectangle on a floured surface. Place one-fourth of pepperoni slices down center of dough leaving a 1-inch border at top and bottom; top with one-fourth cheese mixture. Beginning at short side, roll up dough tightly, jelly-roll fashion; pinch seam and ends to seal. Repeat procedure with remaining dough portions. Place rolls, seam sides down, 2 inches apart on baking sheets covered in parchment paper. Cover and let rise in a warm place (85°), free from drafts, 1 hour or until doubled in size.

5. Preheat oven to 375°.

6. Combine Parmesan cheese and oregano in a small bowl, stirring to combine. Place egg whites in a bowl, stirring well with a whisk. Brush tops of dough with egg whites; sprinkle with Parmesan cheese mixture.

7. Bake at 375° for 35 minutes or until crust is golden brown. Remove from pans; cool completely on wire racks. Serves 12 (serving size: ⅓ of baguette)

CALORIES 141; FAT 3.1g (sat 0.7g, mono 1.1g, poly 0.6g); PROTEIN 3.2g; CARB 25g; FIBER 3.3g; CHOL 27mg; IRON 0.9mg; SODIUM 249mg; CALC 9mg

# KALAMATA OLIVE AND ROSEMARY FOCACCIA

Hands-on time: 30 min. Total time: 1 hr. 50 min.

*A unique blend of potato starch and sorghum, tapioca, and rice flours creates the air pockets and light texture indicative of this popular, flat, oven-baked bread that's as good as any authentic version served in the bistros of Italy. It's a must-have with a bowl of gluten-free linguine and a glass of red wine.*

1 package dry yeast (about 2¼ teaspoons)
1¼ cups warm water (100° to 110°)
3.9 ounces potato starch (about ¾ cup)
3.15 ounces sweet white sorghum flour (about ¾ cup)
3.15 ounces tapioca flour (about ¾ cup)
2.6 ounces white rice flour (about ½ cup)
1 teaspoon xanthan gum
½ teaspoon baking powder
½ teaspoon salt
¼ cup olive oil, divided
3 teaspoons finely chopped fresh rosemary, divided
1 Yukon Gold potato, cooked, peeled, and grated
1 large egg
½ cup chopped pitted kalamata olives
2 garlic cloves, minced
Cooking spray
2 tablespoons grated fresh Parmesan cheese

1. Dissolve yeast in 1¼ cups warm water in a small bowl; let stand 5 minutes.

2. Weigh or lightly spoon potato starch and flours into dry measuring cups; level with a knife. Combine potato starch, flours, xanthan gum, baking powder, and salt in the bowl of a stand mixer fitted with a paddle attachment; beat at medium speed until blended. Add yeast mixture, 3 tablespoons oil, 1 teaspoon rosemary, potato, and egg; beat until blended. Gently fold in olives and garlic.

3. Spoon batter into a large bowl coated with cooking spray. Cover with plastic wrap, and let rise in a warm place (85°), free from drafts, 45 minutes or until doubled in size.

4. Preheat oven to 400°.

5. Turn dough out onto a baking sheet coated with cooking spray; shape into an 11-inch round. Brush top of bread with 1 tablespoon oil. Sprinkle with 2 teaspoons rosemary and cheese. Bake at 400° for 35 minutes or until golden brown and loaf sounds hollow when tapped. Serves 14 (serving size: 1 piece)

CALORIES 165; FAT 6.5g (sat 1.0g, mono 4.4g, poly 0.7g); PROTEIN 2.4g; CARB 25g; FIBER 1.4g; CHOL 14mg; IRON 0.6mg; SODIUM 229mg; CALC 27mg

## a single rise

t i p

Yeast breads using wheat flour usually require a double rise to allow the gluten to develop its elasticity and flavor. In gluten-free yeast breads, only a single rise is needed since there is no need for gluten development.

*Adding grated cooked potatoes adds moisture and sponginess to this focaccia.*

# CRANBERRY ENGLISH MUFFINS

Hands-on time: 12 min. Total time: 1 hr. 55 min.

*During my third year in culinary school, I had the opportunity to work alongside a notable chef from London named Charles. He taught me the secret to making authentic English muffins. After many hours in the kitchen, I was able to convert his recipe to the best gluten-free version possible, with all the nooks, crannies, and cranberries of the original.*

2 tablespoons sugar, divided
1 tablespoon dry yeast
1¼ cups warm 1% low-fat milk (100° to 110°)
9.2 ounces brown rice flour (about 2 cups)
5.2 ounces potato starch (about 1 cup)
4.2 ounces tapioca flour (about 1 cup)
2.3 ounces cornstarch (about ½ cup)
1½ teaspoons xanthan gum

1¼ teaspoons salt
3 tablespoons butter, melted
1 tablespoon canola oil
1 large egg, lightly beaten
⅔ cup sweetened dried cranberries
Tapioca flour, for dusting
1 tablespoon cornmeal, divided

1. Dissolve 1 tablespoon sugar and yeast in warm milk in a small bowl; let stand 5 minutes.

2. Weigh or lightly spoon brown rice flour, potato starch, tapioca flour, and cornstarch into dry measuring cups; level with a knife. Combine brown rice flour, potato starch, tapioca flour, cornstarch, xanthan gum, salt, and 1 tablespoon sugar, stirring with a whisk. Add yeast mixture, butter, oil, and egg; beat with a mixer at medium speed until blended. Add cranberries; gently stir to combine.

3. Turn dough out onto a well-floured surface; knead gently 5 to 6 times. Roll dough to a ½-inch thickness; cut with a 2½-inch biscuit cutter into 14 muffins. Place on a baking sheet lined with parchment paper and sprinkled with ½ tablespoon cornmeal. Sprinkle tops of muffins with ½ tablespoon cornmeal. Let rise in a warm place (85°), free from drafts, 1 hour.

4. Heat a griddle or large nonstick skillet over medium-low heat. Cook muffins 6 minutes on each side or until lightly browned. Cool completely on a wire rack. Serves 14 (serving size: 1 muffin)

CALORIES 225; FAT 4.6g (sat 2g, mono 1.7g, poly 0.6g); PROTEIN 3g; CARB 43g; FIBER 1.8g; CHOL 21mg; IRON 0.6mg; SODIUM 250mg; CALC 33mg

# GARLIC-HERB TORTILLAS

Hands-on time: 38 min. Total time: 48 min.

*This was one of my "just try it and see what happens" recipes that turned out to be a really big hit. These garlicky tortillas can be turned into little pizzas in the oven, rolled with luncheon meats and cheese to make a wrap, or warmed up and buttered for breakfast. My wife ate these every day for two weeks when we first tried them out.*

5.2 ounces white rice flour (about 1 cup)
2.6 ounces potato starch (about ½ cup)
1.15 ounces cornstarch (about ¼ cup)
0.9 ounce flaxseed meal (about ¼ cup)
1 tablespoon brown sugar
2 teaspoons Italian seasoning
1 teaspoon garlic powder
1 teaspoon xanthan gum
1 teaspoon baking powder
1 teaspoon salt
2 tablespoons coconut oil
1 large egg white
½ cup hot water
White rice flour, for dusting
Cooking spray

1. Weigh or lightly spoon flour, potato starch, cornstarch, and flaxseed meal into dry measuring cups; level with a knife. Combine flour, potato starch, cornstarch, flaxseed meal, brown sugar, and next 5 ingredients; beat with a mixer at low speed until blended. Add oil and egg white; beat until mixture is coarse and crumbly. Slowly add ½ cup hot water until dough pulls away from sides of bowl, beating constantly.

2. Turn dough out onto a well-floured surface; divide dough into 8 equal portions, shaping each into a ball. Place on a large plate; cover with a damp cloth and refrigerate 10 minutes.

3. Roll each dough ball into a 10-inch circle on a well-floured surface. Place a 9-inch plate upside down on top of each circle. Cut away excess dough on each using tip of a knife.

4. Heat a large skillet over medium heat. Coat pan with cooking spray. Cook each circle 20 to 25 seconds or until it begins to bubble. Turn circle over, and cook 20 to 25 seconds. Cool completely. Store in an airtight container. Serves 8 (serving size: 1 tortilla)

CALORIES 135; FAT 4.1g (sat 2.4g, mono 0.5g, poly 0.8g); PROTEIN 1.8g; CARB 23g; FIBER 1.4g; CHOL 0mg; IRON 0.1mg; SODIUM 280mg; CALC 35mg

## give it a rest

These tortillas use coconut oil, which is solid at cold temperatures and liquid when warm. Allowing the dough to rest in the refrigerator firms up the coconut oil so the dough won't be too sticky to roll.

# SAUSAGE AND BLACK OLIVE PIZZA

Hands-on time: 17 min. Total time: 1 hr. 33 min.

2 teaspoons granulated sugar
1 package dry yeast (about 2¼ teaspoons)
½ cup warm water (100° to 110°)
3.65 ounces white rice flour (about ¾ cup)
1.4 ounces sweet white sorghum flour (about ⅓ cup)
1.4 ounces tapioca flour (about ⅓ cup)
1.7 ounces potato starch (about ⅓ cup)
0.9 ounce flaxseed meal (about ¼ cup)
1 teaspoon xanthan gum
¼ teaspoon salt
1 tablespoon olive oil
2 large egg whites
1 large egg
Cooking spray
4 ounces turkey Italian sausage (1 link)
½ cup lower-sodium marinara sauce

4 ounces part-skim mozzarella cheese, shredded (about 1 cup)
2 tablespoons chopped ripe olives

1. Dissolve sugar and yeast in ½ cup warm water in a small bowl; let stand 5 minutes.

2. Weigh or lightly spoon flours, potato starch, and flaxseed meal into dry measuring cups; level with a knife. Combine flours, potato starch, flaxseed meal, xanthan gum, and salt in a large bowl; beat with a mixer at medium speed until blended. Add yeast mixture, oil, egg whites, and egg; beat at low speed until combined. Increase speed to medium; beat 2 minutes.

3. Spoon dough onto an 11 x 17–inch baking sheet coated with cooking spray and lined with parchment paper. Lightly coat hands with cooking spray; press dough into an 11 x 12–inch rectangle. Cover with plastic wrap coated with cooking spray, and let rise in a warm place (85°), free from drafts, 30 minutes.

4. Preheat oven to 400°.

5. Bake at 400° for 14 minutes or until bottom is crisp. Cool completely. Increase oven temperature to 425°.

6. Remove casings from sausage. Heat a large skillet over medium-high heat. Add sausage; cook 3 minutes, stirring to crumble. Spread marinara over crust, leaving a ½-inch border; top with sausage, cheese, and olives. Bake at 425° for 12 minutes or until crust is golden. Serves 6 (serving size: 1 rectangle)

CALORIES 309; FAT 11.8g (sat 3.6g, mono 4.7g, poly 2.2g); PROTEIN 15g; CARB 37g; FIBER 3.5g; CHOL 63mg; IRON 1.3mg; SODIUM 564mg; CALC 19mg

# BASIC PIZZA SAUCE

Hands-on time: 6 min. Total time: 41 min.

*In my spare time over the last few years, I have taken up the art and science of gardening. I've found that it is a great way to introduce my boys to the importance of cultivating and eating a variety of fresh vegetables. The past few summer seasons have yielded such a surplus of plum tomatoes that I also had to learn the art of canning. It's definitely been worth all the work, however, because there is nothing like having fresh pizza sauce and marinara all winter long. This recipe is one that mimics that fresh flavor using the convenience of canned tomatoes.*

1 (28-ounce) can whole tomatoes, undrained
  and chopped
1 tablespoon olive oil
3 garlic cloves, minced
1 teaspoon dried oregano
½ teaspoon dried basil
½ teaspoon salt
⅛ teaspoon freshly ground black pepper

1. Place tomatoes in a bowl; crush using back of spoon.

2. Heat a 2-quart saucepan over medium heat. Add oil to pan; swirl to coat. Add garlic; cook 1 minute, stirring occasionally. Stir in tomatoes, oregano, basil, salt, and pepper; bring to a boil. Reduce heat to medium-low, and simmer, uncovered, 35 minutes or until thick, stirring occasionally. Cool and store in an airtight container in refrigerator or freezer until ready to use. Serves 9 (serving size: ¼ cup)

CALORIES 33; FAT 1.6g (sat 0.2g, mono 1.1g, poly 0.2g); PROTEIN 0.9g; CARB 5g; FIBER 1.1g; CHOL 0mg; IRON 1mg; SODIUM 258mg; CALC 37mg

## flavor preservation

Air, heat, and light can cause olive oil to turn rancid and dried herbs to lose their flavor. To prevent both, store them in airtight containers in a cool, dark place (like a pantry or cabinet) where the temperature remains constant.

# FETA AND SPINACH CALZONES

Hands-on time: 36 min. Total time: 2 hr. 16 min.

1 tablespoon sugar
1 package dry yeast (about 2¼ teaspoons)
¾ cup warm water (100° to 110°)
3.9 ounces white rice flour (about ¾ cup)
3.4 ounces brown rice flour (about ¾ cup)
2.1 ounces tapioca flour (about ½ cup)
1.8 ounces flaxseed meal (about ½ cup)
1.3 ounces potato starch (about ¼ cup)
1 tablespoon xanthan gum
½ teaspoon salt
¼ cup plus 2 teaspoons olive oil
2 large eggs
White rice flour for dusting
Cooking spray
½ cup boiling water
2 tablespoons sun-dried tomatoes
1 cup thinly sliced onion
3 garlic cloves, minced
1 pound chopped fresh baby spinach
3 ounces crumbled feta cheese (about ¾ cup)
2 ounces ⅓-less-fat cream cheese (about ½ cup)
1 teaspoon dried oregano
¼ teaspoon salt
¼ teaspoon crushed red pepper
1 tablespoon water
1 large egg

1. Dissolve sugar and yeast in ¾ cup warm water in a small bowl; let stand 5 minutes.

2. Weigh or lightly spoon flours, flaxseed meal, and potato starch into dry measuring cups; level with a knife. Combine flours, flaxseed meal, potato starch, xanthan gum, and salt in a medium bowl; beat with a mixer at medium speed until blended. Add yeast mixture, ¼ cup oil, and 2 eggs; beat at medium speed 1 minute or until blended.

3. Turn dough out onto a lightly floured surface; divide dough into 8 equal portions. Shape each portion into a ball. Coat dough balls with cooking spray; place on a baking sheet. Cover with plastic wrap, and let rise in a warm place (85°), free from drafts, 1 hour and 15 minutes, or until almost doubled in size.

4. Combine ½ cup boiling water and tomatoes in a bowl; let stand 10 minutes or until soft. Drain and chop.

5. Heat a Dutch oven over medium-high heat. Add 2 teaspoons oil; swirl. Add onion and garlic; cook until onions turn golden brown, stirring often. Add tomatoes; cook 1 minute. Place onion mixture in a bowl.

6. Add spinach to Dutch oven, stirring until spinach wilts. Place spinach mixture in a colander, pressing until barely moist. Add spinach, cheeses, oregano, ¼ teaspoon salt, and pepper to onion mixture, stirring to combine. Divide mixture into 8 equal mounds.

7. Preheat oven to 425°.

8. Working with 1 portion at a time, place dough on a floured surface. Pat into a 6-inch circle. Spoon ¼ cup spinach mixture onto dough circle. Fold dough over filling; pinch edges to seal. Repeat procedure with remaining dough and filling. Place calzones on a baking sheet coated with cooking spray. Combine 1 tablespoon water and 1 egg in a small bowl, stirring with a whisk until frothy. Brush egg mixture over calzones. Bake at 425° for 25 minutes or until golden brown. Serves 8 (serving size: 1 calzone)

CALORIES 357; FAT 17.2g (sat 4.4g, mono 8.2g, poly 3.4g); PROTEIN 9.8g; CARB 45g; FIBER 7.2g; CHOL 84mg; IRON 2.9mg; SODIUM 487mg; CALC 126mg

chapter 10

# PUDDINGS, MOUSSES, AND CONFECTIONS

**F**ood is a very basic need but also intertwined with emotion, health, socialization, learning, creativity, and memories. When people hear they must give up categories of food, life can become overwhelming, scary, depressing, even embarrassing. I saw some of this in my household, and over the years have met countless kind, beautiful, and thoughtful people who were also suffering.

While going gluten free is only a small part of anyone's journey, I really want it to be an easy, successful, joyful, and delicious part. This chapter presents some of the miscellaneous ideas, requests, and desires shared by those who found themselves needing to go gluten free and who were looking for a favorite taste of something they thought they might have to give up. I spent many gratifying hours developing, testing, and re-testing these recipes, with the hope that they'll make your life a little bit sweeter.

# CLASSIC VANILLA PUDDING

Hands-on time: 17 min. Total time: 2 hr. 17 min.

*For a quick and elegant dessert, serve this creamy vanilla pudding topped with fresh berries, crumbled pistachio brittle (like the one on page 275), or chopped toffee candy and garnished with a pretty mint leaf.*

4 cups 1% low-fat milk
4 large egg yolks
1 vanilla bean, split lengthwise
½ cup sugar
⅓ cup cornstarch
¼ teaspoon salt
2 tablespoons butter, softened
Cooking spray

1. Combine milk and eggs yolks in a large bowl, stirring with a whisk until frothy. Scrape seeds from vanilla bean. Add vanilla bean seeds and pod to milk mixture.

2. Combine sugar, cornstarch, and salt in a medium saucepan, stirring with a whisk. Slowly add milk mixture, stirring until blended. Cook over medium heat 12 minutes or until mixture comes to a boil and begins to thicken, stirring constantly. Remove from heat; stir in butter. Remove and discard vanilla bean pod.

3. Pour ½ cup mixture into each of 10 (6-ounce) ramekins or small bowls. Cover surface of pudding with plastic wrap coated with cooking spray. Chill at least 2 hours. Serves 10 (serving size: 1 pudding)

**Note:** Substitute 4 teaspoons vanilla extract in place of the vanilla bean, if you like. You'll need to add it with the butter.

CALORIES 138; FAT 5.1g (sat 2.7g, mono 1.7g, poly 0.4g); PROTEIN 4.4g; CARB 19g; FIBER 0g; CHOL 85mg; IRON 0.2mg; SODIUM 126mg; CALC 132mg

## smart egg storage

The best way to store eggs is to keep them in their carton so you can reference the expiration date if needed, and place it in the coldest part of the refrigerator. Avoid the built-in egg containers that sometimes come in refrigerators. The temperature of items stored on the door can fluctuate substantially since the door is opened repeatedly.

# BUTTERSCOTCH PUDDING

Hands-on time: 13 min. Total time: 4 hr. 28 min.

*This fantastic recipe is dedicated to my friend Mike White, who proclaims that butterscotch pudding is "the best food ever invented." The crumbled toffee candy on top gives the creamy butterscotch pudding a crunchy-sweet finish.*

1/2 cup packed dark brown sugar
3 1/2 tablespoons cornstarch
1/8 teaspoon salt
2 cups 1% low-fat milk
2 large egg yolks, slightly beaten
1 tablespoon butter
2 teaspoons vanilla extract
Cooking spray
5 teaspoons almond brickle chips (such as Heath)

1. Combine brown sugar, cornstarch, and salt in a medium saucepan over medium heat. Add milk and egg yolks, stirring with a whisk until smooth. Bring mixture to a boil, and cook 2 to 3 minutes or until mixture thickens, stirring constantly.

2. Remove pan from heat; stir in butter and vanilla. Pour mixture into 5 (6-ounce) ramekins or small bowls. Cover surface of pudding with plastic wrap coated with cooking spray; cool 15 minutes. Chill at least 4 hours. Top each serving with 1 teaspoon brickle bits. Serves 5 (serving size: 1 pudding)

CALORIES 220; FAT 6.6g (sat 3.4g, mono 1.7g, poly 0.4g); PROTEIN 4.8g; CARB 35g; FIBER 0.1g; CHOL 86mg; IRON 0.4mg; SODIUM 152mg; CALC 150mg

# OLD-FASHIONED NO-BAKE RICE PUDDING

*This fragrant stovetop rice pudding is a holiday tradition in our home. The recipe was lovingly passed down from Great Grandma FitzGerald. I hope many more generations to come bring it to the table.*

1½ cups water
¾ cup uncooked medium-grain rice
½ vanilla bean, split lengthwise
1¼ cups 1% low-fat milk, divided
⅓ cup sugar
¼ teaspoon salt
1 large egg, lightly beaten
1 tablespoon butter
⅛ teaspoon ground cinnamon

1. Bring 1½ cups water to a boil in a medium sauce-pan; add rice. Cover, reduce heat, and simmer 20 minutes or until tender.

2. Scrape seeds from vanilla bean; add vanilla bean seeds and pod to rice. Add 1 cup milk, sugar, and salt to rice mixture in pan. Cook over medium heat 15 minutes or until thick and creamy. Remove and discard vanilla bean pod.

3. Combine ¼ cup milk and egg in a small bowl. Slowly add egg mixture to rice mixture; cook 2 minutes over medium heat, stirring constantly. Remove from heat; stir in butter and cinnamon. Serve warm, or pour into a 2-quart dish; cover surface of pudding with plastic wrap, and chill overnight. Serves 7 (serving size: ½ cup)

CALORIES 155; FAT 2.9g (sat 1.6g, mono 0.7g, poly 0.3g); PROTEIN 3.8g; CARB 28g; FIBER 0.3g; CHOL 33mg; IRON 1.1mg; SODIUM 128mg; CALC 61mg

## the right rice

**tip**

Medium-grain rice has more starch than long-grain rice and gives the pudding a creamier texture.

# QUINOA-CINNAMON BREAD PUDDING

Hands-on time: 10 min. Total time: 2 hr 30 min.

2 cups 1% low-fat milk
⅓ cup packed brown sugar
¼ cup granulated sugar
1 teaspoon vanilla extract
½ teaspoon ground cinnamon
¼ teaspoon ground nutmeg
⅛ teaspoon salt
4 large eggs
8 slices Quinoa Bread (page 234), cut into 1-inch
    cubes (about 5 cups)
Cooking spray
3 tablespoons raisins
¼ cup fat-free caramel sundae syrup

1. Preheat oven to 350°.

2. Combine milk, brown sugar, granulated sugar, vanilla, cinnamon, nutmeg, salt, and eggs in a medium bowl, stirring with a whisk.

3. Place cubed bread in an 11 x 7–inch baking dish coated with cooking spray; sprinkle raisins over bread. Pour egg mixture over bread. Press down lightly on bread, using a spatula, allowing bread to absorb egg mixture. Cover and chill 1 hour.

4. Place baking dish in a large roasting pan; add enough hot water to roasting pan to come halfway up sides of baking dish. Bake at 350° for 1 hour or until center of pudding appears set. Cool 20 minutes in pan. Serve with caramel syrup. Serves 12 (serving size: ½₂ of pudding and 1 teaspoon caramel syrup)

CALORIES 315; FAT 10.2g (sat 3g, mono 4.5g, poly 1.8g); PROTEIN 6.6g; CARB 50.1g; FIBER 2.4g; CHOL 98mg; IRON 1.3mg; SODIUM 308mg; CALC 113mg

# TIRAMISU

*This tiramisu is divine! Blending mascarpone cheese with fat-free cream cheese is the key to this phenomenal recipe. The richness and flavor of the mascarpone cheese still shines through but with less saturated fat and fewer calories than traditional recipes.*

1 cup espresso or strong brewed coffee
2 tablespoons Kahlúa (coffee-flavored liqueur)
12 ounces fat-free cream cheese (about 1½ cups), softened
4 ounces mascarpone cheese (about ½ cup), softened
1 cup powdered sugar
½ teaspoon vanilla extract
2 cups frozen fat-free whipped topping, thawed
24 Ladyfingers (page 115)
½ ounce bittersweet chocolate

1. Place espresso and Kahlúa in a medium bowl, stirring to combine.

2. Place cream cheese and mascarpone in a large bowl; beat with a mixer at medium speed until smooth and creamy. Add powdered sugar, 3 tablespoons espresso mixture, and vanilla; beat with a mixer until blended. Fold in half of whipped topping, stirring just until combined. Repeat with remaining whipped topping.

3. Dip 12 ladyfingers in espresso mixture for 2 to 3 seconds each; place in an 8-inch square glass or ceramic baking dish. Top with half of cheese mixture, spreading evenly over ladyfingers. Top with 12 ladyfingers. Brush top of ladyfingers with remaining espresso mixture. Spread remaining cheese mixture over ladyfingers; cover and refrigerate at least 6 hours. Grate chocolate over top. Serves 9

CALORIES 282; FAT 8.6g (sat 4.3g, mono 1g, poly 0.4g); PROTEIN 9.4g; CARB 39.2g; FIBER 0.4g; CHOL 82mg; IRON 0.5mg; SODIUM 331mg; CALC 180mg

Tofu replaces the eggs in this mousse, adding a creamy, smooth texture and almost 5 grams of protein.

# CHOCOLATE MOUSSE

Hands-on time: 8 min. Total time: 2 hr. 8 min.

*Our youngest son, Stephen, is high energy, and by age 3, had already developed a fearless reputation, earning him the nickname "the firecracker." He is also our pickiest eater, at times limiting himself to a rotation of only seven or eight foods in any given week. Nevertheless, he has never turned down a bowl of this chocolate mousse. Since it is a hidden source of soy protein and features fresh raspberries, we're OK with that!*

6 ounces bittersweet chocolate, finely chopped
½ cup sugar
2 tablespoons water
1 tablespoon brewed coffee
¼ cup unsweetened cocoa
½ teaspoon vanilla extract
1 (16-ounce) package silken tofu
8 tablespoons frozen reduced-calorie whipped topping, thawed
3 ounces fresh raspberries

1. Combine first 4 ingredients in a small saucepan; cook over medium heat until mixture is smooth and creamy, stirring frequently. Add cocoa and vanilla; stir until blended.

2. Place chocolate mixture and tofu in a blender; process until blended. Pour mixture into each of 8 (4.5-ounce) ramekins or custard cups. Cover and chill at least 2 hours. Top each serving with whipped topping and raspberries. Serves 8 (serving size: 1 mousse, 1 tablespoon whipped topping, and 3 raspberries)

CALORIES 206; FAT 11.5g (sat 5.4g, mono 2.6g, poly 1.1g); PROTEIN 4.9g; CARB 29g; FIBER 3.2g; CHOL 0mg; IRON 1.5mg; SODIUM 4mg; CALC 24mg

## the many uses of tofu
**t i p**

Neutral-tasting tofu is a chameleon in the kitchen. It's made from soybean curd and readily takes on the flavors of the ingredients it's paired with. You'll find it in silken, medium, firm, and extra-firm varieties. Silken tofu is the softest variety, and it blends smoothly, creating a luscious texture as in this recipe. It also works well in puddings, sauces, and pie fillings.

# PUMPKIN FLAN

Hands-on time: 11 min. Total time: 11 hr. 6 min.

*Pumpkin lends a unique and mouthwatering spin to the classic custard dessert with a soft caramel top. This flan is convenient: It can be made in advance and kept refrigerated until ready to serve.*

³/₄ cup sugar
¹/₄ cup water
Cooking spray
1 cup canned pumpkin
1 teaspoon pumpkin pie spice
1 teaspoon vanilla extract
4 large eggs
1 (12-ounce) can evaporated fat-free milk
1 (14-ounce) can low-fat sweetened condensed milk

1. Preheat oven to 350°.

2. Place sugar and ¼ cup water in a medium, heavy saucepan over medium-low heat; cook until sugar dissolves, stirring gently as needed to dissolve sugar evenly. Continue cooking 7 minutes or until golden (do not stir). Immediately pour into a 9-inch round cake pan coated with cooking spray.

3. Place pumpkin, pumpkin pie spice, vanilla, eggs, and milks in a food processor; process until smooth. Pour milk mixture over caramel in pan. Place pan in a 13 x 9–inch metal baking pan; add enough hot water to large pan to come halfway up sides of cake pan.

4. Bake at 350° for 1 hour and 10 minutes or until center is set. Remove cake pan from water; cool completely on a wire rack. Cover and refrigerate overnight.

5. Loosen edges of flan with a knife or rubber spatula. Place a large serving plate, upside down, on top of cake pan; invert flan onto plate. Drizzle any remaining caramelized syrup over flan. Serves 10 (serving size: 1 slice)

CALORIES 261; FAT 3.8g (sat 1.7g, mono 0.9g, poly 0.4g); PROTEIN 8.9g; CARB 45g; FIBER 1.0g; CHOL 81mg; IRON 0.7mg; SODIUM 115mg; CALC 229mg

# STRUFFOLI

Hands-on time: 39 min. Total time: 1 hr. 39 min.

*Ah, struffoli! These little Neapolitan honey cakes are a Long Island Landolphi Christmas tradition that we start eating at Thanksgiving and really never stop. These marble-sized dough balls are fried quickly to give them a light delicious cake inside and crunchy outside layer. Then they are covered in honey and powdered sugar. Serve with coffee and savor each little indulgent bite.*

3.46 ounces white rice flour (about ⅔ cup)
3 ounces brown rice flour (about ⅔ cup)
1.4 ounces tapioca flour (about ⅓ cup)
1.6 ounces cornstarch (about ⅓ cup)
2 tablespoons granulated sugar
2 teaspoons grated lemon rind
1 teaspoon xanthan gum
¼ teaspoon baking powder
¼ teaspoon salt
5 tablespoons unsalted butter, cut into small
    pieces and softened
¾ teaspoon vanilla extract, divided
3 large eggs
Peanut oil
¾ cup honey
1 tablespoon powdered sugar

1. Weigh or lightly spoon flours and cornstarch into dry measuring cups; level with a knife. Place flours, cornstarch, sugar, and next 4 ingredients (through salt) in a food processor; process 2 times or until blended. Add butter; process until mixture resembles coarse meal. Add ½ teaspoon vanilla and eggs; process until dough forms a ball. Wrap dough in plastic wrap; chill 1 hour.

2. Divide dough in half. Roll each half of dough into 30 (1-inch) balls.

3. Add oil to a Dutch oven to a depth of 2 inches. Heat oil over medium-high heat until a thermometer registers 360°. Add half of dough balls to pan; cook 2 minutes or until golden brown. Remove with a slotted spoon; cool on paper towels. Repeat procedure with remaining dough balls.

4. Add honey to a large saucepan over medium heat; bring to a boil. Boil 2 minutes, stirring constantly. Remove from heat; stir in ¼ teaspoon vanilla. Add fried dough balls to honey mixture, tossing to coat. Cool 2 minutes.

5. Place on a serving platter. Drizzle with any remaining honey, and sprinkle with powdered sugar. Serves 20 (serving size: 3 struffoli)

CALORIES 250; FAT 18.8g (sat 4.5g, mono 7.8g, poly 5.1g); PROTEIN 1.6g; CARB 23g; FIBER 0.5g; CHOL 36mg; IRON 0.3mg; SODIUM 47mg; CALC 11mg

# PIZZELLES

Hands-on time: 6 min. Total time: 32 min.

*When she heard this book was in the works, our friend, Tina Trotochaud, nearly begged for a gluten-free version of pizzelles. I had planned to have her sample them once they were perfected, but my wife ate the whole container in two days! You'll need a pizzelle iron to make these delicate Italian waffle cookies.*

1.3 ounces potato starch (about ¼ cup)
1.05 ounces sweet white sorghum flour (about ¼ cup)
1.05 ounces tapioca flour (about ¼ cup)
½ cup granulated sugar
½ teaspoon xanthan gum
½ teaspoon baking powder
¼ teaspoon salt
¼ cup warm water
2 tablespoons butter, melted
1 tablespoon olive oil
½ teaspoon anise extract
2 large eggs
1 large egg white
Cooking spray
¼ cup powdered sugar

1. Preheat pizzelle iron.

2. Weigh or lightly spoon potato starch and flours into a dry measuring cup; level with a knife. Combine potato starch, flours, granulated sugar, and next 3 ingredients (through salt) in a medium bowl, stirring with a whisk.

3. Combine ¼ cup warm water and next 5 ingredients (through egg white) in a large bowl; stir with a whisk. Slowly add flour mixture to egg mixture; stir with a whisk until smooth.

4. Coat pizzelle iron with cooking spray. Spoon 1 tablespoon batter onto hot iron, spreading batter to edges. Cook according to manufacturer's instructions. Repeat procedure with remaining batter. Top pizzelles with powdered sugar. Serves 22 (serving size: 1 pizzelle)

**Cannoli Shell Variation:** Remove hot pizzelle from iron; wrap around a cannoli mold or the handle of large wooden spoon, overlapping edges of shell. Remove shell from mold; cool on a wire rack.

CALORIES 62; FAT 2.3g (sat 0.9g, mono 1g, poly 0.2g); PROTEIN 0.9g; CARB 10g; FIBER 0.2g; CHOL 20mg; IRON 0.2mg; SODIUM 55mg; CALC 11mg

# CHOCOLATE CHIP CANNOLI

Hands-on time: 16 min. Total time: 12 hr. 36 min.

*Cannoli on a gluten-free diet are practically unheard of. I made it my mission to produce a version that could be enjoyed by all. Add additional chocolate minichips on the ends for garnish, if you like.*

1 cup part-skim ricotta cheese
½ cup powdered sugar
4 ounces ⅓-less-fat cream cheese (about ½ cup), softened
2 tablespoons cornstarch
½ teaspoon grated lemon rind
½ teaspoon vanilla extract
⅛ teaspoon ground cinnamon
¼ cup semisweet chocolate minichips
12 Pizzelles prepared using Cannoli Shell Variation (page 265)

1. Place colander in a 2-quart glass measuring cup or medium bowl. Line colander with 3 layers of cheesecloth, allowing cheesecloth to extend over outside edges. Spoon ricotta cheese into colander. Gather edges of cheesecloth; tie securely. Refrigerate 12 hours. Spoon drained cheese into a large bowl; discard liquid.

2. Add powdered sugar, cream cheese, cornstarch, lemon rind, vanilla, and cinnamon to drained ricotta; beat with a mixer at medium speed until combined. Fold in chocolate minichips; cover and chill until ready to assemble cannoli.

3. Spoon ricotta mixture into a pastry bag fitted with a ½-inch round tip. Pipe 1 tablespoon into each end of prepared cannoli shells. Serve immediately. Serves 12 (serving size: 1 filled cannolo)

CALORIES 151; FAT 7.1g (sat 3.8g, mono 2.4g, poly 0.4g); PROTEIN 4.3g; CARB 18g; FIBER 0.4g; CHOL 33mg; IRON 0.4mg; SODIUM 113mg; CALC 79mg

## a necessary step

t i p

It is important to drain the ricotta cheese to remove any excess moisture. Too much moisture can cause the filling to be runny and the pastry to become soggy.

# GIANT APPLE-RAISIN STRUDEL

Hands-on time: 20 min. Total time: 3 hr.

*Gorgeous layers of sweet apples, raisins, and cinnamon rolled in a gluten-free version of German pastry dough will make this recipe a new favorite.*

2.1 ounces sweet white sorghum flour (about ½ cup)
1.8 ounces oat flour (about ½ cup)
1.3 ounces white rice flour (about ¼ cup)
1.15 ounces cornstarch (about ¼ cup)
1 tablespoon granulated sugar
2 teaspoons xanthan gum
¼ teaspoon salt
2 ounces ⅓-less-fat cream cheese (about ¼ cup), softened
4 tablespoons butter, softened
1 tablespoon 1% low-fat milk
1 large egg
3¼ cups sliced peeled McIntosh apple (about 1 pound)
¼ cup packed brown sugar
3 tablespoons raisins
1 tablespoon fresh lemon juice
1 tablespoon chilled butter, cut into small pieces
1 teaspoon cornstarch
⅛ teaspoon ground cinnamon
White rice flour, for dusting
1 tablespoon butter, melted
1 teaspoon turbinado sugar
1 teaspoon powdered sugar

1. Weigh or lightly spoon flours and cornstarch into dry measuring cups; level with a knife. Sift together flours, cornstarch, granulated sugar, xanthan gum, and salt in a medium bowl.

2. Place cream cheese, softened butter, milk, and egg in a food processor; process until blended. Add flour mixture; process until blended and dough pulls away from sides. Shape dough into a ball; wrap in plastic wrap. Chill 1 hour.

3. Preheat oven to 375°.

4. Combine apple and next 6 ingredients (through cinnamon), tossing to coat apple.

5. Place dough on a baking sheet lined with parchment paper and lightly floured. Cover with an additional sheet of parchment paper. Roll dough into a 13-inch circle; remove top layer of parchment paper. Spoon apple mixture onto half of circle, leaving a 1-inch border around outside edges.

6. Fold dough over filling; press edges together with a fork to seal. Brush top of dough with melted butter; sprinkle with turbinado sugar.

7. Cut three diagonal slits into top of strudel using a sharp knife. Bake at 375° for 40 minutes or until golden brown. Cool completely on pan. Sprinkle with powdered sugar before serving. Serves 8 (serving size: ⅛ of strudel)

---

CALORIES 261; FAT 11.8g (sat 6.2g, mono 3.2g, poly 0.9g); PROTEIN 3.7g; CARB 36.8g; FIBER 3g; CHOL 51mg; IRON 0.8mg; SODIUM 188mg; CALC 32mg

# WINN'S FIG AND PECAN RUGELACH

*This recipe was created for Winnette Berger and her daughters from Colorado. A few years ago, I spent a memorable weekend there teaching them how to prepare delicious gluten-free recipes. This rugelach reflects the perfect sweetness of this generous family.*

2.6 ounces white rice flour (about ½ cup)
1.4 ounces sweet sorghum flour (about ⅓ cup)
1.15 ounces cornstarch (about ¼ cup)
1 teaspoon xanthan gum
½ teaspoon baking powder
¼ teaspoon salt
4 ounces ⅓-less-fat cream cheese (about ½ cup), softened
3 tablespoons unsalted butter, softened
2 tablespoons granulated sugar
2 tablespoons 1% low-fat milk, plus extra for brushing
1 large egg
White rice flour, for dusting
⅓ cup chopped pecans
2 tablespoons brown sugar
⅛ teaspoon ground cinnamon
½ cup kadota fig preserves, melted
1 tablespoon granulated sugar
¼ teaspoon ground cinnamon

1. Weigh or lightly spoon flours and cornstarch into dry measuring cups; level with a knife. Combine flours, cornstarch, xanthan gum, baking powder, and salt in a medium bowl, stirring with a whisk.

2. Place cream cheese, butter, and 2 tablespoons granulated sugar in a large bowl; beat with a mixer at medium speed until blended. Add 2 tablespoons milk and egg; beat until blended. Add flour mixture, beating until blended. Turn dough out onto a well-floured surface; knead until smooth and elastic. Divide dough into 2 equal portions, shaping each into a disc. Wrap each in plastic wrap; chill at least 3 hours.

3. Preheat oven to 375°.

4. Combine pecans, brown sugar, and ⅛ teaspoon cinnamon in a small bowl. Place 1 dough disc onto a piece of well-floured parchment paper. Cover with an additional piece of floured parchment paper. Roll dough, still covered, into a 10-inch circle. Remove top sheet of paper; spread ¼ cup melted preserves over dough. Top preserves with half of pecan mixture. Cut circle into 8 wedges. Beginning with long side, roll up each wedge. Place rolls, point sides down, 2 inches apart on a baking sheet lined with parchment paper. Repeat procedure with remaining dough disc, preserves, and pecan mixture.

5. Combine 1 tablespoon granulated sugar and ¼ teaspoon cinnamon in a small bowl. Brush each rugelach with milk; sprinkle with sugar mixture. Bake at 375° for 24 minutes or until golden brown. Cool completely on pan. Serves 16 (serving size: 1 rugelach)

CALORIES 130; FAT 5.8g (sat 2.5g, mono 1.6g, poly 0.7g); PROTEIN 1.8g; CARB 18g; FIBER 0.8g; CHOL 23mg; IRON 0.3mg; SODIUM 83mg; CALC 22mg

# WHIPPED CREAM PUFFS

Hands-on time: 15 min. Total time: 1 hr. 18 min.

*Potato starch and rice flour make a delightfully tender and flaky, yet chewy, puff pastry. Filled with dollops of creamy whipped filling and topped with powdered sugar, they are a wonderful treat for a shower or party.*

2.6 ounces white rice flour (about ½ cup)
1.3 ounces potato starch (about ¼ cup)
1.05 ounces tapioca flour (about ¼ cup)
½ teaspoon xanthan gum
¼ teaspoon baking powder
⅛ teaspoon salt
1 cup water
3 tablespoons butter
3 large eggs
¾ cup frozen reduced-calorie whipped topping, thawed
1 tablespoon powdered sugar
Fresh raspberries (optional)

1. Preheat oven to 400°.

2. Weigh or lightly spoon white rice flour, potato starch, and tapioca flour into dry measuring cups; level with a knife. Combine white rice flour, potato starch, tapioca flour, xanthan gum, baking powder, and salt in a medium bowl, stirring with a whisk.

3. Combine 1 cup water and butter in a medium saucepan over medium-high heat; bring to a boil. Add flour mixture, stirring well with a wooden spoon until mixture is smooth and pulls away from sides of pan. Remove from heat; place dough in the bowl of a stand mixer fitted with a paddle attachment; beat at medium-high speed 1 minute. Add eggs, 1 at a time, beating well after each addition. Scrape dough off sides of bowl using a rubber spatula; beat 1 minute or until dough is smooth (dough will be sticky).

4. Spoon 2 tablespoonfuls dough 2 inches apart onto a baking sheet lined with parchment paper. Bake at 400° for 15 minutes. Reduce oven temperature to 350°. Bake an additional 18 minutes or until tops are golden brown and puffs sound hollow when tapped. Remove from oven; cool completely on pan.

5. Cut top one-third of each puff horizontally using a serrated knife. Top bottom half of each puff with 1 tablespoon whipped topping. Replace top half of each puff. Sprinkle with powdered sugar. Serve with fresh raspberries, if desired. Serves 12 (serving size: 1 cream puff)

**Note:** When scooping the dough onto a baking sheet, dip the spoon into water after each use to keep the dough from sticking to the spoon.

CALORIES 97; FAT 4.7g (sat 2.7g, mono 1.2g, poly 0.4g); PROTEIN 2g; CARB 12g; FIBER 0.3g; CHOL 54mg; IRON 0.3mg; SODIUM 77mg; CALC 15mg

# CRANBERRY-ALMOND BARK

Hands-on time: 7 min. Total time: 67 min.

*This chocolate confection, shared by our friend Meme Tellier, is a spectacular way to blend cranberries and almonds. However, it comes with a warning: It is addictive.*

**6 ounces semisweet chocolate, chopped**
**½ cup chopped almonds**
**⅓ cup chopped dried cranberries**

1. Place chocolate in a medium microwave-safe bowl; microwave at HIGH 1 minute, stirring after 30 seconds. Spread chocolate in a foil-lined 9-inch square metal baking pan; sprinkle with almonds and cranberries. Chill 1 hour or until chocolate is set.

2. Remove foil from chocolate; break into pieces. Store in an airtight container in refrigerator up to 2 weeks. Serves 25 (serving size: 1 piece)

CALORIES 52; FAT 3.3g (sat 1.3g, mono 1.5g, poly 0.4g); PROTEIN 0.8g; CARB 6g; FIBER 0.8g; CHOL 0mg; IRON 0.3mg; SODIUM 1mg; CALC 9mg

### sweet swaps | tip

Substitute other dried fruits, such as raisins, apricots, figs, or cherries for the dried cranberries.

# GORP CLUSTERS

Hands-on time: 9 min. Total time: 39 min.

*Packed with oats, chocolate chips, pretzels, raisins, and sunflower seeds, these unique clusters offer a sweet, salty, fruity, chewy, crunchy punch all in one bite. Take them along on hikes or long bike rides to provide a pick-me-up.*

1 cup bittersweet chocolate chips
42 gluten-free pretzels (1 ounce), coarsely chopped
   (about ⅟₂ cup)
⅟₃ cup raisins
⅟₄ cup certified gluten-free quick-cooking oats
2 tablespoons unsalted sunflower seed kernels

1. Place chocolate chips in a medium microwave-safe bowl; microwave at HIGH 1 to 1½ minutes or until melted, stirring every 30 seconds. Add pretzels, raisins, oats, and sunflower seed kernels, stirring to coat.

2. Drop mixture by heaping teaspoonfuls onto a baking sheet lined with parchment paper. Chill 30 minutes or until chocolate is set. Store in an airtight container in refrigerator up to 1 week. Serves 30 (serving size: 1 cluster)

CALORIES 25; FAT 1.1g (sat 0.6g, mono 0.1g, poly 0.2g); PROTEIN 0.4g; CARB 3.8g; FIBER 0.4g; CHOL 0mg; IRON 0.2mg; SODIUM 14mg; CALC 1mg

## a good seed

The average sunflower produces between 1,500 to 2,000 sunflower seeds. While their flavor makes them well suited for baked goods or just for snacking, sunflower seeds also supply vitamin E, magnesium, and selenium.

# MINT-CHOCOLATE TRUFFLES

Hands-on time: 30 min. Total time: 8 hr. 30 min.

*I was knee-deep in recipe trials when one of my sons needed a birthday snack for his elementary school classroom. Instead of the usual brownies or cupcakes, I took these insanely decadent and rich truffles. Needless to say, I barely made it out of the teachers' lounge alive!*

½ cup half-and-half
2 tablespoons butter
2 tablespoons corn syrup
12 ounces bittersweet chocolate, finely chopped
½ teaspoon peppermint extract
2 tablespoons unsweetened cocoa

1. Combine half-and-half, butter, and corn syrup in a medium saucepan over medium-high heat. Bring to a boil; cook 1 minute, stirring frequently. Remove from heat; add chocolate and peppermint extract, stirring until smooth and creamy. Pour chocolate mixture into a shallow dish; cover and chill overnight.

2. Place cocoa in a shallow dish. Scoop chocolate mixture by teaspoonfuls; shape into 40 balls using hands. Roll balls in cocoa, and place on wax paper. Store in refrigerator until ready to serve. Serves 40 (serving size: 1 truffle)

**Note:** Store truffles in refrigerator up to 1 week.

CALORIES 66; FAT 4.5g (sat 2.5g, mono 1.1g, poly 0.7g); PROTEIN 0.8g; CARB 5g; FIBER 0.1g; CHOL 3mg; IRON 0.3mg; SODIUM 7mg; CALC 7mg

## enhance the flavor

tip

Before serving, you should remove the truffles from the refrigerator, and allow them to warm to room temperature. They'll have a richer, more pronounced flavor.

# PISTACHIO BRITTLE

Hands-on time: 7 min. Total time: 42 min.

*Using pistachios for your next homemade brittle adds a nice twist on an old classic. Wrap up the pieces in cellophane, and tie with ribbons for a pleasant alternative to Christmas cookies. This recipe is dedicated to Grandpa Don, who loved cashew, almond, and peanut brittle, too.*

Cooking spray
1 cup sugar
½ cup light-colored corn syrup
¼ cup water
⅛ teaspoon salt
1 cup salted shelled dry-roasted pistachios
1 tablespoon unsalted butter, softened
1 teaspoon baking soda
1 teaspoon vanilla extract

1. Cover a large baking sheet with parchment paper; coat with cooking spray.

2. Combine sugar, corn syrup, ¼ cup water, and salt in a medium, heavy saucepan. Bring to a boil over medium-heat until a candy thermometer registers 250°. Add pistachios; cook 15 minutes or until temperature reaches 300°, stirring frequently.

3. Remove from heat; stir in butter, baking soda, and vanilla. Pour pistachio mixture onto prepared pan, spreading evenly into a 12 x 8–inch rectangle. Cool completely; break into pieces before serving. Serves 20 (serving size: 1 piece)

CALORIES 105; FAT 3.5g (sat 0.7g, mono 1.7g, poly 0.9g); PROTEIN 1.3g; CARB 19g; FIBER 0.6g; CHOL 2mg; IRON 0.3mg; SODIUM 110mg; CALC 8mg

## go nuts

Feel free to substitute peanuts, cashews, pecans, or almonds for the pistachios.

tip

# MARSHMALLOWS

Hands-on time: 40 min. Total time: 9 hr. 10 min.

*Our kids love to make these for our big cookouts, where we wind down around the bonfire, roasting marshmallows and enjoying each other's company. Adding cocoa and two types of chocolate chips just increases the excitement.*

2 tablespoons unsweetened cocoa
1 tablespoon powdered sugar
1 tablespoon cornstarch
Cooking spray
1 cup cold water, divided
3 (0.25-ounce) envelopes unflavored gelatin
1 1/2 cups granulated sugar
3/4 cup light-colored corn syrup
1/4 teaspoon salt
2 teaspoons vanilla extract
1/4 cup semisweet chocolate minichips
1/4 cup white chocolate chips

1. Combine cocoa, powdered sugar, and cornstarch in a small bowl.

2. Coat a 9-inch square glass or ceramic baking dish with cooking spray; dust pan with 2 1/2 tablespoons cocoa mixture. Reserve remaining cocoa mixture.

3. Combine 1/2 cup cold water and gelatin in a large bowl; beat with a mixer at medium speed until blended. Let stand 30 minutes.

4. Combine granulated sugar, corn syrup, salt, and 1/2 cup cold water in a small heavy saucepan. Cook over medium heat 5 minutes or until sugar dissolves, stirring occasionally. Increase heat to medium-high; cook without stirring until candy thermometer reaches 244°. Remove from heat.

5. Slowly pour hot sugar syrup into gelatin, beating at low speed until combined. Beat at high speed 12 to 15 minutes or until mixture triples in volume. Add vanilla; beat 30 seconds. Pour mixture into prepared pan; spread mixture in pan using a rubber spatula coated with cooking spray. Sprinkle marshmallows with chips, gently pressing chips with spatula to adhere. Top with 1 1/2 tablespoons reserved cocoa mixture. Let stand, uncovered, at room temperature overnight.

6. Run a knife around outside edge of pan; remove from pan. Cut into 1-inch squares. Serves 36 (serving size: 1 marshmallow)

---

CALORIES 71; FAT 0.9g (sat 0.5g, mono 0.3g, poly 0.1g); PROTEIN 0.7g; CARB 16g; FIBER 0.2g; CHOL 0mg; IRON 0.1mg; SODIUM 24mg; CALC 5mg

# WHOLE-GRAIN CRACKERS

Hands-on time: 40 min. Total time: 1 hr. 30 min.

*Gluten-free crackers are not hard to find on the market, but they're often highly processed, rice- or cornstarch-based, not very nutritious, and expensive. These homemade crackers are teeming with nutrients. Made with high-protein quinoa flour, they are also full of zinc, omega-3s, vitamins, and minerals from pumpkin, flax, sunflower, and caraway seeds.*

2 ounces quinoa flour (about ½ cup)
1.8 ounces oat flour (about ½ cup)
1.05 ounces sweet white sorghum flour
    (about ¼ cup)
¼ cup unsalted pumpkinseed kernels
2 tablespoons flaxseed
2 tablespoons unsalted sunflower seed kernels
1 tablespoon caraway seeds
1 teaspoon Italian seasoning
¾ teaspoon salt
½ teaspoon onion powder
2 tablespoons vegan shortening sticks (such as
    Earth Balance)
2 tablespoons olive oil
1 tablespoon water
1 large egg, lightly beaten

1. Preheat oven to 325°.

2. Weigh or lightly spoon flours into dry measuring cups; level with a knife. Place flours, pumpkinseed kernels, and next 6 ingredients (through onion powder) in a food processor; process until seeds are almost fully ground. Add shortening, oil, 1 tablespoon water, and egg; process until blended and dough pulls away from sides of bowl.

3. Cover a large baking sheet with parchment paper. Place dough in center of paper; gently press dough into a square. Cover dough with an additional sheet of parchment paper. Roll dough, still covered, into a 13 x 10–inch rectangle. Remove top sheet of paper; cut dough into 30 (2-inch) squares. Separate squares on pan.

4. Bake at 325° for 30 minutes or until crackers are golden brown and crispy. Cool 20 minutes on pan. Serves 10 (serving size: 3 crackers)

---

CALORIES 153; FAT 9.9g (sat 2.1g, mono 3.9g, poly 2.4g); PROTEIN 4.2g; CARB 12g; FIBER 2.7g; CHOL 18mg; IRON 1.2mg; SODIUM 189mg; CALC 18mg

# SESAME SEED CRACKERS

*Sesame seeds have a long and established history; they were highly valued for their oil in ancient times. The famous phrase "open sesame" from* **The Arabian Nights** *refers to the unique feature of the sesame seed pod, which bursts open when it reaches maturity. Serve these crackers with hummus, peanut butter, or slices of cheese.*

2.7 ounces almond meal flour (about ³/₄ cup)
2.3 ounces brown rice flour (about ¹/₂ cup)
1.3 ounces potato starch (about ¹/₄ cup)
¹/₂ cup sesame seeds
¹/₂ teaspoon salt
2 tablespoons unsweetened coconut milk
1 tablespoon coconut oil
1 large egg, lightly beaten

1. Preheat oven to 350°.

2. Weigh or lightly spoon flours and potato starch into dry measuring cups; level with a knife. Combine flours, potato starch, sesame seeds, and salt in a large bowl; beat with a mixer at medium speed until blended. Add milk, coconut oil, and egg; stir until a soft dough forms.

3. Shape dough into a ball. Cover a large baking sheet with parchment paper. Place dough in center of paper; gently press dough into a square. Cover dough with an additional sheet of parchment paper. Roll dough, still covered, into a 18 x 12–inch rectangle. Remove top sheet of paper; cut dough into 36 (2-inch) squares. Separate squares on pan.

4. Bake at 350° for 18 minutes or until crackers are golden brown and crispy. Cool 20 minutes on pan. Serves 36 (serving size: 1 cracker)

CALORIES 39; FAT 2.6g (sat 0.6g, mono 0.5g, poly 0.5g); PROTEIN 1.2g; CARB 3g; FIBER 0.5g; CHOL 5.1mg; IRON 0.3mg; SODIUM 40mg; CALC 12mg

# OAT AND FLAX CRACKERS

Hands-on time: 8 min. Total time: 68 min.

*These crunchy crackers are good on their own or paired with dips or cheese.*

3.6 ounces oat flour (about 1 cup)
1 cup certified gluten-free quick-cooking oats
2 tablespoons flaxseed meal
2 teaspoons dried oregano
1/8 teaspoon garlic powder
1/2 teaspoon salt
1/4 cup warm water
2 tablespoons olive oil
1 tablespoon vegan buttery sticks (such as Earth Balance), softened
1 large egg

1. Preheat oven to 325°.

2. Weigh or lightly spoon flour into a dry measuring cup; level with a knife. Combine flour, oats, and next 4 ingredients (through salt) in a large bowl, stirring to combine. Add 1/4 cup warm water, oil, buttery sticks, and egg; stir with a fork until dough forms.

3. Cover a large baking sheet with parchment paper. Place dough in center of paper; gently press dough into a square. Cover dough with an additional sheet of parchment paper. Roll dough, still covered, into a 12 x 10–inch rectangle. Remove top sheet of paper; cut dough into 42 (1-inch) squares. Separate squares on pan.

4. Bake at 325° for 40 minutes or until crackers are golden brown and crispy. Remove crackers from pan; cool 20 minutes on a wire rack. Store in an airtight container up to 2 weeks. Serves 42 (serving size: 1 cracker)

CALORIES 31; FAT 1.6g (sat 0.3g, mono 0.8g, poly 0.4g); PROTEIN 1g; CARB 3.2g; FIBER 0.5g; CHOL 4mg; IRON 0.3mg; SODIUM 31mg; CALC 4mg

## a lactose-free butter option

Fully plant-based vegan buttery baking sticks can work as a replacement for butter in cakes, cookies, and confections. The baking sticks are gluten free, lactose free, vegan, and contain zero grams of trans fat.

# NUTRITIONAL INFORMATION

**How to Use It and Why**

Glance at the end of any *Cooking Light* recipe, and you'll see how committed we are to helping you make the best of today's light cooking. With chefs, registered dietitians, home economists, and a computer system that analyzes every ingredient we use, *Cooking Light* gives you authoritative dietary detail like no other magazine. We go to such lengths so you can see how our recipes fit into your healthful eating plan. If you're trying to lose weight, the calorie and fat figures will probably help most. But if you're keeping a close eye on the sodium, cholesterol, and saturated fat in your diet, we provide those numbers, too. And because many women don't get enough iron or calcium, we can help there, as well. Finally, there's a fiber analysis for those of us who don't get enough roughage.

Here's a helpful guide to put our nutritional analysis numbers into perspective. Remember, one size doesn't fit all, so take your lifestyle, age, and circumstances into consideration when determining your nutrition needs. For example, pregnant or breast-feeding women need more protein, calories, and calcium. And women older than 50 need 1,200mg of calcium daily, 200mg more than the amount recommended for younger women.

## In Our Nutritional Analysis, We Use These Abbreviations

| | | | | | |
|---|---|---|---|---|---|
| sat | saturated fat | CARB | carbohydrates | g | gram |
| mono | monounsaturated fat | CHOL | cholesterol | mg | milligram |
| poly | polyunsaturated fat | CALC | calcium | | |

### Daily Nutrition Guide

| | Women ages 25 to 50 | Women over 50 | Men ages 24 to 50 | Men over 50 |
|---|---|---|---|---|
| Calories | 2,000 | 2,000 or less | 2,700 | 2,500 |
| Protein | 50g | 50g or less | 63g | 60g |
| Fat | 65g or less | 65g or less | 88g or less | 83g or less |
| Saturated Fat | 20g or less | 20g or less | 27g or less | 25g or less |
| Carbohydrates | 304g | 304g | 410g | 375g |
| Fiber | 25g to 35g | 25g to 35g | 25g to 35g | 25g to 35g |
| Cholesterol | 300mg or less | 300mg or less | 300mg or less | 300mg or less |
| Iron | 18mg | 8mg | 8mg | 8mg |
| Sodium | 2,300mg or less | 1,500mg or less | 2,300mg or less | 1,500mg or less |
| Calcium | 1,000mg | 1,200mg | 1,000mg | 1,000mg |

The nutritional values used in our calculations either come from The Food Processor, Version 10.4 (ESHA Research), or are provided by food manufacturers.

# METRIC EQUIVALENTS

The information in the following charts is provided to help cooks outside the United States successfully use the recipes in this book. All equivalents are approximate.

## Cooking/Oven Temperatures

|  | Fahrenheit | Celsius | Gas Mark |
|---|---|---|---|
| Freeze Water | 32° F | 0° C | |
| Room Temp. | 68° F | 20° C | |
| Boil Water | 212° F | 100° C | |
| Bake | 325° F | 160° C | 3 |
|  | 350° F | 180° C | 4 |
|  | 375° F | 190° C | 5 |
|  | 400° F | 200° C | 6 |
|  | 425° F | 220° C | 7 |
|  | 450° F | 230° C | 8 |
| Broil | | | Grill |

## Liquid Ingredients by Volume

| ¼ tsp | = | | | | | 1 ml | | |
|---|---|---|---|---|---|---|---|---|
| ½ tsp | = | | | | | 2 ml | | |
| 1 tsp | = | | | | | 5 ml | | |
| 3 tsp | = | 1 Tbsp | = | ½ fl oz | = | 15 ml | | |
| 2 Tbsp | = | ⅛ cup | = | 1 fl oz | = | 30 ml | | |
| 4 Tbsp | = | ¼ cup | = | 2 fl oz | = | 60 ml | | |
| 5⅓ Tbsp | = | ⅓ cup | = | 3 fl oz | = | 80 ml | | |
| 8 Tbsp | = | ½ cup | = | 4 fl oz | = | 120 ml | | |
| 10⅔ Tbsp | = | ⅔ cup | = | 5 fl oz | = | 160 ml | | |
| 12 Tbsp | = | ¾ cup | = | 6 fl oz | = | 180 ml | | |
| 16 Tbsp | = | 1 cup | = | 8 fl oz | = | 240 ml | | |
| 1 pt | = | 2 cups | = | 16 fl oz | = | 480 ml | | |
| 1 qt | = | 4 cups | = | 32 fl oz | = | 960 ml | | |
| | | | | 33 fl oz | = | 1000 ml | = | 1 l |

## Dry Ingredients by Weight

(To convert ounces to grams, multiply the number of ounces by 30.)

| 1 oz | = | ⅟₁₆ lb | = | 30 g |
|---|---|---|---|---|
| 4 oz | = | ¼ lb | = | 120 g |
| 8 oz | = | ½ lb | = | 240 g |
| 12 oz | = | ¾ lb | = | 360 g |
| 16 oz | = | 1 lb | = | 480 g |

## Length

(To convert inches to centimeters, multiply the number of inches by 2.5.)

| 1 in | = | | | 2.5 cm | | |
|---|---|---|---|---|---|---|
| 6 in | = | ½ ft | = | 15 cm | | |
| 12 in | = | 1 ft | = | 30 cm | | |
| 36 in | = | 3 ft | = | 1 yd | = | 90 cm |
| 40 in | = | | | 100 cm | = | 1 m |

## Equivalents for Different Types of Ingredients

| Standard Cup | Fine Powder (ex. flour) | Grain (ex. rice) | Granular (ex. sugar) | Liquid Solids (ex. butter) | Liquid (ex. milk) |
|---|---|---|---|---|---|
| 1 | 140 g | 150 g | 190 g | 200 g | 240 ml |
| ¾ | 105 g | 113 g | 143 g | 150 g | 180 ml |
| ⅔ | 93 g | 100 g | 125 g | 133 g | 160 ml |
| ½ | 70 g | 75 g | 95 g | 100 g | 120 ml |
| ⅓ | 47 g | 50 g | 63 g | 67 g | 80 ml |
| ¼ | 35 g | 38 g | 48 g | 50 g | 60 ml |
| ⅛ | 18 g | 19 g | 24 g | 25 g | 30 ml |

# INDEX

©2014 by Time Home Entertainment Inc.
135 West 50th Street, New York, NY 10020

ISBN-13: 978-0-8487-4240-9
ISBN-10: 0-8487-4240-0
Library of Congress Control Number: 2014931734

Printed in the United States of America
Second Printing 2014

Be sure to check with your health-care provider before making any changes in your diet.

**Oxmoor House**
Vice President, Brand Publishing: Laura Sappington
Editorial Director: Leah McLaughlin
Creative Director: Felicity Keane
Brand Manager: Michelle Turner Aycock
Senior Editor: Andrea C. Kirkland, MS, RD
Managing Editor: Elizabeth Tyler Austin
Assistant Managing Editor: Jeanne de Lathouder

*Cooking Light. Gluten-Free Baking*
Editor: Rachel Quinlivan West, RD
Art Director: Christopher Rhoads
Project Editor: Emily Chappell Connolly
Junior Designer: Maribeth Jones
Assistant Test Kitchen Manager: Alyson Moreland Haynes
Recipe Developers and Testers: Wendy Ball, RD; Tamara Goldis, RD; Stefanie Maloney; Callie Nash; Karen Rankin; Leah Van Deren
Food Stylists: Victoria E. Cox, Margaret Monroe Dickey, Catherine Crowell Steele
Photography Director: Jim Bathie
Senior Photographer: Hélène Dujardin
Senior Photo Stylist: Kay E. Clarke
Photo Stylist: Mindi Shapiro Levine
Assistant Photo Stylist: Mary Louise Menendez
Production Manager: Tamara Nall Wilder
Assistant Production Manager: Diane Rose Keener

**Contributors:**
Author: Robert Landolphi
Editor: Elizabeth Taliaferro
Designer: Alissa Faden
Copy Editors: Jacqueline Giovanelli, Dolores Hydock
Proofreader: Julie Bosche
Indexer: Mary Ann Laurens
Recipe Editor and Nutrition Analysis:
    Carolyn Land Williams, PhD, RD
Photographer: Jennifer Davick Photography

Photo Stylist: Ginny Branch
Food Stylists: Marian Cooper Cairns, Ana Price Kelly
Recipe Developers and Testers: Jan Smith, Tonya West
Fellows: Ali Carruba, Elizabeth Laseter, Amy Pinney, Madison Taylor Pozzo, Deanna Sakal, Maria Sanders, April Smitherman, Megan Thompson

**Time Home Entertainment Inc.**
Publisher: Jim Childs
Vice President, Brand & Digital Strategy: Steven Sandonato
Executive Director, Marketing Services: Carol Pittard
Executive Director, Retail & Special Sales: Tom Mifsud
Executive Publishing Director: Joy Butts
Publishing Director: Megan Pearlman
Director, Bookazine Development & Marketing: Laura Adam
Finance Director: Glenn Buonocore
Associate General Counsel: Helen Wan

*Cooking Light.*
Editor: Scott Mowbray
Creative Director: Dimity Jones
Executive Managing Editor: Phillip Rhodes
Executive Editor, Food: Ann Taylor Pittman
Executive Editor, Digital: Allison Long Lowery
Special Publications Editor: Mary Simpson Creel, MS, RD
Senior Food Editor: Timothy Q. Cebula
Senior Editor: Cindy Hatcher
Assistant Editor, Nutrition: Sidney Fry, MS, RD
Assistant Editors: Kimberly Holland, Hannah Klinger
Art Directors: Rachel Cardina Lasserre, Sheri Wilson
Senior Designer: Anna Bird
Designer: Hagen Stegall
Assistant Designer: Nicole Gerrity
Tablet Designer: Daniel Boone
Photo Director: Julie Claire
Assistant Photo Editor: Amy Delaune
Senior Photographer: Randy Mayor
Senior Prop Stylist: Cindy Barr
Assistant Prop Stylist: Lindsey Lower
Chief Food Stylist: Kellie Gerber Kelley
Food Styling Assistant: Blakeslee Wright Giles
Test Kitchen Manager: Tiffany Vickers Davis
Recipe Testers and Developers: Robin Bashinsky, Adam Hickman, Deb Wise
Production Director: Liz Rhoades
Production Editor: Hazel R. Eddins
Production Coordinator: Caitlin Murphree Miller
Copy Director: Susan Roberts McWilliams
Copy Editor: Kate Johnson
Research Editor: Michelle Gibson Daniels
Administrative Coordinator: Carol D. Johnson
Editorial Assistant: Alice Summerville
CookingLight.com Editor: Mallory Daugherty Brasseale
CookingLight.com Assistant Editor/Producer: Michelle Klug